A Younger Church in Search of Maturity:
Presbyterianism in Brazil from 1910 to 1959

A YOUNGER CHURCH
IN SEARCH
OF MATURITY:

Presbyterianism in Brazil from 1910 to 1959

by Paul Everett Pierson

TRINITY UNIVERSITY PRESS  San Antonio

Presbyterian Historical Society Publication Series

Vol. I. *The Presbyterian Enterprise* by M. W. Armstrong, L. A. Loetscher, and C. A. Anderson (Westminster Press 1956; paperback reprinted for P.H.S. 1963)

II. *The Presbyterian Ministry in American Culture* by E. A. Smith (Westminster Press 1962)

III. *Journals of Charles Beatty, 1762–1769*, edited by Guy S. Klett (Pennsylvania State University Press 1962)

IV. *Hoosier Zion: The Presbyterians in Early Indiana* by L. C. Rudolph (Yale University Press 1963)

V. *Presbyterianism in New York State* by Robert Hastings Nichols, edited and completed by James Hastings Nichols (Westminster Press 1963)

VI. *Scots Breed and Susquehanna* by Hubertis M. Cummings (University of Pittsburgh Press 1964)

VII. *Presbyterians and the Negro—A History* by Andrew E. Murray (Presbyterian Historical Society 1966)

VIII. *A Bibliography of American Presbyterianism During the Colonial Period* by Leonard J. Trinterud (Presbyterian Historical Society 1968)

IX. *George Bourne and The Book and Slavery Irreconcilable* by John W. Christie and Dwight L. Dumond (Historical Society of Delaware and Presbyterian Historical Society 1969)

X. *The Skyline Synod: Presbyterianism in Colorado and Utah* by Andrew E. Murray (Synod of Colorado-Utah 1971)

XI. *The Life and Writings of Francis Makemie*, edited by Boyd S. Schlenther (Presbyterian Historical Society 1971)

XII. *A Younger Church in Search of Maturity: Presbyterianism in Brazil from 1910 to 1959* by Paul Everett Pierson (Trinity University Press 1974)

To
Rosemary,
Steve, Kathy, Sandy, and David

Preface

Brazilian Presbyterianism is undergoing a serious crisis today. Victim of its success to some extent, it is uncertain as it faces Roman Catholic renewal, political absolutism, the need for radical changes in a rigid economic and social structure, and increasing polarization within both church and society. The Presbyterian Church of Brazil is representative, to a degree, of non-Pentecostal Protestantism in Latin America and perhaps in other areas of the world as well. Thus, a study of its struggles, accomplishments, and failures may facilitate the understanding not only of the situation in which that church finds itself today but of the challenges faced by other younger churches established by the North American missionary movement of the nineteenth century.

During the fifty years under consideration, Brazil changed from a traditional, largely rural society, to one experiencing the pains of rapid industrialization and urbanization. At the same time the modern Protestant ecumenical movement was taking form, and toward the end of the period Roman Catholics began to show concern for renewal and closer relationships with other Christians. But, although the Presbyterian Church of Brazil had grown to over 100,000 communicants and penetrated into various sectors of Brazilian society, it was largely unsuccessful in relating itself positively to either of these important phenomena. This is the key to the present crisis.

One of the reasons for this failure was the type of missionary activity which gave birth to Brazilian Presbyterianism. With their roots principally in small towns and rural areas of North America, the missionaries soon oriented themselves toward Brazil's geographical frontier, away from the growing cities. Another factor was the church's situation as a relatively small "sect" in a nominally Roman Catholic society—a position which led it to take a defensive stance against culture in general and the dominant church in particular. A third reason was the pattern of theological education imported from the United States, which almost inevitably moved pastors and eventually their churches into the middle class, thus alienating them from the most rapidly growing segment of the urban population.

The author spent fourteen years as a member of the Central Brazil Mission of the Presbyterian Church in the U.S.A. (now the United Presbyterian Church in the U.S.A.), engaged first in pioneer evangelism on the geographical frontier and later in theological education in Recife. These years of service stimulated the love and respect for the church and its pastors, missionaries, seminarians, and people which motivated this attempt.

Brazilian orthography changed more than once during the period, and for the sake of consistency modern spelling has been used for Brazilian words and names except in quotes or titles. Although the monetary unit was changed at times, for the sake of simplicity the cruzeiro is used throughout the text. A map and list of abbreviations and Portuguese terms used are available in the Appendix. The two Presbyterian mission boards which worked in Brazil have been designated at times by their location in New York (PCUSA) and Nashville (PCUS). The term "Evangelical" functions as a synonym for Protestant, as it usually does in Brazil.

It is both a joy and obligation to express appreciation to those who have helped in the research and final preparation of this work. I owe special thanks to the Reverend Júlio Andrade Ferreira, archivist and historian of the Presbyterian Church of Brazil and, for many years, professor and Rector of Campinas Seminary. Professor Ferreira not only made the archives and his unpublished manuscript on Erasmo Braga available but spent several hours sharing his insight and experience. The Reverend James N. Wright, Executive Secretary of the Central Brazil Mission, graciously opened the archives of that mission. Dr. David G. Vieira loaned a number of rare books on the struggle against Roman Catholic clericalism, and the Reverend Gerald Gillette of the Presbyterian Historical Society helped discover the relevant missionary correspondence located there. The Commission on Ecumenical Mission and Relations of the UPUSA made it possible for me to complete the work while on regular furlough. Special thanks go to Professor Lefferts A. Loetscher and Dean James H. Nichols of Princeton Theological Seminary for their valuable orientation and criticism.

Finally, I wish to express profound gratitude to my wife Rosemary for her patience, understanding, and support during the many hours when the demands of this work placed an unusually heavy burden on her. To the many others, both Brazilian and North American, who helped in research, I give my thanks. Any shortcomings or errors of interpretation are, of course, the responsibility of the author.

P. E. P.

Table of Contents

A Younger Church in Search of Maturity:
Presbyterianism in Brazil from 1910 to 1959

Chapter One

Religious and Cultural Background

"It is my firm conviction that there is not a Roman Catholic country on the globe where there prevails a greater degree of toleration, or a greater liberality of feeling, towards Protestants."[1] The accuracy of this observation, made about 1840 by a Bible Society agent, is indicated by the existence of over 3,200,000 communicant members in Brazil's Protestant churches today, the largest number in any nominally Roman Catholic country in the world.[2] In order to understand Protestantism and, more specifically, Presbyterianism in Brazil, it is necessary to examine the religious and cultural factors which helped to make that nation receptive to its message.

The Colonial Period: 1500–1822

Portuguese explorers, like the Spanish, brought priests with them to the New World in order to conquer new lands for the church as well as the king, and from the sixteenth to the eighteenth centuries it was inconceivable to authorities that Brazil's religious unity should be broken by "heretics." The attempt to establish a Calvinist colony near Rio de Janeiro in 1555 ended three years later with the execution of the hemisphere's first three Protestant martyrs. With the Dutch invasion of Pernambuco in 1630, about forty pastors entered the country, establishing two presbyteries, but no trace of the work was left after the invaders' expulsion in 1654. Thus, free to imitate Portugal, Brazil attempted to base its political unity on religion. While those of various races and national origins might be admitted, no non-Catholics were acceptable as colonists, and at times friars examined arriving im-

migrants to determine their orthodoxy. Any factor which poten-
tially threatened the link between church and state was feared.
Freyre observed that the identification of Catholicism and nationalism united Brazilians against Protestant invaders to such a
degree that it became difficult to separate the Brazilian from the
Catholic and concluded "Catholicism was in reality the cement of
our unity."[3]

However, the Catholicism which characterized Brazil during
the period was not a unity in itself. Bastide notes that, from the
beginning, two types were present: "the familial Catholicism of
the colonists and the patriarch, and the more Roman and uni-
versalist Catholicism of the religious orders, especially the Jesuits."[4] The latter often alienated colonists because of its attempts to
protect the Indians.

When the Jesuits were expelled by Portugal's Marquis de Pom-
bal in 1759, the Catholicism from the mother country was left to
dominate religious life. As a Brazilian anthropologist has observed, from the beginning this exhibited "a certain softness, tolerance, and malleability which an exalted, turbulent, and hard
Spanish religious character did not know."[5] It was soon modified
by the colonial patriarchal system in which the centers of economic and social life were the plantations. There, in the person of the
chaplain of the "big house," colonial religious life found its typical
representative. The "uncle-priest" was often a younger son of
the plantation owner and lived under his domination. The archi-
tectural arrangement, in which both chapel and priest's quarters
were usually part of the manor house, symbolized the relationship. The church was supported by and subservient to the lord of
the manor. Its ethics were those of the patriarchal society in general, and, following the plantation's easygoing code, the priest
usually fathered numerous children. This Catholicism gave little
attention to doctrine, centering its activities in the *festas*, which
were often a reflection of the cycle of rural life. Thus the chaplain,
along with the religion he symbolized, was "less the representative of Rome than a servant of the lord of the big house."[6]

Brazilian popular Catholicism was also shaped by the presence
of the African slave. Baptized before he arrived or immediately
thereafter, taught the creed, the Ave Maria, and the sign of the
cross, the slave was nominally a Christian. But the church kept

him separate from those of European origin, and he was forced to attend a segregated Mass. Thus, while religion was to some extent a unifying force, it did not fail to remind the Negro of his servitude. It is not surprising that the slaves provided black saints for themselves, continuing to worship their traditional deities, especially certain goddesses whom they rebaptized with Christian names.

Consequently colonial Catholicism was a faithful reflection of the society in which it developed. Dominated by the landowners, it was strongly influenced by the superstitions and religious practices of the slaves. It was festive rather than ethical or doctrinal, and its central figures were the Virgin and the saints. Devotion to Mary, glorified as the Queen of Heaven, became especially strong, and in popular piety she was usually endowed with greater mystical power than either God or Jesus Christ.

Lay leadership played a significant role in religious life quite early, but the scarcity of priests was only one of the reasons. With the rise of cities in the seventeenth century and the greater concentration of population, blacks and mulattoes began to create their own racially separate brotherhoods which were soon assigned places in religious processions according to color and social class. These groups were important, not only in expressing and enhancing the identity of their members, but also in changing the traditional relationship between clergy and laity. Often the societies retained the keys to their own churches and refused to give them to the priests, looking on them as functionaries rather than their spiritual mentors. In Bahia, in 1788, they even demanded formation of a separate Brazilian church.[7] This independent spirit would be an important factor in creating the "Religious Question" which had far-reaching consequences toward the end of the Empire.

By the end of the seventeenth century the rigid racial separation began to break down, and the religious orders were opened to mulattoes, first to sons of priests, then to others. Blacks and mulattoes continued to complain, however, about their place in the processions and the exclusivism of the white brotherhoods.

Despite change, church life continued to be relatively stable during the colonial period. Although its moral and spiritual level was very low, it was closely identified with the life of Brazilian

society. But the disintegration of that close relationship would be
rapid during the short period of the Empire.

The Period of the Empire: 1822–1889

As mulattoes moved into the clerical ranks they began to replace the sons of the patriarchal families, to whom new careers
were now opening, especially after independence in 1822. While
this might have brought a closer identification of the church with
the majority of people, other factors led to quite different tendencies. First, as the poorer classes entered the priesthood, the
clergy became more dependent on hierarchical authority, more
submissive to Rome than to the patriarch, and, in some cases,
more concerned with morality and dogma than the uncle-priests
had been. But if this signalled the beginning of a more elevated
type of Catholicism in Brazil, it was not evident during the greater part of the nineteenth century. The immediate result was
greater alienation of the clergy from the traditional religious life
of the people. A second factor was the decline of the patriarchal
system, a process which would accelerate greatly with the aboli-
tion of slavery, which began at mid-century, and was completed
in 1888. The same tie which bound the Negro to the manor house
in most cases bound him to the chapel, and deterioration of the
former relationship was accompanied, in part at least, by that of
the latter. Finally, with growth of the population and decreasing
prestige of the church, there were never enough candidates for
the priesthood.

The scarcity of priests, often cited as a reason for the church's
weakness in Brazil, became worse during the period. An observer
who called it the nation's most urgent problem stated that in
1800, only 700 out of 1500 priests were active. In a population of
three million this was a ratio of only one to every 4300 Brazilians.[8] But by 1907, according to Freyre, the ratio had fallen to one
to 15,000. In the United States, by way of contrast, there was a
priest for every 867 Roman Catholics.[9]

In 1840 the situation was described by Kidder, the Bible Society agent:

The lack of priests who will dedicate themselves to the cure
of souls, or who even offer themselves as candidates, is sur-

prising. In the province of Pará there are parishes which, for twelve years and upwards, have had no pastor. . . . The Bishop of São Paulo affirms the same thing respecting vacant churches in his diocese, and it is no uncommon experience elsewhere. . . . The numerical ratio of those priests who die, or become incompetent through age and infirmity, is two to one of those who receive ordination. Even among those who are ordained, few devote themselves to pastoral work.[10]

Aggravating the problem were the decadence and ill-repute of the orders. Looked upon as parasites by most people, the monks were envied because of their wealth and distrusted because of their ultramontanism by the secular clergy. The government expressed its hostility in a series of measures immediately after independence. In 1824 a decree prohibited the entry and residence of foreign friars and the creation of new orders while expelling those who obeyed superiors outside of Brazil. Kidder visited three monasteries in Paraíba and found that one, with space for two hundred monks, had only six; a second, one; while the third had become a barracks. Despite government permission to matriculate a limited number of novices, the orders did not succeed in attracting candidates. "Nobody wishes to be a friar" was a common remark.[11] The final move, intended as a death warrant for the orders in Brazil, came in 1855 in the form of a federal decree prohibiting novitiates. By 1891 there was only one Franciscan left in the nation, while the Benedictines were "reduced to half a dozen decrepit old monks."[12]

Among the few priests remaining, the majority showed little interest in the cure of souls. Many devoted their energies to politics and other secular pursuits requiring less effort and paying a better stipend. Just as in the colonial period, few observed their vow of chastity. At times the priest contracted a de facto marriage; frequently he merely had a series of concubines. The Governor of Ceará remarked that the clergy in his province were, with some exceptions, "ignorant, depraved in habits, corrupt in morals, involved in the concerns of the world, and totally forgetful of their heavenly mission." But he also blamed the government for its lack of support and aid to the church.[13]

It is not surprising that Catholic writer Alceu A. Lima speaks of the people's increasing withdrawal from sacramental life during this period.[14] By mid-century, with the rare exception of a few scattered parishes blessed with able and conscientious priests, Brazil's masses had two alternatives. One was an individualistic, non-institutional religion, practiced at home and centered in the *festas* and a favorite manifestation of the Virgin. The other was the more formal Catholicism, focusing on the Mass and the other sacraments, whose official representative, if not absent, was usually distrusted and at times despised. Naturally the great majority chose the former.

Thus, local authority and lay control, so important in shaping North American Protestantism, were also present in Brazil. Stimulated by the brotherhoods, the lack of priests, and the folk nature of popular Catholicism, lay leadership became important in Brazilian religion. A visitor to a plantation in São Paulo in the nineteenth century told of attending evening prayers:

> I had observed a great number of slaves entering, who in succession addressed us with crossed hands and the pious salutation, "Praised be our Lord Jesus Christ." Presently there commenced a chant in the adjoining room. . . . I was told that he (the priest) attended these exercises merely as any other member of the family, the singing and prayers being taught and conducted by an aged black man. . . . This assembling of the slaves, generally at evening, and sometimes both morning and evening, is said to be common on plantations in the country, and is not infrequent among domestics in the cities.[15]

The main duty of the priest, who attended vespers as a member of the congregation, was to celebrate a segregated Mass. It is not difficult to see where lay the greater sense of participation and Christian community for most people.

Another aspect of the nonclerical nature of much of Brazilian religion was seen in messianic movements in Canudos, Bahia, in 1897, and in the Contestado, Santa Catarina, in 1912. The leaders of both were condemned by the church but followed with fanatical religious devotion by thousands of the poor in the hinterland. In these and similar cases, the masses not only organized themselves but implicitly denied the salvation monopoly of the Roman Catholic Church.[16]

It is worth noting that the geographical areas and the groups in which Brazilian Protestantism has grown most rapidly have always been those in which laymen were forced, by lack of pastors, church structure, or other factors, to provide most of the leadership.

The Church and the Government

Government policies also contributed to the weakening position of the church in the Empire. With the invasion of Portugal by Napoleon's troops the royal family fled to Brazil, establishing the court in Rio de Janeiro in 1808. That same year the government began to permit manufacturing and opened Brazilian ports to all friendly nations, bringing closer cultural and social ties with Europe and the United States. The new economic and intellectual contacts which would prepare the way for independence also ended the nation's religious quarantine. In order to attract European industry and agriculture, the government soon offered all acceptable immigrants, not just Roman Catholics or Portuguese, homestead privileges on the same attractive terms previously reserved for those from the mother country.

England's alliance with Portugal against Napoleon led to a commercial treaty between the two nations in 1810. Upon the insistence of the English plenipotentiary, and against strong objections by the papal nuncio, Article XII of the treaty provided freedom for English subjects to build and worship in their own churches and chapels, provided they had the outward appearance of dwelling houses. They would not be allowed to speak against the Roman Catholic Church, nor could they seek proselytes, but it was the beginning of limited religious toleration. Anglican worship was held in Rio beginning that year, and in 1819 the cornerstone was laid for a chapel there, the first Protestant church building in South America.[17]

In 1822 independence from Portugal was declared and the Brazilianized heir to the Portuguese throne, Pedro I, was named first emperor of the new nation. The constitutional convention of 1823, which attempted to restrict political rights to Roman Catholics, was dissolved by the Emperor, and the following year a new constitution, which would remain in effect until 1889, was promulgated. This took another step toward full religious liberty. Although Roman Catholicism continued to be the state religion, other creeds were permitted worship in buildings which did not externally resemble a church. Religious persecution was prohibited, and political rights were extended to non-Catholics.

The motive lay, partially at least, in the desire to stimulate immigration. The founding of the colony of Nova Friburgo in the State of Rio de Janeiro, by Swiss immigrants in 1820, had marked the inception of a systematic policy of non-Iberian European immigration. Although it was stipulated that the Nova Friburgo group should be Roman Catholic, some Protestants were included among them. Four years later the government brought Germans to Rio Grande do Sul, beginning the large Lutheran immigration to that state. In 1855 the new Prime Minister spoke of his special interest in promoting immigration from the Protestant nations which, he said, were the most "evolved," adding that religious liberty was necessary if the program were to succeed.[18] The influence of some foreign Protestants is seen in the impression made by the piety of an English family on the youth José Manoel da Conceição, who would become the first Brazilian Protestant minister.[19] Perhaps this was not an isolated case.

The advantages of the continued establishment of the church were more than offset when the new government followed the Gallicanism of its predecessor. While the clergy was supported by state funds, the Emperor had the right to appoint bishops, distribute benefices, and grant or withhold the exequatur to papal documents and other ecclesiastical decrees. The Vatican, after protest, accepted the arrangement in 1828.

Thus, regalism debilitated an already weakened church. Parish priests were paid a salary which left them in poverty and made the critical problem of vocations worse. The orders were dying while the hierarchy failed to create necessary new dioceses for fear of government influence in nominating their occupants. And as the church accommodated itself to the situation, it lost most of its already eroded apostolic zeal. The former regent, Diogo Feijó, told Kidder that "there was scarcely a priest in the whole province that did his duty as the Church prescribed it, and especially with reference to catechizing children on the Lord's day."[20] Lima observes that the church's attitude during the period was shown by its exaggerated welcome to the protection of the state, increasing ignorance of religious doctrine, and general conformity to the situation. "By the middle of the century," he writes, Catholicism was "so penetrated by worldliness and regalism that it had become a habit more than a conviction."[21]

But the most serious problem lay in the church's domination by a state which was increasingly moving in directions different from those of the nineteenth century papacy. The new ideas against which Pius IX would soon react so violently were finding a hearing among many of Brazil's political and intellectual leaders.

Liberalism in Church and State

Even before independence new currents of thought were entering from Europe and the United States, and the ideals of the American Revolution exerted a strong influence on the abortive independence movement of 1789. But new ideas came in much greater number during the nineteenth century. French Positivism arrived after 1860, capturing the minds of many young army officers, while Liberalism, inspired by contact with the Anglo-Saxon world, was even more important. To a new nation desiring progress and seeking models upon which to pattern itself, Protestant England, with its victory in 1815, its commercial and technical domination, and its political institutions, appeared to provide the needed example. Consequently some looked to English religion as well, wondering if it was not best for progressive peoples. It is no coincidence that there were a number of intellectuals and army officers among the first Brazilian Protestants. Indeed, Freyre accuses men like Abreu e Lima, Joaquim Nabuco, and Rui Barbosa of wanting to make "Brazil march to the rhythm of spiritual progress made by Anglo-Saxons and Protestants."[22]

But such influence was not confined to anti-clericals as a number of leading priests became liberals. Most important among them was Diogo Antônio Feijó who became a deputy in São Paulo in 1826, Minister of Justice in 1831, Senator two years later, and Regent of the Empire from 1835 to 1837 during the minority of D. Pedro II. Apparently blameless in his personal life, but concerned with clerical immorality, he proposed that the province of São Paulo authorize clerical marriage. His suggestion that Moravians be invited to educate the Brazilian Indians brought a strong reaction, which was responsible in part for his forced resignation. Finally, in 1838, he went still further, advocating a national council to separate the Brazilian church from

Rome. It is not difficult to understand why he has been called "the bitterest foe of papal supremacy ever produced by the Brazilian Church."[23]

Coexisting with the Catholicism of the uncle-priests and the demoralized functionaries of the state was a little known but persistent current of Jansenist influence among some of the clergy. The Montpelier Catechism and the Theology of Lyon, both written under the inspiration of this movement, were used in Brazil despite papal attempts to suppress them. While it is difficult to calculate Jansenism's effect on the country, there is little doubt that it stimulated in a number of priests an austere type of piety, love for the scriptures, and a more independent attitude toward Rome. It is known that Feijó belonged to such a group in São Paulo from 1818 to 1824.[24]

The presence of the movement in São Paulo was quite possibly responsible for the use of the Lancastrian system in the principal primary school of that city and for the friendly reception Kidder received there. But it is also important to note that a project, proposed by the Archbishop of Rio de Janeiro, to publish the Bible in Portugese with notes and comments seems to have been motivated by the wish to counteract the activity of the Bible Society rather than a positive desire to make the scriptures more available. It was never realized, perhaps because of the withdrawal of the colporteurs in 1841. A great disappointment confronted Kidder when his proposal to the São Paulo legislature that the Society be allowed to donate copies of the New Testament to every primary school in the province was quietly shelved in committee. How much of the enthusiastic reception originally given to the idea by liberal political and church leaders was due to support for the plan, and how much was typical Brazilian courtesy to a foreigner, is a matter for speculation.[25]

However, despite some signs of interest in the Bible, the attitude of the church's leadership was shown during the period by the first anti-Protestant works published in Brazil. These included a pamphlet by the English priest, William Tylburi, and three books by Fr. Luiz Gonçalves dos Santos, who wrote in violent language from 1837 to 1839.[26] The reaction against General Abreu e Lima in the 1860's demonstrated that this was neither an isolated case nor primarily a reaction against foreign Protestants. The general, who distributed Bibles among his friends in Pernambuco, was accused of giving away "false Bibles" and, upon his death, denied burial in consecrated ground.

But nineteenth-century liberalism made far greater inroads among political leaders than among the clergy. D. Pedro II, Brazil's emperor from 1840 to 1889, and a unique figure in the hemisphere's political history, typified the religious spirit of the leaders of society. He looked on priests as functionaries of the state which paid them and considered their primary task to be the promotion of its welfare. As far as possible he wished to use them as school teachers or university professors. D. Pedro's spirit manifested itself in his warm friendship with Robert Kalley, the Scottish pastor, physician, and missionary, and in his concession of the "Order of the Rose" to Ernst Renan, the French skeptic. Thus, the Emperor's religious attitudes symbolized the liberal Catholicism of many of the nation's leaders, which existed alongside the festive and nondogmatic religion of the masses.

After Pius IX's Syllabus of Errors condemned liberal democratic ideals in 1864 and the First Vatican Council was held in 1870, a number of respected political leaders took a sharply anticlerical stance and began to work toward the separation of church and state. The papacy's struggle to prevent Italian unification and its condemnation of the freedoms which many considered essential for Brazil's progress aroused opposition to the traditional relationship between religion and government. Saldanha Marinho, Grand Master of Brazilian Masonry, argued in Congress in 1874 that since the infallibility of the Syllabus had been declared, the church was no longer that institution which had been recognized as official by the constitution. Therefore, he concluded, the government should immediately end the special relationship between the two.[27]

Other prominent anticlerical Catholics were Joaquim Nabuco, the abolitionist leader, and Rui Barbosa. The latter, born in 1849, distinguished himself at an early age, had a long career in national politics, and is still considered one of Brazil's greatest figures. His reaction to the papacy of Pius IX was shown in his long introduction to the work of Dollinger, Friedrich, and Huber, "The Pope and the Council," published in Brazil in 1877. Attacking papal absolutism on religious grounds, he argued that it was incompatible with modern liberal constitutions and cited the poor conditions in the Papal States as a typical result of ecclesiastical domination. Believing that an established religion was prejudicial to spiritual life as well as to economic and social progress, he praised the ideal of a free church in a free state. "Look at Spain, the ancient Roman states, and Austria until 1870," he wrote. "In all of them, in the people, fanaticism, immorality, and irreligion. Study Holland, the American Union, Canada. They are, one can say, the homeland of sincere religious faith . . . which enters into individual deliberations in the home, in social life."[28] His admiration of public education in the United States led him to advocate the secularization of schools in Brazil. As for religion, Freyre states that for Barbosa and Nabuco, the ideal was: "A Catholicism almost without rites, without processions in the streets, without novenas or saints in the churches. . . . A Catholicism which would be, in Brazil, Anglo-Saxonized into Protestantism . . . just as the laws, the customs, the sports."[29]

The strategic importance of this identification of Protestantism with liberalism and progress was appreciated in Protestant circles. Shortly after his conversion to Presbyterianism, Miguel Vieira Ferreira, member of an aristocratic family, translated and published the work of the Belgian, Emile de Laveleye, "On the Future of the Catholic Peoples."[30] The thesis of the article was that to the nations in which it was dominant, Protestantism had brought education, economic progress, and political liberty, while Roman Catholicism had produced stagnation.

Masonry, the Beginning of Catholic Renewal, and the Republic

Masonry, active in Brazil during the colonial period, exerted its influence in the independence movement and in imposing a degree of religious toleration on the nation's first constitution. A natural ally of liberalism, it included among its members the Emperor, many prominent Catholic laymen, and even some priests. There also existed a little known alliance between Masonry and Protestantism, especially after the arrival of Kalley in 1855 and the Presbyterians four years later.

Ecumenical in outlook and sympathetic toward the old Catholics of Europe in belief, the Masons supported Protestants in a number of cases involving religious freedom during the 1860's. Among the results of their aid was the legalization of Protestant marriage in 1863 and permission for Presbyterians to publish their newspaper, the *Imprensa Evangélica*, in 1864. Police action in Rio in 1860, in which Brazilian Protestants were arrested at worship and jailed, and the confiscation and destruction of "Protestant" Bibles at the instigation of the acting Bishop of Olinda in 1865, kindled a strong reaction in the Masonic press. In 1871 a Masonic member of the Council of State sponsored the petition of the American missionaries requesting incorporation of the Presbytery of Rio de Janeiro. It was refused by Princess Isabel, a devout Catholic and acting Regent in her father's absence, but granted the following year after a new cabinet was formed under the leadership of the Viscount of Rio Branco, a prominent Mason.[31]

The Masonic-Protestant alliance was at least partially responsible for precipitating the famous "Religious Question." This important struggle, the first strong reaction by the church against regalism, marked the beginning of Catholic renewal. It also made the separation of church and state almost inevitable. Just after the Rio Branco cabinet had allowed the Presbytery of Rio to incorporate, the Bishop of that city took harsh measures against Fr. Almeida Martins, a Masonic priest who had preached at Masonic festivities in honor of the Prime Minister. This was the opening shot in a battle which soon became a national issue. Alexander Blackford and other Protestants had been furnishing theological material to the Order's press for some time, and in 1872, when *A Verdade*, a Masonic paper in Recife, published an article by a French Protestant pastor which stated that Mary had other children after Jesus, there arose a great furor. As long as the clergy and pope were attacked, the majority of the public was sympathetic. But in a country where Mary was the central figure of religious devotion and often confused with Negro and Indian goddesses, the Protestant slur on her virginity seemed to many to be an insult to God himself.[32]

D. Vital Gonçalves de Oliveira, Bishop of Olinda, led the public reaction, insisting that all Catholics leave the Masonic Order and that the brotherhoods expel those who refused to do so. When they would not comply, the societies and their churches were interdicted. Appealing to the Crown, they argued that the papal encyclicals which the Bishop had used as his guide had never been approved by the government and thus were not legally enforceable in Brazil. Believing its prerogatives challenged, the state supported the brotherhoods, and when D. Vital, together with the Bishop of Pará, refused to annul the interdiction, the two were condemned to four years of hard labor. (They finally served only one year in prison.)

Strident voices spoke out on both sides, and the affair reinforced the determination of liberals and Masons to bring about the religious neutrality of the state. Most of them agreed with Joaquim Nabuco's 1879 declaration: "I am not an enemy of the Catholic Church . . . of the great majority. . . . But I am an enemy of this political Catholicism, this Catholicism that allies itself with all absolutist governments."[33] Nabuco, along with Rui Barbosa, led the movement for religious liberty, separation of church and state, obligatory civil marriage, and the desacralization of cemeteries. After the Republic was declared in 1889, its first constitution, adopted in 1891, made these measures law.

For the church the "Religious Question" marked the beginning of a new awakening. The long-submissive clergy finally began to defend its authority in spiritual matters and its right to control the faith and morality of priests and members of its brotherhoods. But it received such power only when church and state were separated in 1891. Thus, most Catholic historians would agree with Lima in affirming that separation, "even though it was a doctrinal error, was a great benefit because of the historical circumstances of the Brazilian situation."[34] It brought a freedom of action which the church had never enjoyed during its four centuries in the country. Its institutional development became more rapid as fear of monarchial intervention ceased. New bishoprics and archdioceses were created, and in 1905 the Archbishop of Rio de Janeiro, D. Joaquim Arcoverde de Albuquerque Cavalcante, became Latin America's first cardinal.

D. Vital of Olinda, the leader in rebuilding the new Catholicism, was instrumental in bringing in regular clergy to fill the abandoned monasteries. Beginning in 1889, Capuchins, Benedictines, Carmelites, and Franciscans arrived from Italy, France, and Belgium with the responsibility of reinstituting their respective orders in Brazil. After the Spanish-American War, a number of European priests who had left the Philippines entered the country.

But as the twentieth century began, Brazilians were anything but a block of faithful practicing Catholics. The Redemptorist, Júlio Maria, painted a bleak picture of religion at the time:

Ceremonies that do not edify, devotions that do not show spirituality, novenas that do not reveal fervor, processions that only amuse, "*festas*," finally, that are neither profitable to souls nor give glory to God. It is to this, generally, in Brazilian parishes. that the great, majestic, divine, Catholic worship is reduced. . . . The principal necessity of Brazilian parishes is indoctrination; but our pulpit, if it still speaks, gives off panegyrics and festive sermons, it does not teach. In the parishes the majority of the faithful have no clear idea of that which they believe and practice, they do not know the value of the sacrifice of the Mass; they do not know what a sacrament is. . . . The majority of the national clergy is absorbed, either by agitated worldly concern for position, riches, and pleasure, or by the simple external aspects of religious festivities.[35]

As Azevedo indicates, there were three principal types of Catholics in Brazil: a tiny minority who knew and believed at least a minimum of doctrine and were faithful in religious duties; a much larger group of nominal Catholics; and finally, the "Brazilian" or folk Catholics, stigmatized by the bishops and denounced by the priests.[36] Although the categories overlapped, the great majority of the population, especially the lower-middle class and poor, belonged to the third group. Their non-institutional religion centered in the *festas* and private devotion to the Virgin and saints had almost no contact with the clergy.

At the same time the church, in attempting to improve the situation, faced a difficult dilemma. How could the people be better indoctrinated and Brazilian Catholicism be purified of error without making it, at the same time, less Brazilian? The folk religion of the plantations was syncretistic, but it expressed the life cycle of its society. While the liberal Catholicism of Feijó and others had been anti-Roman, it was closely identified with national aspirations. But the scarcity of vocations made it necessary to bring in a great number of priests from abroad if renewal were to become a reality. Early in the twentieth century over half the regular clergy and nearly that proportion of the secular were foreign. And the new priests, oriented toward Rome, were alien to Brazil's traditions and aspirations. Although they were important in aiding the transition from colonial religion to a Catholicism which was more doctrinal and Roman, the very process of renewal alien-

ated them from significant sectors of national life. Catholicism
became more clerical, more foreign, and more confined to the
church and cloister.

Thus, despite the beginning of renewal, the church in Brazil
had few priests and lacked prestige. During the first two decades
of revitalization, denationalization of the clergy and its alienation
from the masses continued. At the same time many intellectuals,
although formally Catholic, either believed Protestantism to be
the bearer of progress or openly scoffed at all religion. Efforts for
renewal would not begin to bear fruit until the 1920's, but even
then the church's link with the masses remained tenuous, while
efforts to provide an adequate number of priests were never
successful.

Brazilian Catholicism as a Preparation for Protestantism

Brazilian Catholic piety acted as both a positive and negative
factor in preparing people to receive the Protestant message.
Popular religion gave to many some understanding of the basic
terms and concepts of the Christian faith. But the decadence, low
prestige, and alienation of the institutional church impelled a substantial number to seek outside its structures satisfaction for the
spiritual hunger which it often aroused but seldom satisfied. Widespread despair over the situation in the Roman church led many
to reject the institution without totally denying Christian belief.
Protestant preaching must have found a ready audience among
them. The message was not entirely new; it used familiar descrip-
tions of sin and salvation, heaven and hell, and of Jesus Christ
who died on the cross and rose again. When well presented it
must have seemed clearer and easier to grasp than the complicated Catholic sacramental theology. Most important, it offered
religious security to those who, like Luther, were asking, "How
can I be sure of my salvation?"

The small Protestant congregations were often genuine Christian communities, similar to the slave-led vesper services or the
brotherhoods at their best. The prominence of lay leadership in
the scattered rural churches founded by itinerant Protestant
evangelists must have seemed proper to those accustomed to lay-
directed *festas* and absent priests. But Protestant church structure, unlike Roman Catholic, officially recognized lay leadership
and made it legitimate.

The place of the Bible in early Protestant strategy can scarcely be overemphasized. Theoretically at least, the Roman church taught that it was the word of God even though it usually discouraged its distribution and reading, when, indeed, the people were able to read. However, some reading of Roman Catholic as well as Protestant versions took place, and interest in Bible study was not unknown. Where this took place Protestantism often found a hearing.[37] The work of Bible societies reinforced this interest, and usually the colporteurs had no difficulty in placing whatever Bibles they had available for a given locality. The only way the Catholic Church could logically condemn their activities and the scriptures they distributed was to accuse them of printing false Bibles. This it often did.

Both the negative and positive aspects of Brazilian Catholicism's preparation for Protestantism were seen in the conversion of Aníbal Nora, who was to become a great rural evangelist and father of two synods of the Presbyterian Church of Brazil. At the age of seventeen he was disillusioned when he overheard a priest tell his father, "Religion is a way of making a living just like any other. You have your farm, another lives by his business . . . just as I live by religion." The youth soon went to live with a Protestant relative in São Paulo. Overcoming his prejudice against the new religion, he attended a worship service and was amazed to hear of God, Jesus Christ, and the saints, all of whom he thought Protestants despised. He began to read the Bible and soon decided to become a pastor.[38] The same elements were present in the experience of Manoel de Melo, whose story, told by his daughter, illuminates much of early rural Protestantism. Already inclined toward the new religion because of a brother who had been converted through reading the Bible, Melo was disgusted and left the Catholic Church when the local priest, who was also a politician, promised to grant absolution after confession in return for his vote in a coming election. At the same time, replying to the argument that the Protestant Bible was false, his brother tried to convince him that Protestantism was the true fulfillment of the family's religious aspirations:

This story of false Bibles is a fiction of the priest. If our father were not so stubborn he would have compared his Bible with ours already, and today would be a Protestant just as I am. You know very well that in our house there never passed a night without the family reading and hearing a portion of the Scriptures, the Lord's Prayer, and the Creed. The moral standard of our family is Christian. Our father is against the worship of images and he himself has already spoken about this subject. Don't you remember? One day he read the second commandment and commented that he did not know why the Holy Mother Church used such worship when it was prohibited by God. He doesn't have any images in the house. . . . Little brother, our father is a Protestant without knowing it, he is Protestant by the doctrine he confesses. He just cannot tolerate the name because he is a bitter enemy of everything that smells of novelty.[39]

Out of the conversion of Manoel de Melo grew a sizeable Presbyterian community in western Minas Gerais. It seems safe to suggest that similar cases were not uncommon.

But because its roots grew from the soil of Roman Catholic piety in a nominally Catholic nation, Brazilian Protestantism constantly felt the need of defining its nature and mission over against the dominant church. Most Protestants owed more of their religious experience to their Roman Catholic background than they could see. However, the violent break with that tradition which conversion to the Protestant faith involved in the Brazilian context, coupled with the harsh polemic of the Catholic Church against the religious communities and message which had brought them a new sense of liberation and meaning, inevitably led first-generation Protestants to view the church of their fathers in almost totally negative terms. This would not prevent strong interaction between Protestantism and the mentality formed by the Catholic background of its converts. At times it would lead them toward authoritarianism and clericalism, theological conservatism, legalism, and suspicion of innovation—attitudes which often existed in the newly formed congregations alongside the typical Protestant views of education, work, and personal morality. Many of the struggles within the Presbyterian Church of Brazil in the future would center around conflicting definitions of what it meant to be truly Protestant and truly Presbyterian.

Chapter Two

The First Half-Century
of Brazilian Presbyterianism

A twenty-six-year-old graduate of the College of New Jersey
and Princeton Seminary, Ashbel Green Simonton, arrived in Rio
on August 12, 1859 to begin Presbyterian work in Brazil. Even
though his parents had dedicated him to the ministry at birth, he
did not experience conversion until 1855 during a New School
church revival in Harrisburg, Pennsylvania. Although he felt no
special emotion he was intellectually convinced of his need and
resolved "in God's promised strength to go forward and endeavor
to serve Him whether a bright light shines about my path or
not."[1] Simonton was ordained in the Old School church and while
at Princeton heard the call to missionary service through a sermon by Charles Hodge, the greatest exponent of Old School orthodoxy. Thus, in his own experience, Simonton reflected an important characteristic of the future Igreja Presbiteriana do Brasil
—the predominance of Westminster orthodoxy combined with a
churchly spirit which in the Brazilian context became very authoritarian at times.

The founder of Brazilian Presbyterianism died eight years after
arriving in Rio, but he left behind an impressive series of accomplishments. From the beginning he demonstrated a concern both
for the evangelization of individuals and the creation of a church
which would be a missionary community. The results of his orientation were seen in the organization of Brazil's first Presbyterian
church in 1862; the founding of its first Evangelical paper in 1864;
establishment of the first presbytery in modern Brazil in 1865; the
ordination of the first Brazilian Protestant minister the same year;
and the opening of the nation's first Protestant seminary in 1867.

Simonton was joined in 1860 by Alexander Blackford, his

brother-in-law, who did as much to shape the future of the
Presbyterian Church of Brazil as his better-known colleague. Born
of pioneer parents on an Ohio farm in 1829, Blackford demonstrated the rural, frontier spirit which would be typical of most
of his future colleagues. It was Blackford who set his face toward
the interior and made São Paulo a center of missionary activity.[2]
In 1863 he visited the former vicar of Brotas, who had advised his
people to read the Bible. The encounter was decisive in the
decision of José Manoel da Conceição to become the first Brazilian Protestant minister. Two of the first four seminarians of the
infant church were led to profess their faith and enter the ministry through Blackford, and the other two felt his influence and
encouragement.[3] His critical attitude toward Horace Lane and the
American School in São Paulo[4] foreshadowed the deep difference
of opinion between a majority of the Brazilian pastors and many
missionaries regarding educational policy—a dispute which
would bring schism in 1903.

Conceição, the former priest, was most important in opening
the interior of Brazil to Protestantism and bringing into the Presbyterian fold several families from whose ranks future leaders of
the church would emerge. While still a Roman Catholic he had
incurred the distrust of his bishops and been transferred frequently because of his Evangelical ideas. Increasing inner conflict over
his inability to reconcile that which he read in the Bible with the
practice and teaching of his church had led him to settle down on
a farm near Rio Claro, in the interior of São Paulo. It was here he
met Blackford, in an event which Conceição saw as the great
turning point of his life.

As Leonard has indicated, Conceição's experience shows the
impossibility of a purely Brazilian reformation, either within the
Roman church or outside it. It would not have had the necessary
support of the imperial government or of a substantial number of
intellectual leaders; nor would it have attracted significant clerical interest. Not even in São Paulo, where Jansenist influence and
interest in the Bible had been relatively strong, did Conceição attract anything but suspicion for his efforts to preach a more Biblical message within the Catholic Church. Nor was he successful
with churchmen after leaving the priesthood. He was Brazilian,
and his style of life, more akin to that of an itinerant monk than a
foreign missionary, was profoundly identified with that of his own

countrymen. In personality and message he was winsome and irenic, but he was never able to persuade another priest to accept his cause. Thus it is clear that if the Evangelical faith were to enter Brazil it had to come from outside the dominant church.

Conceição professed his faith and was baptized in 1864. He was ordained at the first meeting of the Presbytery of Rio de Janeiro the following year. An active and effective evangelist, he laid the foundation for Evangelical communities in a number of interior towns, especially Brotas, where he had last served as a priest. This became an important center from which the message spread into a number of localities in São Paulo and southern Minas Gerais. Until his death in 1873, Conceição journeyed constantly, traveling great distances on foot, visiting all of his former parishes and other areas as well. Like a modern St. Francis he lived simply, often giving away money or gifts which he received, healing the sick with home remedies, and communicating the gospel through preaching, conversation, and life. At times he was accompanied by missionaries or ministerial candidates, whom he helped and inspired, and occasionally he sent his colleagues lists of converts. But during the last four years of his life, he was increasingly out of touch with the others. Often disappearing for months at a time, he followed his compulsion to preach, traveling over wide areas and suffering persecution and privation. He finally died of exhaustion as he went to Rio, where Blackford had secured a house for him in hopes that he would rest.

Conceição's early death and his isolation from the missionaries during the last four years of his life robbed the infant church not only of its most effective evangelist but of the possibility of a synthesis of Evangelical Christianity and Brazilian culture that would have gone far beyond anything the North Americans and the Brazilians whom they trained were able to construct. Probably because of his own spiritual pilgrimage, his piety and spirit were closer to that of Luther than to nineteenth-century orthodoxy. This fact is especially important in view of certain parallels between the Brazilian Catholicism of the period and that of fifteenth-century Europe.[5]

Four characteristics of the ex-priest qualified him to show the way in which Evangelical faith could be accepted without rejecting much that was good in the dominant, largely Roman Catholic culture. This in turn might have helped Brazilian Presbyterianism avoid the negativism which later developed. First, Conceição was free of the harsh attitude toward Catholicism which became characteristic of Latin American Protestantism as a whole. The irenic and positive tone of the letter of renunciation he sent to his bishop sharply contrasted with the tenor of most subsequent Protestant writing about the Roman church. He was renouncing the religion which had been the inspiration for the best acts of his life, he said, only because he felt it was impossible to maintain in the Church of Rome the liberty of conscience indispensable to the preaching and practice of the gospel. This step was necessary, he was convinced, if he were to live in harmony with Jesus Christ and His message.[6] Second, because of his own long struggle to discover a more Biblical faith, he showed an unusual degree of sensitivity and understanding toward those who held to the simple, often superstitious Catholicism of the masses. He wrote of the need for great care in indoctrinating uneducated people and of the danger in destroying certain beliefs which might be a substitute for the truth itself. "Oh my God," he wrote, "I will respect the religion of the ignorant, the faith of those who have had few opportunities of knowing and worshipping Thee in a worthy way. I will never allow myself to be dominated by vanity and presumption in such a way that I might shatter the pious faith of others by inconsiderate words and actions."[7] Third, his Christocentric piety was akin to that of some of the mystics who represented the best in medieval Catholicism. One of his hymns ends:

> If the Sovereign Monarch of the multitude of men,
> Discerns me, if He marks me in the palm of His hand;
> What importance is it to me, oh world, if you continually
>   misunderstand me!
> Thou, with Thy profound look, Thou, Jesus, Thou knowest
>   me.[8]

Finally, his was not a passive or quietistic faith. In his life and teaching one discovers ethical concerns which went beyond both the traditional religious "good works" of contemporary Catholic piety and the almost purely personal ethic of Protestant morality. Although the heart of his message was trust in what God has done for us, he was not content with a faith reduced to mere dogma and belief, much less to superstition and proper formulas. The purpose of Jesus' sermons and the Apostolic letters, he preached, was to lead men to do works pleasing to God.[9]

However, despite the genuine esteem and love which existed between Conceição and his missionary colleagues, the dialogue which might have prepared the way for such a synthesis apparently never took place. The reasons included the difficulties of cross-cultural communication, Conceição's compulsion to preach as widely as possible, which led to infrequent contacts with the missionaries, and the suspicion the North Americans showed at times toward aspects of Brazilian culture which did not fit into their own tradition, even though these were not necessarily non-Christian. Consequently, important elements in Conceição's piety were largely lost to a more formal and rationalistic Protestant orthodoxy.

The missionaries have been criticized for not capitalizing on the great evangelistic opportunities opened up by the ex-priest. Conceição himself gave no structure or direction to the newly formed Protestant communities, and in areas where no one followed up his preaching with the organization of congregations, his work left no visible results. Speaking of Brotas, Leonard says, "The Protestant movement, which for a time appeared ready to win the whole population, gave origin only to a minority community."[10] Founded in 1865 with eleven adults and sixteen children, the church soon had to fight for survival against a clerical attempt to interdict its meetings. Nevertheless, by 1874 it had grown to one hundred forty adult members and had been instrumental in starting churches in two other localities. The question as to what the missionaries' strategy should have been is a difficult one. During the first three years after Conceição's ordination the number of workers was so small that a missionary could have been sent to reside in Brotas only by removing Simonton from Rio or Blackford from São Paulo. Thus, it was not until 1868, when Lennington arrived, already fluent in Portuguese, that the town received a resident pastor. This was important to the church's development in the interior, but even more important in the long run would be the establishment of strong congregations in the growing cities.

Conceição's work would have brought more lasting results had he been willing to live in Brotas, consolidate the church there, and continue his travel on a less intensive basis. But his tempera-

ment, zeal, and compulsion to preach prevented his acceptance
of such a plan, and much of the potential fruit of his preaching
was lost. It is also quite possible that his reaction against the rigid
authoritarianism and bureaucracy of the Roman church led him
to reject any concern for organization and church structure. Even
so, the statistics for the first ten years of Brazilian Presbyterianism show his influence.[11]

Church	Date Founded	Founder	Membership, 1869
Rio de Janeiro	1862	Simonton	98
São Paulo	1865	Blackford	40
Brotas	1865	Conceição	116
Lorena	1868	"	6
Sorocaba	1869	"	5
Borda da Mata	1869	" (indirectly)	14

Early Theological Education

Simonton and Blackford immediately saw the need of preparing national pastors to form a truly Brazilian church. The latter proposed three of the first converts as candidates for the ministry, and arranged for them to travel with Conceição on various
occasions, both in order to help the ex-priest, and to feel the inspiration of his life and ministry. Miguel Gonçalves Torres and Antonio Trajano, both Portuguese, and Modesto P. de Carvalhosa
from Madeira began their theological studies in Rio in 1867.
Simonton, Carlos Wagner, pastor of the Lutheran church in the
city, and Schneider, the third missionary sent to Brazil by the
New York Board, were their professors. A year later Antonio P.
de Cerqueira Leite, a youth from Brotas, joined them.

For most of the year they followed a course of preparation and
theological study modeled on the North American pattern, and
during vacation periods they traveled as assistants to Conceição
or the missionaries. This represented an attempt to produce a
well-trained ministry, as emphasized by Calvinism, and at the
same time to satisfy the urgent needs of the new areas opened up
by Conceição. While it gave them surprisingly good academic
preparation, it removed the four able, if untrained, workers from
the ranks of active evangelists at a time when rapid expansion
might have taken place in several areas. It seems clear that a sim-
plified academic course, involving shorter periods of formal study

each year and leaving more time for in-service training, would have served the church better at that point in its life.

One must ask why the missionaries did not attempt to discover a pattern of ministry and preparation capable of meeting the urgent need for workers which at the same time could have laid a foundation for serious theological study in Brazil. Could the tradition of lay piety and leadership in Brazilian Catholicism, combined with brief intensive courses and some type of apprenticeship, have provided the basis for such a new pattern? The experiment would have had its dangers and difficulties, especially in view of the widespread illiteracy. But it would have greatly increased the number of men directly involved in evangelistic and pastoral work, augmented lay participation at all levels of the ministry of the church, and impressed Brazilian Presbyterians with the seriousness of the Reformation principle of the priesthood of all believers. It also might have kept pastors and their theology closer to the needs of their parishioners. Later the Baptists would accomplish this to some degree while also depending on traditional methods, but it was the Pentecostals who made it the foundation of their ministerial preparation. Perhaps as a consequence, they achieved a depth of penetration into the masses of Brazilian society unparalleled by that of any other contemporary religious group.

Recognition of the need for a broader pattern of ministry and theological education would never be more than peripheral in the Presbyterian Church of Brazil. The North American theological seminary, developed in the nineteenth century, provided the basic model for Presbyterian ministerial preparation in the country. Even though the original seminary closed in 1870 because of the death of Simonton and the withdrawal of Wagner, an emphasis had been placed on formal theological education which has continued throughout the history of that church. The North American theological seminary, developed in the nineteenth century, was to provide the basic model for Presbyterian ministerial preparation in Brazil although pastors who received other types of training would not be unknown. Once this pattern was established it was not seriously questioned by the church as a whole, even though disputes about location and control of the seminaries were destined to be central in at least two of the crises which it would face in the future.

The Beginning of the Work of the Presbyterian Church,
U.S., and the Formation of the Synod

Simonton came to Brazil under the auspices of the Board of
Foreign Missions of the undivided Old School church, and after
the schism in 1861 the Committee on Foreign Missions of the
newly formed Presbyterian Church in the United States sent its
own missionaries. Their coming was stimulated in part by the
colony of Confederate immigrants who, after the Civil War, had
settled near Campinas, in the Province of São Paulo. Edward
Lane and George Morton arrived there in 1869, established a
church, and two years later formed the first Presbytery of São
Paulo, the members of which were either missionaries or immigrants. Cordial relationships soon developed with the other Presbyterian missionaries. Morton and Lane emphasized education at
first, opening a school in 1870 which they hoped would be a "very
important auxiliary to our work of preaching the Gospel."[12] Although this attempt failed, the more permanent Colégio Internacional opened in 1873.

For over ten years the Colégio absorbed nearly all of their time
and resources, and it was not until 1881 that Lane began extensive evangelistic efforts around Campinas. At the same time their
colleague, John Boyle, began to look toward areas far in the interior where no Protestant minister had ever penetrated. In this
he typified many of his successors. Even though they frequently
moved west before the church was adequately established in the
growing cities, they showed great vision, courage, and perseverance in attempting to evangelize in every geographical corner of
the nation. In 1884 Boyle traveled through Minas Gerais into
Goiás and the area where Brasilia is now located. His report urged
the occupation of that region along with Cuiabá, Mato Grosso,
the banks of the São Francisco and Tocantins Rivers, and finally,
the Amazon Valley. It ended with an appeal to the Committee on
Foreign Missions: "The door to the preaching of the Gospel
stands wide open . . . and if it is not opened down the Tocantins
and the São Francisco, then with the help of God I will open it, or
die in the attempt."[13] But Boyle and Lane both met death in
1892, during a decade that took a heavy toll among the missionaries, many of whom were victims of yellow fever.

John R. Smith, who arrived in Recife in 1873, began the work in northern Brazil. He was joined in 1875 by William LeConte and in 1880 by B. F. Thompson, both of whom died within a year of their arrival. But with the coming of Delacy Wardlaw in 1880 and Dr. George Butler in 1883, the work began to expand. Within five years there were congregations in Recife and Goiana in Pernambuco, and farther north, in Paraíba, Fortaleza, and São Luiz.

Smith shared Simonton's concern for the preparation of Brazilian pastors, and by 1880 he was teaching four young men who worked as parttime colporteurs and evangelists. Three were ordained in 1887, and the descendants of one, Belmiro Cesar, would include at least ten pastors.

The Presbytery of São Paulo was dissolved in 1881 but reorganized six years later as the Presbytery of Campinas and West Minas, this time with one Brazilian pastor and three missionaries as members. The Presbytery of Pernambuco was formed in 1888, and that same year the two judicatories organized by the Southern Presbyterians joined with the Presbytery of Rio to establish the ecclesiastically independent Synod of Brazil. Even though the new body consisted of both Brazilians and North Americans, an anomalous situation arose when the latter continued their membership in separate missions subject to the North American boards. It was clear to the Southern Presbyterians, at least, that such an arrangement was temporary. The thrust toward geographical frontiers and the desire for mission structures totally separate from the national church expressed themselves in the instructions issued by the General Assembly which approved formation of the Synod: "It is further advised that our missionaries, as soon as the native presbyteries can be safely left, push forward as rapidly as possible into the destitute regions beyond, fulfilling the evangelists' office in them."[14]

The versions of the Westminster Confession of Faith and Catechisms currently in use in the mother churches were adopted as the symbols of the newly independent synod. But the changes made in the Confession by the Presbyterian Church in the USA in 1903 were not adopted in Brazil. This indicated not only the greater conservatism of the younger church but foreshadowed future differences in theology and ecumenical relationships between the two.

The twenty-nine years since Simonton's arrival had seen tragedy, the loss of promising workers, misunderstandings, and the lack of vision at times. All made it difficult to take advantage of every opportunity open to the church. But the achievement was impressive, especially considering the hardships and scarcity of workers. The synod was organized with 60 churches and 2,937 communicant members, scattered over twelve states and the Federal District.[15]

The Ethos and Structure of Early Brazilian Presbyterianism

The accomplishments of Simonton and the other pioneers in organizing the basic institutions of the Presbyterian Church in Brazil have already been mentioned briefly. Upon beginning their work they faced questions as to message, type of church structure to be established, proper pattern of and preparation for the ministry, the style of Christian life, and the relationship of the gospel to the culture and life of the country to which they had been called. It is not surprising that their ideal church was the kind they had known in the United States. The American foreign missionary movement of the nineteenth century paralleled similar efforts on the nation's western frontier, and the missionaries, foreign as well as national, attempted to reproduce the schools, colleges, seminaries, church structures, and patterns of ministry they had known previously. Denominationalism, the lack of interest in scientific theology, and concern for moral discipline and righteousness—all found on the American frontier—would characterize Brazilian Protestantism. A contemporary sociologist has pointed out that for the early missionaries:

> . . . eventual success would mean the formation of a congregational life with an associational and institutional life similar to that of a Presbyterian, Methodist, or Baptist congregation in the United States. The existence of these models in the mind of the early missionary may be inferred from their actual projections which indeed bear a remarkable resemblance to American congregations, not as they are now, but as they were half a century ago.[16]

But other factors, peculiar to its own environment, also helped to shape Brazilian Presbyterianism. For example, its defensive attitude toward the surrounding culture must be explained, not primarily by its relationship with the church in the United States but by its status as a tiny minority "sect" attempting to establish itself in a predominantly Roman Catholic ethos. While conversion and Christian experience were stressed in North American Presbyterianism, especially on the "pagan" frontier, they received even greater emphasis in Brazil. One entered a Protestant "sect," breaking with Roman Catholicism and risking persecution and ostracism, only because he was powerfully motivated, presumably by a personal experience of conversion. And the easily understood lines of ethical conduct drawn by the prohibition of certain amusements, smoking, and the use of alcoholic beverages, helped distinguish members of the newly formed congregations from the "world" around them. The nature of the other important Protestant groups in Brazil reinforced this tendency. Presbyterians competed, not with Anglicans and Lutherans, who were not aggressively missionary, but with Baptists, Methodists, and later, Pentecostals. Similar interaction between the message and institutions brought from abroad and the Brazilian mentality and culture shaped the church at other points.

Among the pioneer missionaries, Simonton left the most examples of his preaching. His message presented the grace of God, and in his journal he revealed a deep personal devotion to Christ. But at times, overwhelmed by the low standard of morality around him, especially in sexual conduct, he fell into an emphasis on moralism which foreshadowed much of the preaching of the church he established. In one sermon he told his listeners:

> Here is the narrowness of the gate. In order to enter therein it is necessary to abandon vices, bad thoughts, and impure desires. Before resting in the sacrifice and merits of Christ, it is necessary to feel and confess your guilt. . . . The proud cannot go to Jesus, first he must become humble. The hypocrite cannot enter the way which takes him to life without abandoning his hypocrisy. The man full of vices cannot enter while he continues to carry the burden of them. . . . The true religion is different from all others in severely reprehending evil and the vices of men . . . the Christian life is a continuous struggle against the concupiscence of the flesh, against excessive adherence to worldly things, and against the assaults of the enemy of souls.[17]

John R. Smith, the pioneer in the North, prepared the first pastors in the area and gave twenty-five years of service to theological education in the South. One of his favorite themes, according to reports, was sin and its consequences.[18]

While both Catholics and Protestants believed the main purpose of religion to be forgiveness and release from sin, they differed as to method. In Catholic thought forgiveness came through proper use of the sacraments and rites of the church, while the Protestant message stressed the unmerited nature of grace and the importance of religious experience. But Protestant emphasis on the necessity of a moral life could easily lead those who lived in a Roman Catholic culture to see grace and forgiveness not as the cause but rather as the result of the new life. The depth and richness of the type of piety seen in Conceição, who found the joy of the Christian life in communion with God and its fulfillment in service to others, was certainly present in the missionaries and Brazilian pastors, but too often it was obscured by the more moralistic message.

The implications for ethical thought and a Protestant style of life are also apparent. If the main purpose of religion was to bring not only forgiveness but new life and freedom from sin, and if sin were defined primarily in terms of "vices," it was logical that the main goal of ethical instruction was their abandonment. Vices were usually defined as smoking, drinking, extramarital sex, gambling, and participation in questionable amusements. Reinforcing the moralistic emphasis was an ascetic strain still operative among some practicing Catholics, even though it was not characteristic of Brazilian Catholicism as a whole. In interior cities it is still not unusual to encounter devout Catholics for whom strict religious practice implies nonparticipation in certain amusements and social events. This attitude must have strengthened the tendency toward an individualistic and moralistic ethic which the missionaries imported. Conversely, the same factors, allied with those which forced Brazilian Protestantism into a more sectarian mold, tended to divert attention from concern for a social ethic.

Church government was theoretically a reproduction of North American Presbyterianism, even in its terminology. (New words were coined as session and moderator became *sessão* and *moderador* in Portuguese.) But it was seriously affected by the missionaries' membership in both the Brazilian judicatories and the separate missions, and by financial dependence on the boards. This made it impossible for the church to follow the course advocated by a majority of its leaders on a number of issues. Most crucial was the question of ministerial preparation. Just as churches in the North American colonies, which were dominated ecclesiastically or culturally by European institutions in an earlier period, had seen the necessity of emancipation and independent theological education, so the young Brazilian church, before the end of the century, insisted on establishing its own institution for the preparation of pastors. However, the process was difficult. Even though theoretical emancipation occurred in 1888, the anomalous position of the missionaries made independence a fiction. This was the basic factor in the schism of 1903; it would also lead the church and the missions into the "Brazil Plan" of 1917.

Educational institutions were in operation from the beginning. A number of motives prompted their establishment. The primary reason was, of course, the hope of attracting students and their families to the Protestant message. Second, the church and school had worked closely in founding what was generally considered to be a Christian culture in North America. Ecclesiastical order and the concept of the Christian life in Presbyterianism both presupposed the existence of literate laymen and educated leadership. Third, education was seen, in good American fashion, as the indispensable basis of progress, and the missionaries hoped to contribute to the nation as well as the church with their schools. The appalling lack of educational facilities and low literacy rates must also have been powerful factors. Estimates of the rate of illiteracy during the period range upward from 85 per cent. In 1871, in a total population of over ten million, not even 150,000 attended primary schools in Brazil, and less than 10,000 received secondary instruction.[19] In addition, underlying the establishment of schools was the presupposition that better-educated people would be sufficiently enlightened to throw off Roman Catholic "superstition," read the Bible, and accept the Protestant message.

Institutions such as the Colégio Internacional, which opened in Campinas in 1873, and Mackenzie Institute, which evolved out of the Escola Americana, founded in São Paulo in 1870, received a warm welcome in liberal circles even though they were condemned by the clergy. As their names indicated they represented quite openly the introduction into Brazil of North American educational methods at a time when political and social institutions of the United States were admired as being the most progressive in the world. Consequently such schools soon attracted students from a number of prominent families.

The Protestant schools made impressive contributions to their students, to the areas around them, and to the pedagogy of Brazil. But usually their impact on the growth of the church was disappointing. Especially was this true of Mackenzie Institute. Those who studied in the mission schools were often attracted to North American liberal ideas and frequently became sympathetic to Protestantism, but relatively few became members of Evangelical churches.

Financial problems were greater than anticipated. Missionaries who sometimes assumed that local interest in an institution would be translated into financial aid were disappointed, and the failure of the schools to become self-supporting led to conflict. If they were to grow to a reasonable size and attempt to raise most of their funds through tuition, they would be forced to open their doors to increasing numbers of non-Protestants. The drive for educational excellence also led at times to the employment of non-Evangelical teachers, inviting criticism from pastors and missionaries. At the same time the schools took a disproportionate share of the sparse funds and personnel available to the missions, and evangelistic work suffered greatly. Consequently, the educational institutions, especially those on a secondary and college level, which had been established to aid the church in its work, became focal points of bitter controversy.

The social composition of the church at the end of the century is also worthy of note. Unlike some recently founded churches which counted only the most humble among their adherents, the Presbyterian Church of Brazil soon had a cross section of society reflected in its membership, including members of prominent families. One reason must have been the identification of Protestantism with progress in liberal thought. And in one well-known case, at least, Masonry proved to be a preparation for the gospel.

Leonard has shown that several members of old aristocratic families became Presbyterians in São Paulo and São Luiz, as did a number of *fazendeiros*, or landowners, in other areas.[20] In Araguari, Minas Gerais, Boyle baptized Tertuliano Goulart, the liberal publisher of a local newspaper. On another of his trips the only inhabitant of Cajurú, São Paulo, who would open his door to the missionary was Miguel Rizzo, a Mason and prominent citizen. The encounter led to his conversion. Both families would contribute important leadership to the Presbyterian Church.[21]

Men of unusual ability were attracted to the ministry at this time. Some who made important intellectual contributions to Brazilian life without neglecting the pastorate were Eduardo Carlos Pereira and Otoniel Mota, grammarians; Vicente Themudo Lessa, historian; and Jerônimo Gueiros and Erasmo Braga, educators.

It is clear that such a church, theoretically emancipated from the North American churches one year before Brazil became a republic, would increasingly insist on taking leadership into its own hands and would be quick to react against any attitude of cultural superiority, real or imagined, on the part of missionaries.

The Schism of 1903

The basic cause of the schism of 1903 was the young church's desire to determine its own direction at a time when historical circumstances made it difficult for missionaries and, even more, mission board executives in the United States to understand or sympathize with the need. It was the period of Manifest Destiny in the United States, and probably at no other time was American culture so easily and uncritically baptized as Christian. At the same time the Presbyterian Church of Brazil, organized into an independent synod in 1888, only one year before the nation was made a republic, was becoming increasingly nationalized. Only 40 per cent of the pastors of the newly formed church were Brazilian, while 60 per cent were North American. But the situation would soon be reversed. Several of the most able national leaders coming to the fore would show their deeply Brazilian nature by making contributions to the study of the language and history of their nation, and they were determined that their church should also be profoundly Brazilian.

The struggle centered around three basic issues, all related, and was complicated by a sharp personality clash and the question of Masonry. The first concerned the purpose and place of educational work in the overall missionary strategy and the types of institutions to be maintained. Should they be limited to the primary and secondary levels, or should the missions establish university faculties? Should they be open to all or only to Protestants? Naturally, the answers to these and other questions would depend on the purpose of the schools. If they were to be primarily instruments of evangelism or of implanting the "Christian" culture of North America[22] in order to contribute to Brazil's progress, they would be open to all. If, on the other hand, they were considered inefficient in evangelism but necessary to prepare church leadership, enrollment would be limited to Protestants. In the latter event, how were they to be financed?

The second issue was related to the first: who should direct and control the theological education of the future leaders of the church? It was natural that a church attempting to determine its own future would soon see the preparation of pastors as its most critical need. But it was precisely the measures necessary to meet this need which were frustrated by the missionaries and, especially the New York Board, after 1888.

This was possible because the missionaries were members not only of the Brazilian presbyteries but of the missions, separate organizations subordinate to the American boards. The latter wielded great economic power over the church, which, although emancipated ecclesiastically, was still financially dependent on them. While it was no doubt theologically proper that the North Americans should join the presbyteries, their reluctance to give up their special prerogatives as members of the missions was a third cause of tension. When the New York Board disregarded the wishes at times, not only of the Brazilian Church, but of its own missionaries, the problem became even worse.

A personality clash between Eduardo Carlos Pereira, the most nationalistic and able leader of the church, and Horace Lane, the President of Mackenzie, heightened the dilemma. Pereira, converted through the ministry of Chamberlain in 1881, soon showed interest in a more Brazilian approach to the propagation of the gospel. In 1884, he organized the Brazilian Society for Evangelical Tracts, a national body established to publish works written exclusively by Brazilian Evangelicals, but not limited to Presbyterians. Two years later he devised the Plan of National Missions, designed to make the Brazilian Church self-supporting as rapidly as possible by aiding pastors, teachers, lay evangelists, and seminarians without foreign contributions. In 1888 he was elected pastor of the São Paulo church.

The Escola Americana of São Paulo, and Mackenzie College,

into which it developed, soon became the focus of the educational question. Pereira and several other pastors had little confidence
either in its inclusivist policy of admissions, which they believed
diluted the Evangelical atmosphere, or in President Lane, a man
who had professed his faith only after coming to Brazil as a missionary. In 1892 the struggle led to a number of intemperate acts.
Pereira's session formally admonished Lane for infrequent attendance at worship, and subsequently, Remigio de Cerqueira Leite,
a member of that session, was dismissed from his teaching post at
Mackenzie. Finally, the rival Second Presbyterian Church of São
Paulo was organized by a number of missionaries.

Tension reached a critical point when the New York Board and
some of its personnel refused to cooperate with any project of
theological education not centered in Mackenzie. This attacked
the church at its most sensitive spot. To national leaders it seemed
the board insisted on entrusting the lifeblood of the church to the
care of an institution and, indirectly, to one man, who were
neither subordinate to the church nor trusted by it! While this
conflict continued, death removed a number of the older leaders,
robbing the church and missions of mature guidance and at the
same time making the question of pastoral preparation all the
more urgent.

For two decades after the closing of the original seminary in
1870, an apprenticeship plan had been used to train pastors. The
process of study and work involved often took from five to ten
years, and many candidates failed to arrive at ordination. Several
men, including Pereira and Álvaro Reis, pastor of First Church,
Rio, were prepared in this way, but the total number was far too
small. During the period several requests went to the boards asking for aid in establishing a seminary, but to no avail. John B.
Howell started a school in 1878 which trained several men, but he
was burdened with pastoral and evangelistic work as well. This
neglect of theological education meant lost opportunities for expansion and fired increasing determination by the most farsighted
leaders to fill the need themselves.

The question was discussed at the first meeting of Synod without positive result. The New York Board insisted on including
theological education as a department at Mackenzie and soon
sent Donald MacLaren to open it. As might have been expected,
the national leaders rejected the plan and, allied with mission-

aries of the Nashville Board, voted to open the seminary in Rio. But it was impossible to do so. In 1889 a request from Pereira and Trajano for $3,000 to help launch a one-year theological class in São Paulo, while arrangements were being made for a more permanent institution, pointed the way to an alternate pattern of ministerial preparation.

> The state of the work is such that it cannot wait five or six years. . . . We deem it, in view of the critical circumstances of our churches, to be urgently necessary to bring together immediately in São Paulo, from the various churches of the Presbytery, believers already proven to possess some qualifications for evangelistic work, and give them a year's course of exclusive Bible instruction; give them opportunities every week of directing meetings under direction, and thus put their studies to a practical test, and afterwards send them into the field as "provisional auxiliaries," to evangelize.[23]

The boards ignored the request.

After various failures the seminary finally opened in Nova Friburgo, a small town of difficult access, north of Rio. Classes for its three students began in November, 1892, with John R. Smith and J. M. Kyle as professors. That same year the missionaries of the New York Board submitted a plan by which they would withdraw from the Brazilian presbyteries and end their organic connection with the national church while continuing to work in educational institutions and in unevangelized areas. The proposal, which might have alleviated the tension, was refused by the Board.[24]

São Paulo, the most logical site for the seminary, had been avoided because of Mackenzie and the Lane-Pereira clash. But in December, 1892, Pereira, eight other pastors, and twenty-three elders and deacons, published their "Plan of Action." Expressing the church's long frustration over twenty-two years of waiting for an institution to prepare its pastors and seeing little future in the Nova Friburgo Seminary, they announced the establishment of a theological institute in São Paulo. They also began publication of the *Estandarte*, a purely Brazilian Evangelical paper, to replace the mission-sponsored *Imprensa Evangélica* and the now defunct *Evangelista*. An assertion of Brazilian over North American leadership in determining the crucial question of theological education, the move had as its central issue the freedom of the national church to establish its own seminary without being hampered by missionary rivalries or decisions made in the United States. Synod action in 1894 confirmed this. The Nova Friburgo Seminary was transferred to São Paulo and absorbed into the *Instituto teológico* with Pereira, Cerqueira Leite, and John R. Smith as its professors. "In attention to the interests of the Protestant College,"[25] the New York Board withdrew its cooperation and unsuccessfully pressured the Nashville Board to do the same. But the following year the seminary enrolled thirteen students and embarked on a financial campaign for the construction of its buildings.

The high-water mark of Pereira's influence came with the Smith Motion, voted by the 1897 Synod. It passed with nearly unanimous support by the Brazilians and the votes of five missionaries, only one of whom was under the New York Board. Six missionaries opposed the motion, which requested that whatever aid the mother churches wished to provide be used: "in the great work of evangelization by the most direct methods, including the work of education and preparation for the ministry in accordance with the plans of the Synod, and in sustaining parochial schools for the children of believers."[26] At the same meeting the Synod refused the request of William A. Waddell, who was linked to Mackenzie, for permission to withdraw from the Presbytery of São Paulo, now in the hands of the nationalists, and transfer to a North American judicatory.

The rift between Pereira and other important Brazilian leaders arose over his proposal in 1897 to enlarge the seminary's preparatory course by opening it to younger boys who were not necessarily preparing for the ministry, transforming it into an official secondary school. Pereira's hope was that the enlarged school would provide enough income to aid the theological institution. But it was interpreted as a direct attack on Mackenzie and rejected by a majority of the seminary's Board of Directors, including Kyle, one of the few missionaries under the New York Board who had previously supported Pereira. Although the plan was to limit enrollment to children from Protestant families, most felt it would have led inevitably to the admission of non-Protestants as

well, inviting the problem which had been criticized in Mackenzie. The defeat, which killed much of Pereira's interest in the
seminary, was the primary cause of his resignation from its faculty the following year.

The unfortunate introduction of Masonry into the controversy
in December, 1898, only served to further divide the nationals
and missionaries who were interested in forming a genuinely
Brazilian church, while it confused a clear-cut and basic issue
with one which was at best secondary. It was ironic that Masonry,
long the champion of nationalism and liberalism in Brazilian
political life, should now, in the Presbyterian Church, be seen as
an ally of those accused of hostility toward ecclesiastical nationalism. Heightening the irony was the Masonic defense of Protestants against clericalism and persecution and its fight for religious
freedom and separation of church and state. On both issues Masons were in accord with Brazilian Protestants, which explains why
so many national pastors were members and why they defended
their liberty to remain so. While Pereira, in accusing Masons of
subscribing to a deistic faith, had strong theological arguments
on his side, sentiment and loyalty to the Order because of its contribution to the Brazilian Republic worked against him.

After a series of articles by a prominent member of Pereira's
church appeared in the *Estandarte*, the question as to whether or
not a Christian could be a Mason was taken to the Presbytery of
São Paulo in 1899 and to the Synod of 1900. The latter recognized
the right of each believer to his own opinion but denounced
propaganda for or against membership in the Order as prejudicial
to the work of the gospel. The discussion did not end, however,
and Pereira's *Plataforma*, published in 1901, hastened the crisis.
The document's three demands indicated how Masonry had complicated the problem. It insisted on the withdrawal of missionaries from the presbyteries of the Brazilian Church, a declaration
of the incompatibility of Masonry and the gospel, and urged
adoption of a policy of "the education of the children of the
Church in the Church, by the Church, and for the Church."[27] It is
almost certain that had Masonry not become an issue, the nationalists would have won the first and third points without schism.
The missionaries had already tried several times to withdraw
from the presbyteries, and indications were that board secretaries
in the United States were beginning to see the necessity of such

action, given the situation which had developed.[28] If this had been done, the church could have determined its own educational policy, with or without mission aid.

However, when the Synod of 1903 opened its meeting, animosities were already so great that none of the problems could be discussed rationally. Personal feelings overshadowed issues, and the church split over the Masonry question. A motion refusing reconsideration of the 1900 decision passed with fifty-two in favor, while seven pastors and ten elders were opposed. The minority, led by Pereira, left both the meeting and the Synod to constitute the Independent Presbyterian Church, taking about one-third of Brazil's Presbyterians with them.

Founded on the basis of nationalism and anti-Masonry, the *Independente* Church would lose the first issue to the Presbyterian Church of Brazil with adoption of the Brazil Plan of 1917. Through the years it therefore concentrated on the latter as the primary reason for its separate existence. Despite Pereira's promising attempts to nationalize literature through the Tract Society, and his early campaign for new patterns of theological education and pastoral support, the nationalism of the new church was limited to ecclesiastical independence from the missions. Never did it involve theology or the relationship of the faith to Brazilian culture. Three decades later, when Eduardo Pereira de Magalhães, grandson of the Independente leader, made one of the first attempts by a Brazilian Evangelical to interpret the gospel in terms more meaningful to the newer generation, he was rejected by his church and finally left the ministry. Other Independentes had similar experiences.

The continuing Presbyterian Church carried on the struggle to establish a seminary and strengthen its organization, and, in 1906 and 1907, Synod prepared for formation of the General Assembly in 1910. The church had come through schism and would now begin its second half-century of life with forty-two Brazilian pastors, nearly ten thousand communicant members, ninety-one organized churches, three hundred preaching points, seven presbyteries, and two synods.[29]

Chapter Three

Organization and Expansion: 1910-1917

The Presbyterian Church of Brazil faced a herculean task as it began its second half-century in 1910. The largest Protestant church of missionary origin and orientation in the nation, it had only ten thousand communicant members scattered from Santa Catarina in the South, to Pará and Amazonas in the far North. With nearly twenty thousand other Evangelicals,[1] it faced the task of evangelizing a nation of over twenty million people, scattered over an area larger than the continental United States. Having come through controversy, schism, and bitter rivalry with the dissident group, it confronted the tasks of evangelistic expansion and the organization and consolidation of the institutions necessary to its life.

Most urgent was the need to strengthen the seminary and prepare pastors, in order to make up for the deficit in leadership caused by four decades of mission-church rivalries over theological education. Related to this was the quest for greater national unity, made difficult by the great distances involved, poor transportation, and strong regional differences. It was also essential to evangelize the larger cities, now beginning a period of rapid expansion, without neglecting the work in growing rural areas.

Organization of the General Assembly

In 1910 the original synod was divided, and the General Assembly of the Presbyterian Church of Brazil, comprising two synods and seven presbyteries, was organized. Working within the geographical and ecclesiastical bounds of the presbyteries were four North American missions: the South Brazil Mission (SBM) of the Presbyterian Church in the USA (PCUSA), with personnel in the states of Rio de Janeiro, São Paulo, Paraná, and Santa Catarina; the North Brazil Mission (NBM) of the Presbyterian Church in the US (PCUS), working in the immense North and Northeast; the East Brazil Mission (EBM), also of the PCUS, with workers in São Paulo and Minas Gerais; and the West Brazil Mission (WBM) of the same church, working in São Paulo and soon to move into Minas Gerais. The latter favored direct evangelism over the institutional emphasis of the EBM. A fifth group, the Central Brazil Mission (CBM) of the PCUSA, had separated from the SBM in 1897 and worked in Bahia and Sergipe. By 1910 it had already removed itself and its fields from the Presbytery of Bahia-Sergipe.

Looking to the past as well as the future, the General Assembly celebrated the 400th anniversary of the birth of John Calvin in a special worship service and paid a visit to the Island of Villegaignon where three of the first Calvinists to arrive in Brazil had been martyred. There they prayed together, "Lord God, give us Brazil for Christ," and added, "May all the Evangelical denominations cooperate in the most complete union toward this end."[2] The desire to cooperate with the church elsewhere, both as a receiving and sending body, was evident in other actions. A protest went to the Edinburgh Conference denouncing its exclusion of Latin America from consideration as a mission field, and the Moderator, Álvaro Reis, was sent to the United States to appeal to the boards for more missionaries. He went on to Edinburgh as an observer[3] and returned by way of Portugal.

The General Assembly organized several institutions to strengthen both its scope and internal life but soon discovered that it was considerably more difficult to maintain them than to vote them into existence. The size of the church, its relative poverty, the sporadic nature of voluntary giving in Roman Catholic Brazil, and regionalism complicated the problem, and most of the projects were slow to bear fruit. An orphanage was established in Lavras, Minas Gerais, but after a precarious existence it was closed in 1915 and reorganized four years later on an unofficial basis with the help of two wealthy laymen.[4] The church took a bold step in sending its first foreign missionary to Portugal. A committee named to publish a Presbyterian hymnal to replace the commonly used *Salmos e Hinos* of the Congregational churches never completed the project. At the same time the

Synod of the South agreed to cooperate in publication of *O Puritano*, a venture of First Church, Rio, in a plan to establish one official paper.

The Struggle to Consolidate the Seminary

Apparently well on its way to becoming firmly established in 1895, the seminary lost its strongest professor and several students during the crises of 1898 and 1903. Moving to Campinas in 1907 with John R. Smith and Erasmo Braga as professors, it again requested the cooperation of the New York Board. Despite the opposition of the CBM, led by Waddell,[5] the SBM now attempted to rectify past errors and voted unanimously to assign Dr. Thomas Porter to the institution. The Synod had requested his services in 1891 and 1894, but the board's opposition had blocked the assignment.[6] Even now, after the schism caused primarily by the board's attitude, Dr. Speer concurred with the mission's action only after several strong letters from the field. Porter complained that a leader of the church had told him:

> The policy of the Board toward the Church is incomprehensible. . . . For twenty years we have been asking. We cannot wait any longer. Why is it that the Board cannot give weight to our own judgment as to our own needs? The American name in the world stands for organization and foresight. Where is the foresight? Where is the wise preparation . . . in this strange reluctance to help us prepare a ministry?[7]

Finally, thirty-eight years after the original seminary in Rio had closed its doors, the New York Board allowed one of its missionaries to cooperate in the official Seminary of the Presbyterian Church of Brazil.

The seminary struggle also involved an attempt to unify the church around its most important institution. Several obstacles loomed. Poverty left the institution and its students in constant financial straits, and the lack of secondary educational facilities made it extremely difficult for young men to complete their preseminary preparation. A third barrier was the belief that indifference and even opposition to the seminary continued among some of the missionaries. Lennington wrote in 1912 that the church feared the mission was about to withdraw Porter. He added, "Where they got this notion I cannot see, unless some unwise remark has been made outside of mission meetings."[8] In 1914 the SBM voted to leave Porter in Campinas, putting those fears to rest.[9]

From the beginning the Brazilian church attempted to follow the Calvinistic tradition of piety combined with learning and to establish a high academic level in its theological education. Miguel Rizzo, Jr. wrote in 1915 that while piety was most important to a minister, intellectual discipline was equally so, because a pastor had to compete intellectually with the advocates of other doctrines.[10] The prescribed theological course took three years and included the full spectrum of subjects given in a North American seminary.[11] Prerequisites for admission were the same as those for a university, with provision being made for special students without the necessary qualifications. Naturally few young men were sufficiently prepared for the full course in a country where schools were so scarce that over 80 per cent of the population was illiterate. Because a majority of the ministerial candidates came from the impoverished interior where even fewer schools existed than in the cities, the candidate usually underwent years of pre-seminary study in an area far from home, and his support became a problem. The only places where future pastors could complete their secondary course, as a rule, were mission schools such as the Colégio Internacional, now located in Lavras, which prepared a number of men for seminary during the period. Mackenzie, on the other hand, because it provided little scholarship aid and was distrusted by the presbyteries, produced few candidates.

Despite problems, the seminary grew stronger. By 1915 it had a faculty of two Brazilians and two North Americans, while the student body fluctuated between ten and fifteen. It was not an unimpressive achievement for a young church struggling against a host of problems, and Brazilian Presbyterians could take pride in the evaluation made of the institution at the Panama Congress in 1916: "This is probably the best developed seminary in Latin America."[12] However, the special situation of the church in northern Brazil would hinder efforts to unify theological education in Campinas.

Regionalism and the Problems of the North

The common saying that there are two Brazils reflects a reality which has always created tensions and hindered unity in both the church and the nation. Distance, allied to the lack of adequate transportation and communication, isolated the North from the South, and problems which were great in the latter were staggering in the North. Extreme poverty, drought, illiteracy, and disease burgeoned in a society that was feudalistic, conservative, and, at times, fanatically against innovation. The Presbytery of Pernambuco pictured its situation in 1913:

> This presbytery occupies more than half the Brazilian territory, leaving less than half for the other seven. It includes almost all of the zone punished by drought . . . and includes also the vast basin of the Amazon. . . . The means of transportation are extremely scarce and expensive, the workers few. . . . The states of Piauhy, Maranhão, and Amazonas and the territory of Acre do not have any minister of our denomination and almost none of any other.[13]

Internal migration often robbed the northern churches of leaders and members who sought new opportunities in the South. During 1914 and 1915 the church in Belém, located in an area suffering economically because of the war and a drop in the rubber market, lost three elders and one deacon.[14] The following year, Natanael Cortez, the pastor in Ceará, wrote that three flowering interior congregations had been dispersed by drought.[15] Finally, in cities like Recife, Salvador, and São Luiz, a strange combination of pride in their intellectual and economic leadership of the past, coupled with a feeling of inferiority and frustration because of present poverty and decadence, led to extreme conservatism and suspicion toward outsiders from other parts of the nation.

Northern problems often affected the church's structure and program. The Presbytery of Bahia-Sergipe was not represented at the first General Assembly because of financial difficulties, while the delegates from Pernambuco arrived late. In order to have a quorum the assembly named John R. Smith, a member of the Presbytery of Pernambuco now teaching in Campinas, and two pastors recently transferred to the South who were still members of Bahia-Sergipe, to represent their respective judicatories.[16] The biennial meetings of the northern synod, which stretched from Rio to the Amazon, also constituted a financial burden for the poorer churches, and there were proposals that synods be abolished.[17] General Assembly refused, giving no reason except that they were an integral part of the Presbyterian system.[18] On a number of occasions the northern judicatory failed to meet for lack of a quorum.

The North also published its own newspaper, continuing to do so at intervals until 1958 when the *Norte Evangélico* and the *Puritano* combined to create the *Brasil Presbiteriano*. Delay in arrival and distribution of the paper from Rio was one reason for the separate publications. Another was the content of the *Puritano*. It reflected the concerns and life of the church in the South, while the *Norte Evangélico*, with news of its area, became an important element in uniting the poor and often persecuted Presbyterians scattered from Alagoas to Amazonas.

The most important manifestation of regionalism was the North's insistence on conducting its own theological education instead of supporting Campinas Seminary. There were a number of valid reasons. The trip of over two thousand kilometers from Recife to Campinas was expensive, and the few students who might undertake the venture could not be used in northern churches during vacations. The North, with greater poverty and fewer schools, had even greater difficulty than its counterpart in finding men prepared for the regular seminary course. If the required preparation were to be obtained in Recife or elsewhere it would involve another long, costly delay for a church which could scarcely support its pastors, let alone its seminarians. Even more crucial was the great difference in cultural and economic levels between the two areas, which made it doubtful that students who studied in Campinas would return north. If the church had succeeded in taking well-trained men from the South to the North, and from the coastal cities to the hinterland, it would have reversed a trend which was very strong in Brazilian society, but there is no evidence that this was possible. Even among pastors trained in the North there would be a large number who would exercise most of their ministry in the South, but almost none went in the opposite direction.

The Central Brazil Mission, working in Bahia and Sergipe, was more isolated from the church than any other mission during the period. Waddell's presence was a contributing factor. An able and strong-willed person, he had clashed with Brazilian leaders in São

Paulo until his transfer to Bahia in 1899. In 1903, still refusing to cooperate with the official seminary of the church, the mission granted funds for theological education in Bahia.[19] Waddell, who had been sent to Brazil to teach in the theological course in Mackenzie, never to be accepted by the national church in that capacity, was put in charge. The plan involved more than a system of apprenticeship, for in 1909 Waddell wrote to Speer that the school, located in the interior at Ponte Nova, had two middlers and one junior in theology with seven in the preparatory course. He added that this surpassed enrollment in Campinas.[20] When Waddell went to São Paulo in 1914 to become president of Mackenzie, the Bahia students were sent, not to Campinas, but to the school in Garanhuns.[21]

In 1891 the Presbytery of Pernambuco had requested that the Synod establish a seminary in the North but without success.[22] Consequently, when responsibility for his aged parents made it impossible for Jerônimo Gueiros to go south to study as planned, Butler initiated a theological class in Pernambuco. But the deeper motives were those already discussed. The only Brazilian pastors working in the North were those who had studied there under Smith. The first youth sent from the North to study in the South had never returned, while the second had died before returning.[23]

In 1899, classes started for Gueiros and one other student in Garanhuns, Pernambuco, with Martinho de Oliveira and, later, George Henderlite as the professors. Thus began both the Presbyterian Seminary of the North and the Colégio Quinze de Novembro, the two institutions which would prepare the great majority of Presbyterian pastors who served in the North.

Hardships were staggering, and when Oliveira died suddenly in 1903, Henderlite had to maintain the institution as well as his evangelistic work. But despite its precarious nature, the seminary educated a number of men who gave impressive service to the church.

The school in Garanhuns was called a "short-cut Bible school" by churchmen in the South and was accused of endangering the unity of the church.[24] In 1911 the Synod of the North, dominated by the Presbytery of Rio, declared the school "inconvenient" to the life of the church,[25] and in an obvious attempt to fuse the two institutions, the General Assembly of 1912 designated Henderlite as Smith's replacement on the Campinas faculty and named

Gueiros to its board of directors.[26] The northerners, who had already lost their pioneer missionary and theological educator to the South, denounced the plan. The proposed withdrawal of Henderlite, they objected, would make it impossible to train men in the North and seriously curtail the work.[27]

In an apparent compromise the following year, Pernambuco voted to dissolve its seminary but requested that the North Brazil Mission maintain a "theological school" in Recife which Henderlite would direct. The presbytery accepted five new candidates for the ministry at the meeting, including Cícero Siqueira and Natanael Cortez, and attempted a further compromise in voting to send two youths to Lavras to prepare for Campinas while the older men continued to study in the North. It also appealed for more workers, requesting the return of Mota Sobrinho, the missionary to Portugal, and urging Américo Menezes of Lavras to accept a call to Piauí.[28] But Lavras had no place for the two candidates, and the need for more workers went unmet. The Seminary of the North continued its precarious existence in Garanhuns until 1920, when it was transferred to Recife and reorganized.

Criticism of the northern seminary was only partially valid. Its academic level was low, but necessarily so. As one professor wrote, in the backward North candidates came from among the ignorant country folk and had to learn to speak their own language properly while they began to study the Bible. After that they learned polity and homiletics and, in some cases, Greek and Hebrew.[29] Despite such handicaps the area produced a number of outstanding leaders and evangelists. But the excessively narrow theological position of the northern seminary would create tension in the future. Not only its isolation, but also Henderlite's dispensationalism, reinforced the conservatism of the area.[30] Thus the seminary, which in itself was a product of geographical and cultural isolation from the main body of the church, reinforced the tendency toward regionalism.

It is clear, however, that the institution was a necessity. Without it the church in the North could have done little more than exist precariously in a few coastal cities, and many strong interior churches, which contributed a number of leaders to the church elsewhere, would never have been established. It is unfortunate that vision and resources were not sufficient to support it adequately.

Evangelistic Expansion

Rio de Janeiro

The center of power and influence in the life of the church during this period was Rio de Janeiro, the nation's capital and largest city. While the Independente movement had robbed São Paulo of its largest congregation and several outstanding pastors, in Rio there were almost no losses. The city was also blessed by the pastorate of Álvaro Reis, the most effective Evangelical preacher in Latin America during the first quarter of the century. The son of Roman Catholic parents who were converted to Protestantism, he completed his preparation for the ministry in 1888. When he was called to the historic Rio pulpit in 1897, Presbyterianism in the immediate area consisted of the central church with 400 communicant members, a weak daughter church in the suburb of Riachuelo, and an unorganized *congregação* in Niteroi.[31] Because of his personality as well as his position, Reis soon emerged as the major rival to Eduardo Carlos Pereira and, after 1903, the most prominent leader in the church. A charismatic personality, a powerful presence in the pulpit, a penchant for polemics, and friendship with José Carlos Rodrigues, liberal publisher of the *Jornal do Comérico*, soon made Reis well known. For years he carried on a constant debate in pulpit and press with Fr. Júlio Maria, and congregations of over 1500 people crowded the church to hear his replies to the Roman Catholic polemicist. Reis also founded the *Puritano*, which became the church's major paper, and under his staunchly orthodox preaching fourteen men were called to the Presbyterian ministry, including Guilherme Kerr, the future rector of Campinas Seminary, and Victor Coelho de Almeida, a former Catholic priest and seminary professor.

But it was as an evangelist that Reis excelled. He built his church into the largest Protestant congregation in Latin America and established new work at a number of points in the city. By 1917, twenty years after his arrival in Rio, he had received 1512 adults on profession of faith,[32] and First Church numbered over 1300 communicant members.[33] In addition, the Riachuelo Church was reorganized, and five other daughter churches and eight *congregações* came into being.[34]

Despite the impressive ministry of Reis and others, Rio de Janeiro, with a population nearing one million, counted only 5,000

Protestant believers of all denominations in 1913.[35] Opportunity
was great and growth was impressive, but there were still too few
workers and resources to meet the needs. In 1915 the Presbytery
of Rio asked the South Brazil Mission for the services of R. F.
Lennington, who had been born in Brazil and was fluent in Portuguese. He was to establish new congregations in rapidly growing urban areas in strategy emphasizing the importance of the
city. The mission declined because of insufficient personnel to
cover its vast fields in the interior, even though it did ask the
New York Board for additional workers.[36] But the Brazil Plan,
established in 1917, would make it impossible for the mission to
fill the request. Thus was lost an opportunity for the missionaries
to remain in closer contact with the Brazilian Church and to aid
in the evangelization of Brazil's largest city.

Eastern Minas Gerais and Espirito Santo

The area where Brazilian Presbyterianism was to have its
greatest growth included the eastern part of the state of Minas
Gerais and extended into Espirito Santo. A number of factors
coincided there to make Protestantism dominant in several communities. The first was the European background of a number of
the early settlers. Another was the newly opened frontier which
prospered as coffee was planted. This gave rise to a society composed of those who had forsaken the tightly knit family structure
and *compadre* relationships which were a strong force in maintaining traditional religious patterns in older areas. Smith shows
the region to be one of the most rapidly growing rural areas in
the nation from 1920 to 1940, with a population increase of over
90 per cent in the two decades.[37] In addition, most of the settlers
belonged to the rural middle class with neither minifundia nor
latifundia predominant. Willems notes that this group often
played a strategic role in the adoption and dissemination of Protestantism. Many not only accepted the new message but were instrumental in establishing preaching points and helping build
new churches.[38]

A fourth factor was the leadership supplied the church in the
area by a number of unusually energetic, able, and courageous
pastor-evangelists, including Matatias Gomes dos Santos, Aníbal
Nora, Samuel Barbosa, Cícero Siqueira, and Synval Moraes. Com-
plementing the outstanding pastoral leadership was a high level

of lay activity, made necessary by the large number of widely scattered congregations. The churches which grew up often provided the deepest experience of community life in a region where it was rare, and they pioneered in opening schools in several localities.

Protestantism moved into the area from Nova Friburgo, settled in 1820 by a group from Switzerland. Despite the agreement that immigrants be Roman Catholic, three hundred were Protestants. Five years later they were joined by a group of German Lutherans accompanied by a pastor.[39] In 1891 J. M. Kyle, a missionary of the New York Board, arrived and established a Presbyterian congregation with Lutheran cooperation and began to evangelize the countryside. Several Protestant families from the city had moved to the region of Manhuassu, Minas Gerais, in 1868 to plant coffee in the rich land now available. While the majority were religiously indifferent, a group of committed Protestants, led by Henrique Eller, son of the founder of Alto Jequitibá, sent out a call for a pastor. The first to answer was Solomão Ginsburg, a converted European Jew who was one of Brazil's greatest Baptist evangelists. Disagreeing with him over baptism, the group requested a visit from the Lutheran pastor in Nova Friburgo. When he failed to respond, they appealed to Kyle, who arrived in 1897 and was instrumental in sending Matatias Gomes dos Santos, just out of seminary, to reside there in 1902.

Alto Jequitibá, where the young pastor and his wife lived, had only eighteen primitive houses at the time, and the area was a haven for fugitives from the law. Persecution was strong but was diminished both by the good will the pastor inspired and by pressure from Masons in Rio through the efforts of Álvaro Reis. The work progressed rapidly, and the church, organized with 104 communicant members in 1902, became a center from which the message spread to other localities, including São José do Calçado, Espirito Santo. When Santos was called to the Salvador church in 1906, the fields of East Minas and Espirito Santo received visits from pastors residing in the state of Rio de Janeiro. This continued for three years, and by 1908 the Alto Jequitibá church had 525 communicants.[40]

The church in São José do Calçado was attacked and its building destroyed by a mob led by the local priest and deputy sheriff in 1909. But the same year Samuel Barbosa, a tireless and effective evangelist in the few years of life left to him, went there as pastor. Assuming leadership of the churches of Campos and Sana as well as Calçado in May, 1909, he added 632 people on profession of faith in less than four years, baptizing nearly the same number of children.[41] Traveling constantly by horse and on foot, under the tropical sun and rain, through forests and mountains, he preached and catechized, baptized and served communion, and counseled and disciplined believers in isolated farms and towns. On a typical journey Barbosa preached thirty-three times in forty-four days, holding worship and evangelistic services in homes, on farms, out of doors, and even in a Spiritist temple, as well as in church buildings. On his last trip he traveled 320 miles on horseback. Arriving home ill with typhoid, he died in February, 1913, at the age of thirty-two, lamenting the fact that he had done so little for the gospel.[42]

Aníbal Nora, pastor of the Alto Jequitibá field from 1908 to 1927, laid the foundation for two future synods. His pastoral reports show that during his first years in the area approximately half of those whom he baptized had German-Swiss names such as Gripp, Storck, Herringer, Sathler, and Emerich. Several members of the latter two families became pastors. At the same time many of Portuguese and mixed descent entered the church, and names such as Oliveira, Veiga, and Souza appeared frequently.[43]

By 1912 his field included five organized churches and thirty-four unorganized ones in an area measuring 140 miles in diameter. His pastoral report for that year described the field:

> The church of Inhapim . . . is twenty-five leagues from our residence. This church, which requires more than a month for a satisfactory visit, has various preaching points: Jango, Serra, Pedras, Onça, Bradão, Bicários, Bom Jesus, and Entre Folhas, with the next to last *congregação* eight leagues from the church and the last, five. Not counting the others of less importance we have eight preaching points here with calls to five other places.
>
> The Manhuassu church is five leagues from Jequitibá, and its *congregações* are Manhuassu, Manhuassuzinho, Barra, São Pedro, Santa Helena, and Sacramento, the latter five leagues, and the next to last, seven, from Manhuassu. Besides these six preaching points we have other places more or less distant which offer us good opportunities.

The Santa Margarida Church is six leagues from the center and includes the central church together with José Barbosa, Matipó, and Garimpo, four and five leagues away. The São Sebastião da Barra Church, five leagues from Jequitibá, has as its points, São Sebastião, Braço do Rio, and São João, two and a half leagues from the central church.

The Alto Jequitibá Church has the following *congregações*: Caparaó, two and a half leagues; Jacutinga, one; José Pedro, three; Pouso Alegre, four; Lessa, two and a half; Ouro, one; Santana, seven; Paulinos, nine; São Domingos, ten; Mantimento, twelve; Angelim, thirteen; Batista Freire, fifteen; Laginha do Mutum, twenty-five; and Divino, seven leagues from Alto Jequitibá.[44]

Nora concluded with the laconic observation that neither work nor opportunity was lacking. On a typical two-week trip he traveled 240 miles, preached fourteen times, received seventeen people on profession of faith, and baptized eighteen children.[45] During his first five years in the field he received 551 adults on profession of faith and the five churches under his care grew to include 1190 communicant members.[46]

In 1912 a cattle buyer, Eusebio Cabral, came from Espirito Santo to live in the new village of Figueira do Rio Doce, on the bank of the Doce River, north of Nora's field. Convinced of the truth of the Protestant message, Cabral began to evangelize his neighbors and distribute Bibles. On Nora's first visit there in 1914 he baptized Cabral and thirty-one other adults. The following year newly ordained Octavio de Souza was sent, and in 1917 a church was organized in the growing town,[47] which would later be called Governador Valadares. This marked the beginning of Protestant work in the Valley of the Rio Doce, the area where Brazilian Presbyterianism has grown most rapidly.

São Paulo

The controversy at the end of the century, the concentration of the resources of the New York Board in Mackenzie, and the Independente movement had made a shambles of the Presbyterian Church in the city and state of São Paulo. This occurred just when the area was beginning to see the rapid growth which would make it the most important in the nation. The population of the city grew from 239,820 in 1900 to 579,033 in 1920.[48] But nearly half a century after Blackford had established work there, it counted only three struggling Presbyterian communities, in addition to the historic First Church, which had followed its pastor into schism. These were the Unida Church, formed in 1900 by the anti-Pereira faction, the Italian or Brás Church, and the Pinheiros *congregação*. The three, with the aged Modesto Carvalhosa as pastor, had a total of less than 150 communicant members. To make matters worse, the Italian Church was soon dissolved, victim of the Pentecostal movement which arrived in 1910 with Louis Francescon, a former Presbyterian who made some of its leaders the nucleus of the Congregação Cristã do Brasil.[49]

A strong evangelistic thrust was desperately needed in the growing metropolis. But efforts to place more workers there met little success. This area had suffered from the schism more than any other. Many interior churches were split, with small Presbyterian and Independente groups alongside each other, each clamoring for care from pastors whose ranks had been thinned by the division. And the North American missions gave almost no aid.

In 1913 Matatias Gomes dos Santos, the pioneer of Alto Jequitibá, came to the Unida Church to replace Carvalhosa and began to rebuild Presbyterianism in the city. He found the evangelical cause there nearly paralyzed, growing very slowly, and losing ground in comparison with the progress made by the city. But a few encouraging signs began to appear. Porter aided the Pinheiros Church on weekends, and in 1913 it began to construct the first church building put up by Presbyterians in the city since the 1870's.[50] The Brás Church was reorganized in 1914, with André Jensen becoming its pastor the following year. Unida, still using a dark warehouse for its services, soon began to expand and build under Santos' leadership.

But three factors prevented the North American missions and boards from aiding evangelistic work in the city, even when they were repeatedly asked to do so. First, the controversies of the past had caused mutual suspicion and widened the rift between the missionaries and the national church, especially in São Paulo; second, the New York Board continued its strategy of pouring a disproportionate amount of its resources into Mackenzie; and finally, the movement toward the geographical frontier which was to be formalized in the Brazil Plan of 1917 dominated the thinking of the missions.

In 1910 the presbytery requested a man from each board for direct evangelistic work in the city. While the West Brazil Mission responded that it could not send anyone,[51] the SBM sent C. A. Carriel but assigned him to the chaplaincy of Mackenzie and recommended that he remain outside the judicatory of the national church.[52] His work with the presbytery was limited to the new congregation in Lapa, which was dissolved in 1914.[53] Presbytery's request in 1915 was no more successful. The SBM sent a capable young pastor to open work in the far-western state of Mato Grosso but regretted that lack of personnel made it impossible to cede anyone to São Paulo.[54] The overriding concern for the western frontier was apparent the following year in a resolution to consult the General Assembly "as to whether or not the interests of the Gospel in Brazil would not be served best by adequately manning its work in the outlying and frontier territory before concentrating on the large cities."[55] The same year the mission, having again refused the request from São Paulo, made plans to send a man to the tiny isolated city of São Luiz de Cáceres, not far from the Bolivian border.[56]

The Mission in Portugal

The General Assembly of 1910, answering a petition signed by 132 people in Lisbon, launched its first foreign missionary venture. Presbyterianism in Portugal dated from 1866, when Robert Stewart, a Scot, began work there, but it had suffered from discontinuity and lack of leadership. The country's new political atmosphere (it had become a republic in 1910) and the promise of changes which would bring religious freedom and fresh opportunities for Protestantism gave impetus to the renewed effort. The Brazilian church also felt a strong sentimental tie to the mother country. A number of its early pastors had been Portuguese, and Álvaro Reis and Erasmo Braga, who proposed establishment of the mission, were both sons of Portuguese immigrants.[57]

Volunteering for the task, much to the regret of his church and presbytery, was João Marques da Mota Sobrinho, the capable young pastor of the city and state of Paraíba. Upon arriving in Lisbon in 1911, he found a church with only eighty-nine members and no building, its work seriously limited by lack of funds.[58] Within four years, membership had grown to over one hundred, attendance had doubled, and two new congregations and a school had been established.[59]

Lack of support from Brazil brought this phase of the mission to an end. In 1921 Mota found it necessary to return his family to Brazil because he could not support them,[60] and two years later he joined them. The mission, abandoned by the General Assembly, would be reorganized as a voluntary society by Erasmo Braga in 1924.

The North and West

The needs in the North were so overwhelming and the workers so few that the missionaries in the area, even more than elsewhere, were torn between evangelizing and alleviating social problems. George Butler, a physician and pastor, combined evangelism with the only effective medical service in a large area of interior Pernambuco and established a strong church, a hospital, and a school in Canhotinho. He gained the respect and love of the residents despite initial persecution and an attempt on his life instigated by a priest.[61] Henderlite concentrated most of his efforts in the theological school in Garanhuns, while W. M. Thompson worked with literature and the Colégio Quinze de Novembro. Since the other five members of the North Brazil Mission worked in schools, presbytery wrote to Nashville in 1913 with a request for two more ordained missionaries. It had 2200 members scattered through nine states, with only seven pastors to serve them. But no one could be sent, and the mission continued to work almost entirely with its institutions.[62] Consequently, many congregations with promising beginnings were closed for lack of pastoral care.

The Central Brazil Mission, operating in Bahia and Sergipe, soon moved into the interior. Rural people seemed more open to the Protestant message and the church usually grew more rapidly there. In addition, most missionaries assumed that once the church had been established in the coastal cities, they should move on to the hinterland, even though the congregations they left behind were still small and struggling for survival.

But Bahia presented a special problem for missionary strategy —one apparently not perceived early in the century when patterns which would determine much of the future were established. Unlike growing Paraná and Santa Catarina, where the SBM worked, and the Minas Triangle and Goiás, into which the WBM was moving, Bahia and Sergipe were losing ground in comparison with the rest of the nation. While the population of Brazil as a whole rose 2.2 per cent annually from 1890 to 1940, that of Bahia and Sergipe grew at a rate of 1.4 and 1.1 per cent respectively. Thus, while the region had 15.57 per cent of Brazil's population in 1890, its share had dropped to 10.79 in 1940,[63] with the greatest demographic density in the coastal areas which the mission had left to the undermanned national church.

The missionaries often had reason to be optimistic about the work in the interior. Waddell had received seventy-six people on profession of faith in 1907. Two years later, he wrote that his interior field would produce a completely new parish, approaching self-support, every twenty-four months, while others should do the same.[64] In 1910 the Presbytery of Bahia-Sergipe ended the year with 1389 communicant members, having received 184 on profession of faith that year.[65] But because of the constant exodus from the area the number of strong churches established scarcely reflected the size of missionary effort. Those who became Protestants were often more prone to seek better opportunities elsewhere than were those who followed traditional religious beliefs. Apparently there were two reasons for the phenomenon. Those who were already seeking new ideas and directions in life were often more willing to listen to the missionaries in the first place. And once the message was accepted it often helped to create a new mentality, dissatisfied with the traditional life style and more concerned with education and new opportunities. Both stimulated the migration of church members to cities on the coast and in the South.

The call of the interior, so strong in Boyle and other pioneers, found its most fervent exponent in Waddell among missionaries of the New York Board. He was one of the most capable and certainly the most forceful missionary in Brazil during the period, and his voice captured attention in New York. It was his orientation toward the West which led the CBM to open work in Goiás and Mato Grosso even though it was failing to man the coastal cities. In 1913 the mission sent F. F. Graham on an epoch-making trip across the heart of the nation, from Bahia to the Bolivian border. The resolution clearly indicates the strategy:

> Resolved: That Mr. Graham make a tour in Goyaz and Matto Grosso in '13–'14, starting as soon as possible;
> That his special duty be to choose sites for stations for the general evangelization of that part of Goyaz that belongs to us, and Matto Grosso;
> That at least one of these sites be for a school on the Ponte Nova basis with physician and evangelist resident.[66]

It took Graham and his companion, ministerial candidate Antonio dos Santos (who received twenty-two Greek lessons during the trip) from March 5 to October 14 to travel from Caetité, Bahia, to Cuiabá, Mato Grosso. On the way they passed through the future Federal District, where, in 1922, Graham would establish the first Protestant work.

Remaining in Cuiabá a year, Graham baptized eight adults and five children, organizing a congregation which he related to the Presbytery of Bahia-Sergipe, 2000 kilometers away. The following year, Philip Landes, the son of missionaries, arrived in the city. He soon became well-known as a polemicist, evangelist, and teacher. Anti-clerical sentiment was strong, and when the Franciscans began to attack Protestantism in their weekly paper, A Cruz, Landes was able to reply in the liberal press. He also accepted the chair of English in the local ginásio and made many friends in educational circles. The polemics, which included addresses in the main square and a running debate with the Bishop, who was appointed governor that year, attracted too much attention and were finally discontinued by the Catholic clergy. In the process, the young pastor gained public sympathy, the church grew in the city, and congregations were established in other towns.

But as the pioneers Graham and Landes pushed into the sparsely populated interior, their missions apparently never questioned the strategy which led them to do so at a time when the burgeoning coastal cities were left tragically undermanned. While requests for workers for Rio and São Paulo were refused, Landes was sent to a state which, although over twice as large as Texas, had only 0.68 per cent of the nation's population in 1900.[67] (Even in 1960 it still had less than one inhabitant per square kilometer, and its total population was only one fourth that of the city of São Paulo.)[68] The demographic density of the area of Goiás to which Graham would be sent was no greater.

The reluctance of the missions to cooperate with the national church in theological education and evangelization of the large cities, combined with the movement toward the West, would soon widen the chasm between missionaries and nationals, leading to a radical change in the structure of Brazilian Presbyterianism and to the creation of new problems in the future.

Chapter Four

Relationships with Other Churches: 1910-1917

Brazilian Presbyterianism, like any other institution attempting to define itself, had to do so in relationship to, or reaction against, other groups which shared its purpose. From the beginning some were considered antagonistic while others were looked upon as competitors or collaborators in a common task, but from 1910 to 1917 a number of events forced the church to reevaluate carefully its relationship with other ecclesiastical bodies. The Book of Order, which stated that Presbyterian government was Biblical and necessary for the perfecting of the Body of Christ but not essential to its existence, opened the door to ecumenical relationships. It concluded, "All those denominations which maintain the Word and the Sacraments in their fundamental integrity should be recognized as true branches of the Church of Jesus Christ."[1]

Following this principle the Presbyterian Church of Brazil initiated a movement toward closer cooperation with other Protestant groups and attempted, unsuccessfully, to unite with Methodists and Independentes. It was challenged to reexamine its attitude toward Roman Catholicism, while the entrance of Pentecostalism into the country constituted a new factor which might have led Presbyterians to reflect on their inherited pattern of the ministry. But, although they were the most ecumenical among Brazilian Protestants at the time, their concept of the faith would not allow them to accept the Roman Church or the Pentecostal groups as sister institutions. During the same period church-mission relationships underwent complete restructuring, and through the Panama Congress Brazilian Presbyterians became more aware of the Evangelical movement throughout Latin America and received a strong impulse toward cooperation and unity in the following decade.

The Attitude Toward the Roman Catholic Church

José Manoel da Conceição could say that the Roman Catholic religion had been the inspiration for the best acts of his life. Thus he maintained an irenic attitude even while leaving it to preach a more Biblical message. Most Brazilian Protestants, however, could not make the same affirmation. The traditional church had not inspired the best in their lives. Rather it had given them a little known and infrequently practiced religion and a mixture of superstition almost devoid of Biblical truth. When they did encounter the living Christ in a Protestant congregation and begin a new life, the dominant church condemned and, at times, persecuted them. In common with most Brazilians, Protestants criticized the immorality, avarice, and indifference of many members of the clergy. But more important, because of its condemnation of their own activities, Evangelicals believed the Roman church to be the greatest obstacle to the propagation of the gospel and thus to be apostate.

North American missionaries contributed to development of this attitude since they brought with them the anti-Catholicism typical of their home churches. Because most Presbyterian missionaries in Brazil were from the more conservative and evangelical wing of the sending churches and came from the rural areas of the Midwest or South of the United States, they probably represented a stronger anti-Roman attitude than did the mother churches as a whole. But for reasons inherent in the Brazilian situation, the attitude of their national colleagues was almost always more anti-Catholic than that of North Americans.[2]

The antagonism toward Catholicism by Brazilian Protestants is not surprising. It was the reciprocation of a similar and usually prior attitude by the Catholic clergy. Despite the liberalism of a few priests the church as a whole condemned Protestant work and, at times, reacted with violence. In comparing the persecution of Brazilian Protestants with that in sixteenth-century Europe Leonard doubted that the hierarchy had instituted any pre-established plan of harassment.[3] Nevertheless, persecution, often instigated by priests, was common and included name calling, accusations that conversions were bought,[4] social and economic pressure, ostracism, destruction of buildings, stonings, beatings, and even assassination. While such action could not exterminate the Evangelical communities and in some cases even stimulated their growth by arousing interest and sympathy,[5] the victims were convinced that had it not been for the liberties guaranteed by the Constitution, their situation, especially in the interior, would have been precarious indeed.

Among the few cases of assassination of Brazilian Presbyterians the best known was that of Manoel Vilela, the companion of Dr. Butler, who in 1897 saved the missionary's life by taking the knife thrust intended for him. At the trial the murderer was defended by the local priest, who called him an "angel sent by God."[6] Protestantism was frequently called the religion of the devil, and the faithful were forbidden to read "Protestant" Bibles, even though no other version was accessible to them. At times, mobs led by priests drove out Protestant congregations, sacked their churches, and threatened to kill them.[7] Public polemics and holy missions against "heresy" were also common and usually brought a response in kind. When such a mission in Natal received the support of the Governor, Jerônimo Gueiros responded from his pulpit to a full house.[8] Polemics such as those between Álvaro Reis and Júlio Maria were frequent.

In most cases authorities protected the constitutional rights of Protestants. But there were enough exceptions during the first three decades after 1889 to create fear that if Catholicism ever became the official religion again, it would be difficult for Protestantism to survive. After a mob in São José do Calçado, instigated by the priest and led by a police chief, sacked and burned the local Presbyterian church, state authorities refused to act, perhaps, as O Puritano charged, because the campaign of persecution was in reality directed by the Bishop, who was a brother of the Governor.[9] From 1912 to 1916, in Lage do Canhoto, Alagoas, a foreign priest made it impossible for Presbyterians to hold services. Their building was stripped, armed mobs were told to kill the visiting pastor, and on one occasion seminarian Cícero Siqueira had to flee from hired killers. In several instances the local police, despite orders from the state government, left at convenient times to avoid involvement.[10]

A more basic reason for criticism of the dominant church lay in the religious experience of the first generation of Protestant church members. Most of them had grown up as nominal Catholics, sharing the usual reverence for the church and its teachings, combined with indifference or hostility toward the clergy. Rarely had they come to a personal experience of the grace of God in Christ or received religious instruction that might orient their lives. As a contemporary priest working in Latin America has observed, the masses had accepted the Christian faith as a cultural heritage but had not been "exposed to the good news of salvation by a personal Savior as a first hand experience."[11] When this life-changing event came through the preaching and example of the Protestant congregations which were springing up and, at the same time, were denounced as heretical by the priests, it became inevitable that Protestants should condemn Catholicism as apostate.

The theological position of the Roman church and its lack of moral leadership also met severe criticism. Not even Catholic observers could discover much Biblical content in the life and message of popular religion during the period. The *Puritano* complained that while Roman Catholic leaders said Brazil was a social and moral ruin, they combated Protestant efforts, whether evangelistic or social, because, they said, the nation was Catholic.[12] Others noted that priests left the most notorious sinners undisturbed; yet anyone who repented of his sins and confessed Christ in an Evangelical church was condemned.[13] Worst of all, Catholic doctrines and ceremonies appeared to Protestants to hide and distort, rather than proclaim, the gospel. They considered the Mass a "pagan falsification"[14] of the Christian Eucharist, accused the Pope of attempting to usurp the place of Jesus Christ, thus becoming the anti-Christ,[15] and charged that Romanism had banished the gospel from its message.[16] Brazilian Protestants, with their emphasis on proclamation of the word of salvation, the Bible as the rule of faith, and high personal moral standards, found the dominant religion, with its liturgy in Latin, popular devotion centered in the Virgin and saints, discouragement of Bible reading, and apparent indifference to ethics, hopelessly corrupt. Replying to Speer about the proper attitude toward Roman Catholicism in Brazil, Reis wrote that because it was a child of the devil, a champion of Christ must fight against it with the two-edged sword of the Spirit.[17]

Nationalism and political loyalty also contributed to hostility. The actions of many priests, often foreigners who were unsympathetic to the constitutional provision for separation of church and state, civil marriage, desacralization of cemeteries, and secular education, infuriated both Protestants and liberals. Commenting on the case in Lage do Canhoto, the *Norte Evangélico* emphasized the fact that it was a foreign priest who showed his contempt for Brazilian laws by attempting to "spill the blood of our countrymen."[18] In a number of cases priests defied the law by refusing to allow Protestants to be buried in local cemeteries,[19] while bishops denounced "those illicit unions, cloaked with the name of civil marriage."[20] Although Protestant churches were careful to perform religious ceremonies only for couples already legally married by civil authorities, priests failed to make that requirement. At times they were accused of performing the sacrament of matrimony for couples even when one was legally married to someone else.[21] This attitude appeared to be a dangerous attack both on the Constitution and the spirit which had produced it. A newspaper in Curitiba, oriented by the clergy, even defended the Inquisition, insisting that it was "absolutely necessary for the Church, founded by Jesus Christ, to have the power to destroy those who opposed themselves to its progress."[22] Protestants had good reason to fear any resurgence of clericalism.

The actions of the Roman church on the international scene, especially its failure to condemn the invasion of Belgium during World War I, confirmed the widespread suspicion that its primary motivation was institutional self-interest. In a conversation with Pascoal Pita an Italian priest defended the papal attitude because, he said, if Germany were victorious, she would restore temporal power to the papacy.[23] To those who believed in republican ideals and considered them essential for progress, this attitude on the part of an institution which claimed to be the spiritual and moral mentor of the people was inexcusable.

It has already been noted that the Synod of 1888 adopted the version of the Westminster Confession used by the Presbyterian Church in the USA at the time, with no subsequent modifications being made. Thus, added to other factors which led Brazilian Presbyterians to consider the Roman church apostate was Chapter XXV, Article VI, of the Confession, which called the Pope "that anti-Christ, that man of sin and son of perdition, who exalts himself in the Church against Christ and against all that is called God."[24] While this passage was not a primary cause of Presbyterian condemnation of Catholicism, it reinforced and confirmed the attitude already held and made any change in outlook more difficult. The seventeenth-century position of the Confession fit much better into the historical context of twentieth-century Brazil than that of contemporary Europe or North America.

Protestant fears of Catholicism intensified in the second decade of the century with the growing strength and influence of the Catholic Church. The movement of Catholic renewal which had begun with D. Vital in the 1870's and become introverted after establishment of the Republic, again became stronger as more priests, with better preparation, came from Europe. At the same time the two greatest secular opponents of clericalism, positivism and liberalism, went into decline. Political influence of the clergy was growing, and several priests served as congressmen or governors. Bishops were again becoming indispensable at public functions, and there was even talk of a Roman Catholic political party. A eucharistic congress was convened in São Paulo in 1915, and construction began on the city's cathedral. The nationality of the new Bishop of Florianopolis, who was Portuguese, in contrast to his German predecessor, indicated that the Catholic Church was adopting wiser strategy.[25]

The Controversy Over Roman Catholic Baptism

An opportunity for Presbyterians to reexamine their attitude toward the dominant church arose in 1915 when the young pastor, Solomão Ferraz, decided he could not conscientiously rebaptize converts who had already received Roman Catholic baptism. The issue had been decided previously by Presbyterians in Brazil and the United States, but their positions had already begun to diverge.

The Old School General Assembly of 1845 had voted almost unanimously to oppose the position of the Reformers and reject the validity of Roman baptism, with Charles Hodge against the measure and J. H. Thornwell strongly in favor.[26] The PCUSA then partially reversed the decision in 1875 when the Assembly voted to leave the matter to the discretion of each local session.[27]

Simonton had rebaptized his first convert from Catholicism but wrote that if others did not desire it, he and his colleagues would "refrain from disturbing their consciences." Most Presbyterians followed the example of Robert Kalley, who had arrived in 1885 to establish Brazil's Congregational churches, in his insistence on rebaptism.[28] The question apparently did not arise formally in any Brazilian judicatory until the Synod of 1891, when a committee composed of J. R. Smith of the PCUS, D. G. MacLaren, G. A. Landes, and J. M. Kyle of the PCUSA, and one Brazilian, elder F. Rodrigues, who was under appointment as a missionary of the PCUS, gave its report. The exact content is unknown but may be surmised from Synod's response: "Upon a motion, however, the report was not accepted and this synod resolved to pronounce itself clearly against the validity of said baptism. Permission was given to Mr. Kyle to register his protest."[29] This was only the first of several occasions on which Brazilian leaders expressed disapproval, believing that some missionaries and the churches they represented, especially the PCUSA, were not sufficiently rigorous in their anti-Catholicism.

Solomão Ferraz, a second-generation Protestant, conceived of Presbyterianism in broader terms than most of his colleagues. In contrast with sectarian, intolerant Roman Catholicism, he said, Presbyterianism represented the liberal historical Catholicism of Paul, Augustine, and à Kempis.[30] But even though the Roman church was guilty of gross error, it was still part of the Body of Christ and its adherents were brethren, he added. Thus the justification for Protestant activity in Brazil lay not in the apostate nature of Catholicism but in the spiritual needs of the people, and the task of Evangelicals was not to attack Rome but to manifest more clearly the words and spirit of Christ. He pleaded with his brethren to remember their own faults and be humble in criticizing the dominant church, warning that the attitude of unconditional opposition to Rome prejudiced their own ministry. Finally, he wrote:

> . . . to curse the Roman clergy because of their faults is a task which requires neither great souls nor elevated principles. . . . Those who cry most passionately against tyrants, if they are not proceeding according to the same norms already, are usually prepared to do so upon the first opportunity. . . . The maximum heresy . . . is that of the heart and the character, the lack of magnanimous love.[31]

In keeping with his theological principles, Ferraz rejected the implicit Donatism of his church and began to receive converts from Catholicism into full communion without rebaptism. His presbytery soon prohibited the practice and affirmed its adherence to the 1891 decision, arguing that:

> . . . even though the Roman Church has the name of Christian, baptism is a sacrament and can only be administered by a minister of God, and the priest is not a minister of God because he claims for himself the right of Christ Himself, usurping His priesthood which is eternal. Heb. 8:24.[32]

Ferraz agreed to obey the ruling until the General Assembly could act on presbytery's overture: "What attitude should the presbytery assume when one of its members, conscientiously, for reasons which appear just to him, does not consider himself to have the right to reject the validity of Roman baptism?"[33]

A number of voices spoke out in the ensuing discussion. The only one partially in favor of Ferraz's position was that of Porter, editor of the *Revista das Missões Nacionaes* and professor of history in Campinas Seminary, who had voted with the majority in 1891. He suggested that the question be left to the discretion of each local session,[34] spurring an attack from Gaston Boyle, a missionary of the PCUS, who quoted Thornwell's arguments against Hodge.[35] The debate raged on, with prominent leaders, including a number of future seminary professors, unanimously condemning Ferraz's point of view. Criticizing the North American church because of its "softness" toward Catholicism, Herculano Gouvêa charged that the Roman church shrewdly hid its ultimate purpose in Protestant North America while revealing it in Brazil. He followed Boyle in condemning the action of the 1875 General Assembly of the PCUSA, even to the point of criticizing Hodge. When Ferraz cited the position of Luther and Calvin on the question, Gouvêa replied that the Reformers were *muitíssimo confusos* (very confused) in their teaching on the sacraments and were not proper guides.[36] The implication was that in Brazil the Reformation had reached its fulfillment, going beyond the point to which it had progressed elsewhere.

The first argument used against Ferraz was that the Roman church was not Christian in any sense and therefore had the right neither to ordain clergy nor to administer the sacraments. Consequently, even if it were admitted that one might find saving truth in Catholicism, baptism by a priest was still invalid because it was essentially baptism by a layman and a contradiction of proper church order.[37] But the basic argument against acceptance of the Roman church as Christian was expounded by Antônio Trajano, one of the two oldest pastors in the Presbyterian Church of Brazil. For him Ferraz's position implied condemnation of sixty years of work by missionaries and pastors because it cast doubt on the legitimacy of Protestantism in the nation. If the Roman church is Christian, he wrote, why evangelize Roman Catholic nations?[38] It was a manifestation of the continuing concern which had prompted the protest to the Edinburgh Conference.

Several judicatories protested against Ferraz's position and his own presbytery for failing to discipline him.[39] Rio de Janeiro included criticism of Porter for permitting the *Revista das Missões Nacionaes* to become a vehicle of opinions offensive to the resolution of 1891. As was inevitable, the 1916 General Assembly voted to continue the traditional practice.[40] Pressures were great, and Juventino Marinho, a pastor in the North, wrote that any other decision by the assembly would have triggered another schism.[41] But, unfortunately, the action implied the rejection of any serious attempt to restudy the church's relationship to Roman Catholicism. And it made it very difficult to deal with the possibility of Catholic renewal in the future.

The difference of opinion between some North American missionary leaders and Latin American churchmen became more evident in the Panama Congress on Christian Work in Latin America. There the rift between Latin Americans and mission board leaders from the United States foreshadowed great differences in attitude toward the ecumenical movement in the future.

Ferraz, continuing his quest for a church which was both evangelical and catholic, became an Episcopalian in 1917. In 1936 he helped establish the Free Catholic Church of Brazil and became its bishop. In 1960 he entered the Roman Catholic Church and, although married, was accepted as a bishop without diocese.[42]

Presbyterians and Other Evangelical Churches

Permanent Methodist work began in Brazil in 1876, and Southern Baptist missionaries came from the United States in 1881.

They were welcomed by Presbyterians, who aided in their orientation and language study. Brazil was huge, and it was clear that
there was room for all. An early attempt at a comity agreement
with the Baptists in Bahia[43] foundered in the face of aggressive
and wide-ranging evangelistic efforts by both groups. The Baptists' natural rejection of Presbyterian baptism and their refusal to
receive other Evangelical believers at Communion or transfer
their members to sister Protestant churches also frustrated con-
ciliation, as did the accusation that they failed to respect the discipline of other denominations.[44] Situations often arose in which
Presbyterians, newly arrived in an area where there was Baptist
work but rebuffed in their efforts to be accepted in that church
without rebaptism, formed their own congregations and asked for
aid from a mission or presbytery. The strong Baptist polemic
against the Roman church and the early practice of baptizing
new converts publicly in rivers or at beaches were often criticized
for attracting adverse attention to the Evangelical cause.

Polemics between Baptists and Presbyterians were minimal.
Controversy over baptism received expression in the *Puritano* and
Jornal Batista from 1911 to 1914. Replying to Baptist charges that
Presbyterian baptism was invalid, writers in the first paper denounced the *hydrolatria* of their brethren and called their insistence on immersion "ridiculous, anti-hygienic, and almost im-
moral."[45] At the same time some Baptist pastors, especially in the
interior, did not hesitate to proselytize active and disciplined
members of other churches, and one even warned that those who
received Presbyterian baptism were lost.[46] On the whole, however, the two groups went their own ways despite local and sporadic clashes.

While some problems existed with the Baptists, relationships
were relatively good with Congregationalists and Episcopalians.
Presbyterians turned over their only church in Rio Grande do Sul
to the latter before the end of the century, while intercommunion
and transfer of members from one to another was enjoyed between Presbyterians and Congregationalists.

Despite strong denominational feeling and occasional controversy, the Presbyterian Church led in attempts to achieve greater
cooperation and unity among Protestants and made specific attempts to unite with Methodists and Independentes. The Synod
of 1888 approved a motion, made by Pereira, nominating a com-

mission to enter into contact with "all of the existing Evangelical denominations in Brazil" to establish the basis for an alliance.[47] A project agreeable to the Methodists was drafted in 1891, and nine years later a commission of the two churches concluded a comity agreement. The plan specified that no city of less than 25,000 inhabitants was to be occupied by more than one group, there would be no proselytizing, discipline would be mutually respected, and a commission would be established to resolve future problems. Among the few specific agreements made, one in 1902 reserved the region along the Northwest Railroad in the interior of São Paulo for the Methodists and turned over Serra Negra to the Presbyterians. But the refusal of the Independentes to respect such agreements soon led to their repudiation.[48]

The Synod of 1907 proposed a plan of union to the Methodists which they refused on the basis of differences in doctrine and form of government,[49] the Methodist paper suggesting that the two churches follow a parallel march. When the subject of cooperation again arose in 1913, Porter deplored the waste of effort and resources involved and indicated that attempts at cooperation had brought few positive results: "It is this parallel march which takes both churches into the same small places, with expensive trips of evangelists, rivalries between believers, and at times, little discipline of the weak, and stumbling blocks for the unbelieving."[50]

Despite disappointments, interest in cooperation and even unity continued to grow. Álvaro Reis wrote from Edinburgh in 1910 that upon his return to Brazil he hoped to work for union of the Evangelical churches and greater solidarity in the conquest of the nation for Christ.[51] In 1915 a Methodist missionary bishop suggested that the two churches work together in preparation of ministers,[52] and the same year a national Sunday School convention and a congress of the Evangelical Alliance were held. The General Assembly of 1915 voted to recommend that members who moved to localities without Presbyterian churches cooperate with other denominations if they were members of the Alliance and accepted letters of transfer.[53]

Attitudes Toward the Newer Protestant Sects

As they struggled to find their own place in Brazilian society, Presbyterians reacted negatively to the Darbyites, Adventists, and

Pentecostals who were becoming active during this period. Darbyite thought, which entered the Congregational churches after 1870 through Richard Holden, a former Anglican,[54] created problems for Presbyterians and Baptists in Espírito Santo. Aníbal Nora denied that they were even Christians.[55]

The Adventists, who had arrived in Brazil at the end of the previous century, were a much greater problem because of their widespread activity and strong institutions. Álvaro Reis wrote a number of strong articles, condemning them as false prophets,[56] and the General Assembly of 1912 declared that they were not to be considered brethren in the faith because they subverted fundamental Christian principles.[57]

Pentecostalism, which was destined to become the biggest Protestant group in Brazil,[58] entered the country in 1910. That year Louis Francescon arrived from Chicago, where he had helped establish the Italian Presbyterian Church. Preaching Pentecostal doctrines in the Italian Presbyterian Church in São Paulo, he took most of the small group with him in the ensuing split. Thus began the Congregação Cristã do Brasil, which by 1969 would be the second largest Protestant group in the nation. According to the *Puritano*, these "fanatics" taught that it was not necessary to have ministers and that the presence of the Holy Spirit was manifested through physical movements, miracles, and "speaking in tongues."[59]

The same year, two Swedish-American Baptists, Daniel Berg and Gunnar Vingren, arrived in Belém. Aided by a young Presbyterian in their language study, they lived and worked in the local Baptist church, which was without a resident pastor, until the group expelled them and their followers over the question of "tongues." As a result they established the Assemblies of God in Brazil, a movement of remarkable growth and vitality, which has become the largest Protestant church in Latin America.[60]

The group came to the attention of Presbyterians elsewhere when the *Norte Evangélico* reported the expulsion of a member of the Belém Church for joining a sect known as the "Latter Rains."[61] A number of articles denouncing the group appeared in the papers of the more traditional churches. Its proselytism, ignorance, and the noise and apparent lack of order in its worship services came under fire. A Presbyterian in Belém described a meeting he had attended out of curiosity. The preacher, who spoke incorrect Portuguese, read a Psalm, led a hymn, and gave a short exposition of the text which included much repetition of the phrase "Glory to Jesus." Then came a frenzied prayer for the healing of a woman who appeared to be blind, all accompanied by "infernal noise." Following this were testimonies which repeated the theme "Jesus is good, He saved me, He cured me. Glory to Jesus." The writer concluded that the meeting was blasphemy.[62] Both Jerônimo Gueiros and Henderlite, adhering to dispensationalist theology, admonished that scripture taught there could not be another baptism of the Holy Spirit or revival in the last days, as the Pentecostals claimed, but that increasing wickedness would predominate in the world.[63] For sociological as well as theological reasons the reaction of Presbyterians and other Protestants to Pentecostals was totally negative, even to the point of their being classified with Spiritists as non-Christian.[64] It is probably too much to expect that the situation could have been any different. Presbyterians and Methodists, especially, were attempting not only to evangelize within a hostile environment but to demonstrate to society as a whole that Protestantism was intellectually respectable. Pentecostalism was both an embarrassment and an attack on their left flank at the same time. And while they were struggling to establish churches and seminaries modeled on those in North America, it was too much to expect them to perceive the new pattern of ministry and the penetration into the most neglected and numerous segment of Brazilian society which was being initiated by the despised group.

The Approach to the Independent Presbyterian Church

After the schism of 1903 the relationship between the continuing Presbyterian Church of Brazil, called the *Sinodais* because it remained loyal to the Synod, and the Independentes, was bitter. Working hard to win individuals and congregations to its cause the dissenters succeeded in taking about one third of the total membership of the church. Congregations in important cities such as Curitiba, Campinas, São Luiz, Natal, and Fortaleza were split, and a violent polemic was carried on in the *Revista das Missões Nacionaes* of the *Sinodais* and the *Estandarte* of the Independentes. The latter exhorted believers to choose between Christ and

Masonry, calling Masons heretics, while a synod publication compared Pereira and his followers to Loyola and the original Jesuits.[65]

The first step toward reconciliation came when the Synod of 1907 invited an Independente pastor to be seated as a visiting member and passed the following resolution: "The Synod, out of love for peace and Evangelical Brotherhood, counsels the members of the Presbyterian Church of Brazil to abstain from Masonry."[66] However, the Independent Church continued to forbid pulpit exchange and intercommunion with the *Sinodais*, alleging that its refusal to declare Masonry incompatible with the gospel implied denial of the mediation of Christ. At the same time, the *Puritano* complained, ministers of the Methodist, Episcopal, and Congregational churches, some of whose pastors were Masons, were allowed to preach from Independente pulpits.[67] Pereira showed his vehemence about the matter in 1910 when he received an inquiry from Speer concerning the possibility of union between the two churches. He denounced as "criminal incoherence" any idea that the Independentes should return. "It is evident that when God removes the obstacles to full solidarity between the two branches of national Presbyterianism, we will not be the ones who must return, it will be the synodical Church which must take the first step and join the Independent Church."[68] Clearly the possibility for union was not great!

A new era in the relationship between the two churches began when pastors from both groups met at Mackenzie Institute in August, 1915, not to discuss principles or attitudes toward Masonry but to pray, remove offenses, and restore mutual confidence in a quest for greater cooperation. Along with Waddell, who apparently was responsible for the meeting, M. G. dos Santos and André Jensen were present from the Presbyterian Church of Brazil, while Pereira, V. T. Lessa, Bento Ferraz, and five laymen from the Independent Church attended.[69] The same group, joined by others, met the following October, requesting the Presbyterian General Assembly to declare that "it has never recognized and does not recognize either the compatibility or the incompatibility of Masonry with an evangelical profession, and that all previous deliberations of the General Assembly of the Presbyterian Church of Brazil be interpreted in this sense."[70] The Independentes present promised that if such a resolution passed they would work toward free communion between the two bodies.

Hopes were aroused on both sides. The *Puritano* reprinted an article from the official bulletin of the Independent Church in which one of its pastors expressed the desire for union, a position with which the newspaper agreed.[71] After long discussion the 1916 General Assembly unanimously approved the October proposal, thus hoping to remove obstacles to union. Only two delegates expressed reservations about certain phrases in the resolution, while one abstained.[72]

But there were still dissenters, especially among the Independentes. Even before the General Assembly met, an article in *O Estandarte* called upon it to go further and remove the "stumbling stone" which had caused the separation and declare the profession of Masonry in the Church of Jesus Christ to be a transgression of the spirit and letter of the gospel.[73] And during debate on the conciliatory measure which it finally approved, the Assembly received a strong protest from three laymen in São Paulo arguing that the church's acceptance of such a humiliating peace would be a revolt against the Holy Spirit. The only way the schismatics could return, they concluded, was as prodigal sons.[74]

An understandable resentment against this analogy in Independente circles was one of the reasons the efforts failed. But a deeper motive lay in the rationale developed by that church to justify its separate existence. Having begun as a genuinely nationalistic movement, it had soon de-emphasized the missionary question, making anti-Masonry its rallying point. Perhaps this was a more plausible and easily propagated issue, especially in areas where missionaries were highly regarded. The question soon became a battle cry and the "witness against Masonry" was often cited in Independente literature. The thirty-first of July, the anniversary of the schism, was chosen as the date for the annual special offering, designed to support the institutions of the church. To generate interest, *O Estandarte* inevitably evoked the memory of July 31, 1903, as a new Exodus. Pereira and his colleagues had left the Synod, the paper said, in order to stand up for the "Royal Crown of the Savior," an action which implied the repudiation of Masonry. The missionary issue was scarcely mentioned. Thus the need for institutional preservation and support, as well as the necessity of defining itself over against the Presbyterian Church of Brazil, imprisoned the Independent Church in its own rhetoric and led it to concentrate increasingly on a peripheral issue. In doing so it betrayed the more profound questions which had led to the division.

The problem is illustrated in the warning offered by Bento Ferraz, an Independente leader, after the 1916 General Assembly. "Ardent and convicted anti-Masons fear that the hoped and planned for union implies the repudiation of the cardinal principles of our church."[75] Even Pereira, who had encouraged the desire for union, began to talk only of intercommunion and finally led in the action which ended the hope of reconciliation. The Independente Synod of 1917 reaffirmed the incompatibility of Masonry and the gospel and adopted an intransigent position toward the General Assembly. It accepted the statement that the sister church did not, at the present time, espouse an official policy concerning Masonry and the gospel but rejected its claim that it had never said they were compatible. It finally limited itself to accepting pulpit exchange and intercommunion with Presbyterians, just as with other Protestants, while maintaining restrictions against Masons of any communion.[76]

Although there would be sporadic attempts by the Presbyterian Church to create an acceptable plan of union in subsequent decades, the Independentes always stopped short of a positive response. Neither side would completely abandon its stance of 1903, and this, added to the reluctance of the smaller body to be absorbed into the larger, frustrated all such efforts.

The "Brazil Plan" of Church-Mission Relations

The other side of the attempts to achieve greater unity among Brazilian Evangelicals was the realization that the church must become independent of foreign missions and boards. With the growing suspicion of North American "imperialism," it was even more important to avoid the appearance that Protestantism was maintained or dominated by the colossus of the North. Álvaro Reis made it clear in 1915: "The blessed future of the missionary task is in its complete nationalization. Without the help and cooperation of the national, native element, no people will be truly and permanently evangelized."[77]

This could have been accomplished either by increasing the

Brazilian majority's control of the church, even while the mission-aries remained within it, or by complete withdrawal of the North Americans from the national judicatories. The first would have insured closer contact between all workers, resulting perhaps in better use of personnel and resources from abroad despite the danger to national self-sufficiency posed by the missionary pres-ence. However, the combination of a desire to work independent-ly of the national body and a missionary strategy which gave priority to the geographical frontier led to separation of the mis-sions and their resources from the Brazilian church. In the Brazil Plan of 1917, a number of parallel Presbyterian ecclesiastical or-ganizations were established, usually with little or no contact be-tween them.

Ecclesiology was part of the issue. If unity of the church is taken seriously, all pastors and believers in a given country should, as far as possible, be members of one institution with pri-mary authority in planning and executing overall strategy and use of personnel and funds from various sources. In this case the principal relationship of the missionary would be to the church in which he worked, not to the body which sent him. This ap-peared to be the desire of the missionaries of the PCUSA and their board from the beginning, but the stated policy of the PCUS was different. Shortly before organization of the Synod, repre-sentatives of the latter church had not yet formed presbyteries with their Brazilian colleagues, a practice which, in the opinion of one writer, "was aimed at keeping the native element in a sub-ordinate position."[78] When the PCUS missionaries did form mixed judicatories, it was noted as an exception to board policy.[79]

Workers from the PCUSA had been members of mixed presby-teries from the beginning. However, a serious problem arose over their unwillingness to accept either the implications of ecclesiasti-cal unity or the orientation of the church after their Brazilian col-leagues had become a majority. The issue became increasingly complex as the missionaries and national churchmen took oppos-ing sides on a number of questions. Early in its history the Synod was caught in an unequal conflict with several missionaries and the New York Board, which refused Brazilians the right to de-termine use of resources sent from North America. Aggravating the struggle was the parental if not paternalistic feeling toward the church on the part of some missionaries—this, just when it was attempting to assert independence, even though it still needed North American aid.

The tensions which erupted in schism were not created primarily by the conflicting opinions or missionary membership in the judicatories of the national church as such. Controversy arose with the efforts of some missionaries to work outside the judicatories, using the power of the missions and boards to thwart the plans of the church. Thus, the cause of friction was the organization of the missionaries into separate structures which often acted independently of, and contrary to, the wishes of the church, rather than North American membership in the presbyteries. This became clear in several decisions made by the Synod shortly after its organization. At the first meeting it declared that the mother churches had the right to choose evangelistic and institutional projects which it wished to aid in Brazil, "but only if nothing were done against the express will of the highest council of the Church in Brazil."[80] Because the missions did not always observe the measure, proposals soon called for all ordained Brazilians to become members of the missions or for the latter to be absorbed into the Synod. When the North Americans rejected these suggestions, the Synod of 1891 requested placement of every missionary under the control of a Brazilian presbytery, from which only concurrent action by that body and his mission could remove him. The boards rejected this recommendation.[81] It was ironic that the Brazil Plan removed the missionaries from the presbyteries, where they had remained in close contact with the church, while it allowed them to remain in the more objectionable mission organizations. In adopting the scheme, the North Americans avoided serious consideration of ecclesiology on the mission field.

While ecclesiology indicated that missionaries and nationals should be members of the same church with equal voices in its government, traditional missiology, with its emphasis on the development of a self-governing, self-propagating, and self-supporting national church, moved in another direction. A frequently used illustration conceived of the mission not as an integral part of the church building but as a scaffold, external to the structure and destined for removal when construction ended. This concept necessarily raised the question as to when, where, and how removal should take place. Should the missionary withdraw after establishing one small church in a city of over half a million? Did the missions have the responsibility of aiding in the preparation of pastors, or was this to be left to the church which was now "established" in a country, even though it did not have the resources necessary for the Calvinistic ideal of an educated ministry? These and similar questions were never considered in depth as the church and missions moved inexorably toward separation.

The first cause was the explicit policy of the PCUS that missionaries should not normally become members of Brazilian presbyteries.[82] A second powerful impetus was the conflict leading to the schism of 1903, stimulated largely by the insensitivity of a number of missionaries of the New York Board. But despite the problems national churchmen had suffered with the missions, there is no evidence to indicate that the Brazilians initiated the separation. Rather it was the North Americans, especially those of the Central Brazil Mission, who were most eager for complete division of work. They wished to be free of the presbyteries, which they feared would tie them too much to the established work in older areas.

Thus, a third factor, which has been ignored by historians, was the orientation of most North American missionaries and the sponsoring churches toward the geographical frontier. Waddell was undoubtedly the strongest voice urging the missions to turn their backs on the coastal cities and move farther into the interior, but the emphasis did not originate with him and he was not alone in it. The tendency was natural for most missionaries since they came from small towns or rural areas, mostly from western Pennsylvania, the Mid-West, or South, where memories of the frontier were still fresh during their formative years.[83] At times they seemed to equate virtue with a rural environment and sin with the city.[84] The foreign missionary movement in North America was a continuation of the impulse which had established home missions on the frontier, and the thrust toward the West in vast Brazil was almost inevitable. Many North Americans were convinced that the greatness of their own nation would depend on development of the region beyond the Allegheny Mountains, which for Christians implied rescue from "barbarism" through establishment of the church and the institutions which perpetuated Christian culture. Perhaps this was in Waddell's mind when he said the battle in Brazil would be won by country preachers trained in backwoods seminaries.[85] It is also possible that North

American Presbyterians, realizing that their church had lost its
dominant role in the United States because it had been too slow
in moving into the expanding frontier, were determined not to
make the same mistake in Brazil. At any rate it is indisputable that,
for missionaries, the analogy between the North American West
and the Brazilian interior was powerful in guiding their strategy.[86]

Because two factors were apparently ignored, few realized that
the analogy was false. In the United States the church had been
relatively well established in the eastern cities before the period
of westward expansion began. The frontier preachers did not
leave behind them cities which were almost totally unevangelized
when they went to the sparsely populated West. But in Brazil, as
the missionaries moved west they abandoned Protestant churches
which were still tiny minorities in the major centers of population.
In addition, the North American frontier traditionally meant a
place of new opportunity to which the young, able, and adven-
turesome hastened, while in Brazil the opposite was the case.
Despite a certain mystique about its vast area and potential, the
interior, as the hinterland of Brazil is usually called, has almost
always been the region of greatest poverty, with little apparent
opportunity, from which the young, able, and successful escape
to the cities. The negative attitude was partly in response to the
region's geographical features, but it also reflected a fundamentally different approach to the land from the beginning of
colonization. Viana Moog has pointed out that while the first
English settlers in North America turned their backs on Europe
to establish a new fatherland and were "colonizers, not conquer-
ors," the opposite was true in Brazil. The Portuguese went to the
New World seeking riches to take back to Europe. Thus, the first
men to be called Brazilians were not inhabitants of the new country, but fortune hunters who had gone there and returned to Portugal. Later, the *bandeirantes*, adventurers who claimed Brazil's
interior, went west not to settle but, like their predecessors, to
find easily removable riches before returning to the coast.[87] Thus,
population growth was much greater in the eastern cities than in
the hinterland.

Country people were often quicker to accept the Protestant
message, and it is possible that the missionary felt more at ease
with the dispossessed of the interior, where he immediately had

status, than he did in the sophisticated cities. Certainly it was true that converts were won more rapidly in the rural areas, and workers often expressed great optimism regarding the possibility of establishing self-supporting churches in a short time, even though migration to the cities made this more difficult than imagined. The report of the New York Board in 1890 said: "The fruitfulness of these fields seems to be in the ratio of the distance from the seaboards or the great commercial centers, and . . . this serves to emphasize the importance of evangelistic work in the more destitute portions of the country. . . . The work which seems the most hopeful for the future is that of frontier evangelization."[88] In 1904 the General Assembly of the PCUSA urged the Central Brazil Mission to make a special effort in that direction.[89]

The westward thrust was clear in the statement of the SBM made in 1913, three years before the Brazil Plan was proposed to the General Assembly: "The South Brazil Mission is looking forward to entrusting to the Brazilian Church the work in the states of Santa Catarina and Paraná in accordance with the long expressed policy of the board. The future extension of our work will be towards the North in the states of Goyaz, Mato Grosso, Northern Minas, and the far northwestern part of São Paulo, which has never been evangelized."[90] The same year the mission sent to the Presbytery of Rio a request for permission to send a man to open new work in Mato Grosso before fulfilling Presbytery's demand for a man to be assigned to the nation's capital.[91]

Apparently few asked if the only kind of frontier in the twentieth century was geographical, but there were some dissenting voices. Lennington, who had been raised in Brazil, protested to Speer that they should never have left the cities for the interior and that Santa Catarina should have been left to the Episcopalians, who had wanted to enter that state. The Brazilian church was protesting too, he added, and at a recent synod meeting, he was frequently asked: " 'Why do you give up São Paulo?' All in Rio say we should have missionaries there," he concluded, "for the field is large and it is the center of Brazil."[92] In Recife, Antônio Almeida wrote that concentration on the cities, the meeting places of people, was the Biblical method. "If then we have erred," he continued, "it is where we left the centers from which the Gospel might have radiated out around, centralizing our work in rural areas." He noted that the Presbyterians had organized their first congregation in Recife in 1878 and, while maintaining only one church there, had made the interior town of Garanhuns their center. But the Baptists had established their school and seminary in Recife, evangelizing the interior from there. As a result they now had more churches in both the city and the interior than did the Presbyterians.[93] But such arguments, although they came from able and mature leaders, were not able to halt the march to the interior by the missions.

It is ironic, in the light of later history, that most Brazilian churchmen wanted the North Americans to remain in the national judicatories, while the missionaries of the PCUSA insisted on separation.[94] Except for Daffin, the PCUS personnel, whose official policy implied separation of church and missions, apparently were not concerned about the question during the period. From 1892 to 1902 a number of attempts to withdraw from the presbyteries, made by missionaries of the PCUSA, brought a negative response from their board.[95] However, the path of the future became evident in the 1903 meeting of the CBM, five months after the schism. Even though Synod had just voted overwhelmingly, with the missionaries abstaining, that the latter should remain as members of the national judicatories, the mission voted to advise its members "who are connected with the Brazilian presbyteries to sever their relations with same and unite with some presbytery in the States."[96] The same body took action to begin theological education in Bahia, implying greater isolation from the seminary and controversy in the South as well as an orientation toward the interior.

The next step, a logical implication of the separation of North Americans from the presbyteries, was the adoption in 1907 of the "Modus Operandi" between the CBM and the Presbytery of Bahia-Sergipe, formed that same year. Waddell described the plan, which was the basis of the new structure to be adopted in 1917, to Speer:

> It amounts to assuming a "Home Board" relation to the native churches from the first, with its provision for (1) the gradual emancipation of the native church, (2) the ultimate withdrawal of foreigners, (3) the full recognition of the right of the church to control its own development as to the ministry; it renders the development of nationalism improbable and by the separation between mission and presbytery, it renders

any such feeling impotent. It would have saved us all the more had it been put in force 30 years ago.[97]

The SBM moved toward the same position in 1912, recommending that its missionaries in São Paulo, Rio, and Campos remain outside the local presbyteries, a resolution with which the Presbytery of Rio concurred.[98] The completeness of the separation envisioned is shown by the stipulation that as long as he remained a professor in the seminary, Porter would be considered an associate missionary, receiving his salary from the board but having no vote in the mission. The same year Porter and Smith, the only North Americans in the institution, expressed a desire to be replaced by national professors.[99] The following year the mission voted that its men should withdraw from the Presbytery of the South as soon as a sufficient number of Brazilian pastors entered it,[100] adding that the pastoral relationship between missionaries and churches in that judicatory must cease on June 30, 1915.[101]

At first few Brazilians expressed themselves on the issue. But in 1914 Erasmo Braga, concerned about the primary responsibility of the missionaries to their boards, urged administrative harmony, suggesting that the membership of North Americans in Brazilian presbyteries had produced an anomalous situation which should not continue beyond the first phase of the work. Now the time had come, he said, "of collaboration in evangelistic work without authority or responsibility on the part of the missionaries, who would work in parallel organizations, while avoiding construction of a state within a state." He cited the Modus Operandi in Bahia and the resolution of the Presbytery of Rio approving the SBM plan as examples of the new period coming.[102]

Some dissenting voices spoke out. Álvaro Reis, who in 1913 had voted with his presbytery to approve the SBM policy, reversed himself the following year and advocated continued missionary membership in the presbyteries. He was afraid the new policy would lead to what Braga had warned against—creation of a state within a state, with the North Americans placed beyond national church discipline. Such a system, he said, would not be Presbyterian.[103] When A. C. Salley sought dismissal from the Presbytery of the South in accordance with the new policy, his

Brazilian colleagues asked him to remain for at least one more year.[104]

The question came before the General Assembly in 1915 with the introduction of a motion lamenting the withdrawal of SBM personnel from the southern presbytery. The measure passed after the term expressing regret in the original motion had been replaced by a weaker one.[105] When J. P. Smith of the West Brazil Mission asked the assembly to speak openly regarding the membership of missionaries in the presbyteries, a second motion was passed: "The General Assembly resolves to communicate to the Board of Foreign Missions in New York and the Committee of Foreign Missions in Nashville, that it is entirely agreeable for the missionaries to remain as members of the presbyteries in Brazil, if, and while that is agreeable to those corporations and to the missionary brethren."[106]

While the strongest advocates of the new structure were the missionaries of the PCUSA, the Brazilians who had become convinced of its necessity were among the most respected leaders in the church. Consequently, the 1916 General Assembly approved the report of a committee headed by M. G. dos Santos, who had been pastor in Salvador when the Modus Operandi was adopted in Bahia and was now closely associated with Waddell in Mackenzie. It declared that the situation of the missionaries who "were members of missions and, at the same time, under the jurisdiction of national judicatories, had become anomalous for both, and for that reason it was judged to be more practical that they be independent of those judicatories, there being established a plan of cooperation."[107] Santos chaired a committee composed of Belmiro Cesar, Waddell, H. C. Anderson, C. E. Bixler, A. C. Salley, R. F. Lennington, S. R. Gammon, Robert Daffin, and William Thompson, nominated to study the matter. It is significant that Santos, Waddell, Bixler, and Anderson had been involved in formulating the CBM-Bahia plan, while Daffin was the first missionary of the PCUS to request transfer to a presbytery in the United States.

After long discussion the Brazil Plan, which closely followed the Modus Operandi of 1907, was adopted by the 1917 General Assembly. The resolution began by noting the goal of the missions to be establishment of an autonomous national church. Although this had been accomplished in Brazil, the existence of vast regions and great multitudes still unreached by the gospel justified the continuation of missionary work. The purpose of the plan was to harmonize the interests and define the fields of the various bodies, and although the entire nation was declared to be the responsibility of the church as well as the missions, the fields presently occupied by each would be considered their own. No worker could belong to both church and mission at the same time, except upon request for a specific task and for a definite period, and under no circumstances was any minister to belong to two presbyteries simultaneously. The presence of Porter and Smith in the seminary was recognized as desirable, however, and was to be continued. Missionaries would have full authority in their fields, with national presbyteries possessing jurisdiction over all ministerial candidates. When agreed upon by the church and a mission, a field of the latter would be transferred to a presbytery, and if the field had not yet reached self-support, the mission might agree to subsidize it for a specified period, with reductions in the amount of 8 per cent each year. A permanent Modus Operandi Committee, composed of six missionaries and six Brazilians, was to meet annually to oversee administration of the plan, serve as an intermediary between the missions and the General Assembly, and promote the unification of evangelistic efforts.[108]

Reaction against the scheme was strong in the North. Almeida wrote that the problem of dual membership and loyalty on the part of the missionaries was theoretical, not real. He added that if there were differences between nationals and missionaries, they would be intensified with the separation caused by the new structure. He also feared that the church would lose disciplinary power over missionaries working in evangelistic fields and, even more serious, in its seminaries.[109] Objections also hinged on financial considerations. The Presbytery of Pernambuco, the largest in area and poorest in resources, cautioned that if its work were to continue to expand, the increasing number of workers would require greater, not smaller, subsidies. The alternative would be to confine the church to a few large cities, mainly on the coast.[110] New evangelistic work depended on the cooperation of the North Brazil Mission and would do so for some time.

Consequently, the Presbytery of Pernambuco protested unanimously because the resolution of the 1916 General Assembly which called for withdrawal of the missionaries had been voted without previously consulting the presbyteries. Complaining that it was the action of a small group of ministers in which the only representative of Pernambuco had been absent from the North for over twenty years, the judicatory requested the assembly to either reconsider the action, exempt Pernambuco from the plan, or allow it to adopt the new structure at a future date when circumstances permitted.[111] Natanael Cortez, who represented the North in the 1917 meeting, noted that when he protested the plan on the floor of the assembly, missionaries who appeared to dislike the work of his colleagues in Garanhuns and who did not know the problems of the North argued against him. The assembly did grant one small concession to Pernambuco in allowing missionaries who had pastorates within presbyteries to retain them as long as both the national judicatory and the mission involved so desired.

Perhaps some plan for division of territory and jurisdiction was necessary, given the existing situation, the controversies of the past, and the concept of missionary strategy accepted by most of the North Americans. But it is probable that if the Central and South Brazil Missions had not been so insistent, the pattern already in effect would have continued. If this had happened and if, at the same time, the missionaries had shown greater sensitivity and discretion in their relationships with national colleagues, the continuing structure would have brought greater flexibility in the use of North American personnel and facilitated their serving under the orientation of the church in the burgeoning cities as well as in the interior. At the same time careful policies in the use of missionary funds and workers could have stimulated the growing self-reliance of the church.[112]

Praised for having fostered independence and eliminated friction between the church and the missions,[113] the plan, without doubt, brought a series of unfortunate consequences.[114] The Edinburgh Conference had warned of the temptation "for the foreign missionary to stand aloof, throwing the whole burden upon the infant church."[115] Braga concluded his article in 1914 with the admonition that in any new structure it would be the missionaries' duty "to attend the meetings of judicatories, maintain interest in points of common concern, and avoid isolating themselves from the overall work."[116] In a paper written over ten years later he saw the role of the Protestant missionary movement as that of a catalyst which would stimulate new currents of spiritual power while the indigenous church generated mass movements.[117] But the new plan did precisely that which Edinburgh and Braga had warned against. It threw the burden of work in the most rapidly growing areas on the church while isolating the missionaries from it and, by thrusting them into the most backward regions of the nation, made it almost impossible for them to continue as agents of change in the larger centers.

The new structure, allied with the thrust toward the geographical frontier, locked the missions out of the cities just when their growth was accelerating and the church was requesting missionary aid in Rio and São Paulo. The municipalities containing Brazil's capitals, which were its most urbanized areas, enjoyed a rate of growth between 1920 and 1940 which was almost double that of the rest of the nation. The gain in the areas around the capitals was 62.9 per cent, while that in the rest of the country was only 31.9. Belo Horizonte, the new capital of Minas Gerais, saw a growth of 281 per cent, while the population of the rest of the state increased by 12.9. São Paulo and Rio expanded about three times as rapidly as the rural areas of their states.[118] But the progress of the Presbyterian Church fell behind that of the Baptists in virtually all of the coastal cities. In 1959, eighty-eight years after work had begun in Salvador, there were still only two Presbyterian churches there compared with ten Baptist congregations.[119] Like other cities in the area, Salvador had been left too soon without missionary personnel and resources. In 1931 the Presbytery of São Paulo asked the West Brazil Mission for a man to be placed in Santos, the busiest coffee port in the world.[120] The request was refused, and in 1959 there was still only one Presbyterian church in that city of 200,000.

The isolation of the missions from the church was accompanied by a lack of understanding which sometimes produced a mutual lack of sympathy with each other's problems. The separation envisioned by some missionaries was so great that the Brazil Council, representing the two missions of the New York Board, proposed in 1938 that, henceforth, if a missionary became a professor in the Presbyterian Seminary, he should "cease to hold any relation to the Board of Foreign Missions, as employee or beneficiary."[121] Porter objected, and the recommendation apparently was not accepted. The Modus Operandi Committee, theoretically established by the plan, had not yet been formed in 1927.[122] In 1926 M. G. dos Santos complained that the missionaries paid scant attention to the plans and programs of the General Assembly and gave them little support.[123]

Coming at a time when Brazil was changing from a predominantly rural, agricultural society to an urban, industrial nation, the isolation thus imposed not only decreased evangelistic growth but increased the tendency to emphasize a rural ethos. While it enabled the church to make a positive impact in many interior areas, this trend left it unprepared to discover a style of life and worship suited to the urban environment, or even to see its necessity. The missionaries traveled widely through the interior, where most people were illiterate, but they remained isolated from the great centers of the nation and thus experienced little in-depth exposure to Brazilian culture. This magnified the isolation of the national church from its own society, especially since a disproportionate number of the ministerial candidates came from rural mission fields and studied in mission schools before going to seminary. When they became pastors they tended to reproduce the rural ethos and style of life, along with the negative attitude toward some aspects of Brazilian culture, which was typical of interior churches. The separation also intensified the separation of the Brazilian Church from world Christianity and contemporary theology. Most missionaries showed little interest in the development of the ecumenical movement and in new currents of theology. They were too overburdened with large evangelistic fields or heavy institutional responsibilities to look beyond their own areas, and some were suspicious of the new ideas. But their introduction into the national judicatories of the church would at least have been a reminder of the worldwide nature of the church and perhaps prevented some of the narrowness that developed later.

Finally, there is evidence that the plan attenuated the missionary spirit of the church. Jorge Goulart wrote that "for a long time the national church felt that the obligation to expand the work belonged to the foreign missions alone."[124]

The Panama Congress, 1916

The Congress on Christian Work in Latin America, held in Panama in February, 1916, resulted from a serious omission in the

Edinburgh Conference of 1910. That gathering, generally considered the beginning of the modern ecumenical movement, limited participation to those involved with missions in "non-Christian" countries, a price paid in order to secure the attendance of some continental and Anglican societies.[125] Consequently, Latin America, except for its Indian population, was not considered a legitimate object of the missionary movement and was not officially represented at the conference. It is worth noting that much of the reluctance which Latin American Protestant churches later showed toward participation in the World Council of Churches and other manifestations of the ecumenical movement had its roots, if not in this act, at least, in a deep fear of the attitude toward the Roman Catholic Church which inspired it. It is ironic that the exclusion probably strengthened anti-Catholic sentiment among Latin American Protestants by putting them even more on the defensive, not only against Catholicism but toward the world Protestant community. They understandably felt that to accept Rome as a sister church would imply the validity of the Edinburgh Conference's assumption. And if Latin America were not a proper mission field, serious doubt was cast on their legitimacy as churches.

The General Assembly of 1910 pronounced the conference's attitude "incredible," voting to register its "energetic protest against this unjust discrimination which had no reason to exist . . . and moreover to declare its conviction that Roman Catholics need the Gospel of Christ just as all other peoples of the world."[126] Álvaro Reis, sent to Edinburgh as an observer by the New York Board, was favorably impressed by the concern for greater Christian unity and proclaimed his "ardent desire" to see it in Brazil. He warned though that he preferred disunion to concessions not "in conformity with the Divine Word."[127]

Speer was so disturbed by Edinburgh's exclusion of Latin America that he immediately initiated plans for a meeting to deal with the missionary task in that area. With the Panama Canal opening in 1914 and the war raging in Europe, North Americans also began looking more to the South. An important step came in 1913 when the Committee on Cooperation in Latin America was formed by the Foreign Missions Conference of North America. Unfortunately, the CCLA showed a certain ambivalence unacceptable to Brazilian churchmen from the beginning. As Hogg wrote: "The new body was concerned, not to convert Roman Catholics, but to survey the needs of Latin America's unevangelized millions, and to coordinate Protestant efforts to meet these needs."[128]

Tensions soon arose because Latin American Protestants evaluated the situation quite differently. The problem which some North Americans apparently refused to face was that the "unevangelized millions" were nearly all nominal Catholics and claimed as such by the dominant church. On the other hand most Latin American Protestants believed that all Roman Catholics, both nominal and practicing, were unevangelized and thus believed their primary task was to convert them. The attitude was not entirely without justification. Added to the reasons already discussed was the difference between Anglo-Saxon and Latin American Catholicism, a contrast to which Brazilian writers often referred. Which was the "true Catholicism" and which an aberration due to special historical circumstances was a matter for dispute. It is important to remember as well that the historical context of Latin America vis-à-vis the Roman Catholic Church, was closer to that of sixteenth- or seventeenth-century Europe than that of twentieth-century North America. Thus, an attitude which appeared toward Roman Catholicism, one which would secure the cooperation of all the North American Protestant mission boards and forestall greater hostility on the part of the Roman church, was likely to be unacceptable to Latin American Evangelicals.

The dilemma of the missionaries on this question showed itself clearly when the 1915 convention of the Evangelical Alliance voted two to one to consider the Roman church a "branch which had apostacized from Christ."[129] Virtually all of the Brazilians present voted with the majority, and the North Americans with the minority. In the opinion of one writer, probably Porter, who described the meeting, the difference was more apparent than real. His personal concern had been that the term apostate would offend the North Americans and hinder the cause of missions. But the conviction was universal, he said, that the time had come for a strong appeal for more missionaries and that its basis was the testimony of Brazilian Evangelicals—"We fled from the Roman Catholic Church in order to find eternal life. Whatever it might be elsewhere, when we were in it here, we were in darkness and sin."[130]

The apprehensions of the Latin Americans did not ease in 1915, when the committee preparing for the Congress stated in Caldwell, New Jersey:

> It shall be the purpose of the Panama Conference to recognize all the elements of truth and goodness in any form of religious faith. Our approach to the people shall be neither critical nor antagonistic, but inspired by the teachings and example of Christ. . . . In the matter of Christian service we will welcome the cooperation of any who are willing to cooperate in any part of the Christian program. We should not demand union with us in all our work as the condition of accepting allies for any part of it.[131]

The concern became greater when some Roman Catholic leaders were invited to attend,[132] even though none did so. The reality of the situation south of the Rio Grande soon appeared graphically when the Bishop of Panama decreed excommunication for anyone attending the Congress.[133]

North Americans predominated overwhelmingly in both the planning and attendance at the Congress. Of the 230 official delegates, 145 resided in Latin America, but only 21 were nationals.[134] The makeup of the various commissions showed the same composition. Delegates from the Presbyterian Church of Brazil were Alvaro Reis and Erasmo Braga, the brilliant young seminary professor who was to become Latin America's most important leader in Evangelical cooperation. Independente leader E. C. Pereira also served as a delegate.

The structure of the Congress stifled the few Latin American voices. Motions and amendments could come to the floor only upon a two-thirds vote of the business committee, chosen in advance in New York and chaired by John R. Mott, but the committee was not required to report on papers which it rejected. When a report did reach the floor the chairman had forty-five minutes for its defense, while other speakers, who had to indicate their desire to speak on the previous day, were limited to seven and, later, to five minutes.[135] While this might have been the only efficient way to handle commission reports, it made serious debate impossible. John Fox, a delegate from the Bible Society, wrote that the "real bone of contention" was whether or not the Congress should make a definite pronouncement on the relationship between Protestantism and Romanism and, if so, what it should be. Álvaro Reis made a public appeal for discussion of the question, and three papers on the issue, including one from Pereira,[136] were submitted to the business committee. Apparently, however, it decided that the Congress should remain silent on the issue.[137]

Even though the Latin Americans were unsuccessful in bringing the matter to the floor, their voices, in chorus with those of the missionaries, made it clear that any expressed desire for eventual cooperation with the Church of Rome would cause far more division than unity, arouse suspicion and resentment, and stimulate greater fragmentation of the Protestant churches. Consequently, although the initial report of the Commission on Cooperation and the Promotion of Christian Unity recommended that Catholic cooperation be sought, it was modified to read: "When the inevitable question is raised, whether at any point or in any form we may expect cooperation with the Roman Catholic Church, the usual reply is that such an expectation is hopeless."[138] However, the continuing difference of opinion was unmistakable in a statement by Charles Thompson, Chairman of the Commission:

> In response to a general demand from the field, we have modified our report so that it declares that there is not now any hope of cooperation of any kind, or in any degree, with the Roman Catholic Church as an organization. . . . We accept it as a present fact, we do not accept it as an ultimate fact. . . . We even dare to cherish the hope of an ultimate union of Christendom.[139]

The official position of the Congress represented only a tactical retreat for the North American leaders, but it continued to be a matter of principle for Brazilian Presbyterians, who considered the Roman church apostate.

The necessity for greater Protestant cooperation and unity was a point which generated no friction. The Committee on Cooperation in Latin America received authorization to carry out the spirit of the conference discussions, with one of the stated goals being "to secure eventually, a national church to which all the

Evangelical Christians" in a given country would belong.[140] Specific recommendations for Brazil included establishment of a committee on cooperation, a union seminary, and union training schools on a lower level; joint preparation of literature, comity agreements, and greater coordination of the courses of study in Evangelical schools and colleges, including organization of the various faculties into a Protestant university.[141] In keeping with attempts to establish union seminaries all over Latin America at this time, it was suggested that the proposed union between Methodist and Presbyterian theological education include all Evangelical denominations in Brazil and that, if possible, two union seminaries be established, one in the North and the other in the South. This would be the best way, the argument went, to destroy prejudice between the churches and prepare for union.[142]

Four regional conferences met in South America after Panama: in Lima, Santiago, Buenos Aires, and Rio, with the latter including Baptists, Methodists, Episcopalians, Presbyterians, Independentes, Congregationalists, and representatives of the YMCA. In addition to approving the recommendations made in Panama, the Rio conference emphasized the need for more workers, both national and foreign, and made a more definite proposal for the formation of a union seminary. While the majority envisioned an institution of high academic level, Ginsburg, the Baptist, advised the establishment of a number of Bible institutes to prepare lay preachers. The Rio Congress also adopted a strong statement on the desirability of organic union among Brazil's Protestant churches, urging that preparatory steps be taken immediately. It is interesting to note that the delegates feared the missionaries' antagonism to such a move for reasons connected with their own history, but foreign to the church in Brazil. If the nationals were left alone, they believed they would be in favor of union.[143] While the argument appeared logical, the reality would prove to be quite different.

As the delegates moved farther south, the anti-Catholic sentiment of the Latin Americans, muffled in Panama, became more vocal. Erasmo Braga described the continuing concern over the North American attitude:

> In Buenos Aires, more than in any other place, the "Caldwell Declaration," already mentioned, produced profound agita-

tion. In Evangelical circles there was even a tragic abstention of many precious elements . . . who refrained from participating in the work of the Congress. The question of the attitude toward the Church of Rome occupied a large part of the first session, full liberty of expression being given to the house . . . Thus pastor Juan Varetto of the Baptist Church of La Plata presented to the Congress a long exposition of the motives which make impossible and undesirable any attitude toward the Church of Rome except the condemnation of her because of her history and doctrines.[144]

The Rio Congress approved Pereira's paper on Catholicism in which he attempted to avoid what he called the two extremes of Anglo-Saxon tolerance and timidity and Latin American combativeness.[145] He recognized the Roman church's accomplishments: profession of the great dogmas of the faith, production of some saintly characters, perpetuation of the idea of Christian unity, and service to humanity through its missionaries. There was, however, a negative side. It had added many pagan elements to its worship and belief, imposed religious tyranny, and threatened public morality, civilization, and progress. He urged Protestants to show sympathy toward the Christian elements within it while rejecting those which were anti-Christian, attempting to be constructive even while giving testimony against error.[146] But despite his recognition of Biblical elements within it, he finally concluded that the Roman church was not "of our Lord Jesus Christ' because it had apostatized from its norms of faith and practice."[147] After the *Puritano* printed Pereira's article it received a number of letters criticizing its "romanophile concessions."[148]

The growing threat of Roman Catholic clericalism, aggravated by the long-standing hostility between Catholics and Protestants in Brazil, was to close the door to any serious consideration of the favorable aspects of Pereira's analysis. But despite the failure of the Panama Conference to enlarge the church's thinking on that question, it did arouse hopes for Protestant cooperation and perhaps even unity in the future.

Although the missionaries, in an action that was unfortunate both for ecclesiastical relations and evangelistic strategy, had isolated themselves from the Presbyterian Church of Brazil, that body still appeared to be more open to cooperation than any other group in the nation. There was reason to hope it would lead others in that direction. However, the depth of that concern would soon be tested by the United Seminary, one of the most important institutions to arise from the Panama Conference, and one which would become the focus of the most bitter struggle in the church since 1903.

Chapter Five

The Message and Life-Style of the Church

The Protestant message frequently wrought a striking difference in the lives of its adherents in Brazil, the congregations
which were subsequently formed making a strong impression on
their neighbors, especially in rural areas. The Christian life, as
they understood it, should include personal piety, active participation in the life of the church, support of the congregation and
its pastor with one's time, money, and prayers, attempts to evangelize others, and a high standard of personal morality and conduct,[1] all of which were uncommon in Brazilian society. According to a Roman Catholic observer, Presbyterians and Baptists in
Pernambuco often lived up to the standard:

> The Evangelical, reading the Bible everywhere, in the shop,
> the barracks, and at home, has some notion of the Christian
> religion, the morals of which enter into all of his acts. This
> brings a salutary effect in ordinary life. We see the Thirty-
> fourth Battalion of Infantry composed of Evangelicals, be-
> come the most moral and best disciplined of all the troops
> stationed in this city. The marriage judges note that the
> Evangelicals always attempt to observe the precepts of civil
> law, thus avoiding harm to spouse and children. Among
> Evangelicals, cases of common-law marriage are rare.[2]

Thus the picture of Protestants in Brazil has been one of sober,
honest, industrious, literate, law-abiding citizens, who usually
avoided the sexual immorality, drunkenness, and gambling which
were common in the society as a whole.[3] And because their piety
emphasized the Biblical hope of eternal life through Christ, a note
of joy as well as austerity often enriched their lives.

But alongside this positive witness, rejection of the dominant religion and its manifestations in Brazilian culture, and of the vice and corruption rampant in many areas of life, often led to negativism and the isolation of Protestantism from the society in which it lived. The Evangelical message, which came as one of grace, with a gospel bringing freedom and new life, at times became legalistic and dogmatic in its emphasis. Although there was widespread belief that the acceptance of Protestantism would automatically lead to liberalism and progress in political, economic, and social life, an attitude of authoritarian conservatism was often produced in the church which resisted all innovation in either form or content. The confidence that the new faith would stimulate progress was warranted in some situations, but because of its assumption that personal morality and education alone would solve social problems, Presbyterianism failed to discover the deeper roots of injustice in the nation and undertook no special mission in the political sphere other than calling for honesty in public life.

The Shape of the Church's Piety

The Presbyterian Church of Brazil was a product of Old School Presbyterianism, and a majority of the early missionaries were graduates of Princeton and Western seminaries in the northern United States, and Union (Richmond) and Columbia in the south. The church emphasized Westminster orthodoxy and piety and often taught the Shorter Catechism to adults as well as children. One of the first theological works translated and published in Portuguese was A. A. Hodge's "Commentary on the Confession of Faith,"[4] while the theologians most quoted were Charles Hodge, J. H. Thornwell, and R. L. Dabney, all champions of Old School orthodoxy.

Examination of the preaching and teaching of Brazilian Presbyterianism reveals a positive Christocentric emphasis much of the time. Álvaro Reis' sermons on the words from the cross sounded the notes of love and forgiveness and focused on Christ as Messiah, Intercessor, and Mediator. The exposition of the words to the dying thief made clear the present reality of salvation and the assurance of the Christian hope, which the preacher contrasted with the uncertainty inherent in Spiritism and Roman Catholicism.[5] The *Puritano* told of the pastor who, speaking of the death of his mother, witnessed to his hope in the words of the popular chorus:

> Since Jesus is mine I'm completely happy,
> I'm going to Heaven, my beautiful country,
> I do not deserve it, vile sinner that I am,
> But because I believe, I know Jesus as Savior.[6]

Emphasis on the life to come resulted both from the theology which the church adopted, and the situation of its members, who were usually poor, despised, ostracized, and, at times, persecuted. The man who asked his friends to sing the hymn containing the following line at his funeral expressed an attitude common among his brethren.[7]

> The world I despised, its profit and its praise,
> And for my Shield and Defender, God I took.

It sounded the valid note that a believer could trust God completely and should put Him first. But the piety it expressed could also degenerate into a selfish concern for one's own salvation in the life to come and a religion indifferent to the needs of others in this world.

Perhaps as a consequence of its reaction against Roman Catholic sacramentalism, the worship of the church never exhibited the balance between Word and Sacrament which Calvin had intended, and it often lost its corporate nature. Almost all Brazilian Presbyterians held Zwinglian views on the Lord's Supper, and, because of the missionary situation in which the church existed, the majority believed the main purpose of the worship service to be evangelization, moral exhortation of believers, or continuation of the polemic against rival religious groups. The pastor was more a preacher than a leader of worship, and the sermon was usually emphasized to the detriment of aspects of the service involving congregational participation. A congress sponsored by the Evangelical Confederation in 1936 reported that most Protestant services still followed a routine which included three hymns (read aloud beforehand for the benefit of illiterates who might be present), three prayers, scripture, the offering, the sermon, and the benediction. It added: "There are places where any change in this pattern . . . almost causes scandal."[8]

The necessity of proclaiming the gospel in a nominally Roman

Catholic society, often in the face of Catholic polemics, led the church at times to lose the positive note in its message. The Reverend Richard Mayorga, an ex-priest, preached a sermon attacking auricular confession, the doctrine of purgatory, the Mass, indulgences, and the "idolatry" of the Roman church.[9] And lists of the "false doctrines" taught by Catholicism appeared sporadically in the Protestant press. One writer's understanding of his church, and his misunderstanding of history, became evident in his comment: "We are called Protestants, because we protest against the errors of the Roman Catholic Church." Then he listed seventeen "errors" of that church, including the supremacy of the Pope, auricular confession, clerical celibacy, worship of images and saints, the idea of sacrifice in the Mass, use of Latin in the liturgy, and the place accorded to Mary. But nowhere did he include the point which was crucial to the sixteenth-century Reformers, the question of justification and how it was to be received. The writer concluded that because such doctrines were not of divine origin, one must protest against them.[10] Anti-Catholicism was so extreme that the church prohibited the use of pictures of Biblical figures in religious education[11] and in the North, at least, even rejected the use of the term "Holy Week."[12]

It seems clear that for many Protestants, as well as for most Catholics, religion was seen as a list of revealed dogmas which should lead to proper conduct. Protestants believed their doctrines to be Biblical and those of the dominant church to be false, and they strove for a high moral standard, while, too often, popular Catholicism had almost no impact on personal conduct. The difference between them, however, was not in their concept of religion as such but in the content of their doctrines and the quality of moral life. Many Protestants failed to perceive the radically different understanding of the Christian faith and life which the Reformers had rediscovered and expounded as an implication of justification by faith. Thus, a large number of Brazilian Presbyterians fell into the error of seventeenth-century Scholasticism, reducing the gospel to a list of doctrines and defining faith as belief in them. This invited the danger of a new institutionalism in which, in extreme cases, the rigid, legalistic Roman Catholic piety was transferred to the Protestant church with little change in basic attitudes.[13]

Brazilian Presbyterianism embraced a strongly conservative

theological position from the beginning. Several factors explain this: its roots in Old School Presbyterianism in the United States, the fact that missionaries usually came from the more conservative wing of the mother churches, and the relatively large proportion of Southern Presbyterians in the total missionary force in the nation. But the Brazilian church took a theological stance still more conservative than that of most missionaries, at times criticizing them and the North American church for their "liberalism." Gammon commented: "I am from the South. I belong to the most conservative part of the Synod of Virginia. I was raised in the most orthodox manner, by the most orthodox teachers. I have always considered myself 'sound in the faith,' but the conservative orthodoxy of these Brazilian brothers is such that I fear for my orthodox skin!"[14]

It is clear that the Protestant orthodoxy which came with the missionaries interacted with the Brazilian concept of religion, formed largely by the Roman Catholic Church, to reinforce the conservative trend. While most of the lay and folk Catholicism in Brazil was quite liberal and undogmatic, after the 1870's, clergymen and laymen who worked for Catholic renewal conceived of religion in increasingly traditionalistic and rigid terms. This Roman Catholic dogmatism helped form the Brazilian concept of what genuine religion should be, even for Protestants who had never been practicing Catholics. Porter alluded to this in his plea for tolerance toward Pentecostals, when he denounced the common prejudice toward innovations and warned that the Roman concept of a static church was permeating Presbyterianism. Worse still, he added, was the conviction that Presbyterians were so wise that God had called them to anathematize brethren. He concluded: "It seems that in the breast of each believer . . . there reigns a lordly pope." The *Puritano* reacted against this manifestation of "liberalism" by the missionary and criticized him for advocating "innovations" in the church.[15]

Presbyterian piety put great stress on the scriptures, and they were read and expounded not only in the church, but often in the homes. New believers frequently learned to read in order to study the Bible, which, except for the hymnal, was often the only book in a humble home.[16] As a result one common nickname for Protestants was *Biblias*. It was understandable that Brazilian Presbyterians emphasized the authority of the Bible. Not only had they found its message liberating, but, like Protestants of the sixteenth and seventeenth centuries, they were caught in a struggle against papal authority and tradition. Any departure from Biblical literalism appeared to imply erosion of scriptural authority and therefore of the whole basis of Protestant Christianity.

Álvaro Reis saw the First World War as the direct result of the "apostasy" of Rome allied with that of the Protestant liberalism and rationalism which, he said, had begun with higher criticism.[17] Some accused the PCUSA of being loose in doctrine and less Christian than the Brazilian Church because of its apparently decreased opposition to the papacy, implied when the clause calling the Pope the anti-Christ was removed from its version of the Confession of Faith in 1903.[18] The Brazilians made no changes in their version of the Confession, not even adding the chapters on the Holy Spirit and the love of God and missions. However, the action of the 1916 General Assembly of the PCUSA which reaffirmed the "essential doctrines of the Word of God," the first of which was "the inspiration, without error, of the Scriptures," brought a favorable response in Brazil.[19]

An example of Biblical literalism carried to the extreme was the controversy over the use of individual cups in place of the traditional common chalice in the Lord's Supper. Reis accused those who advocated this "innovation" of implicitly denying the divinity of Christ. The Synod of 1903 had left the matter optional, but the discussion became so heated in 1914 that some spoke of schism.[20]

Conservatism in the North, reinforced by the defensive stance of a feudal society fallen into decadence, was even stronger. There, too, the dispensationalist theology of a number of pastors intensified both anti-Catholicism and the suspicion of anything new. Jerônimo Gueiros taught that the apostasy predicted by Jesus and Paul had become a reality in the Church of Rome. At the same time the fear of apostasy in Protestantism became apparent in frequent condemnations of "innovations" and "worldliness" in the church, and true Presbyterianism was implicitly identified with sectarian conservatism.[21]

The Ethical Emphases of the Church

A number of factors in the Brazilian situation reinforced the emphasis on personal morality which came with the missionaries. When nominal Catholics, for whom the teaching of the church had little influence in daily life, accepted the Protestant message, religion usually became related to morality for the first time in their experience. The society in which they lived, especially in the interior, was often violent, and many of the social events and religious *festas* provided occasion for drunkenness, gambling, fighting, and sexual immorality. Thus it was inevitable that much of the Protestant ethic should be negative, rejecting the conduct which caused so much suffering. It was also necessary that moral instruction be pointed and simple for new converts, who, in most cases, could not understand the subtleties of sophisticated ethical distinctions. Thus, in a society where inebriation and its resulting misery were common and where it was understood that men had almost no limitations on their sexual conduct, the issue was clear for the new Protestant communities. The confining of sex to marriage and abstention from excessive and public use of alcoholic beverages or, in most cases, total abstinence became the norm of conduct for Evangelicals. Even those who rejected the new faith were scandalized if a believer drank or was guilty of fornication. Thus the society in which Brazilian Presbyterianism was planted needed and reinforced the ethical emphases of late-nineteenth-century North American Puritan Protestantism.

Secondly, piety which usually considered this world, with its problems and its temptations, as a sphere from which one should flee in life and escape at death naturally produced an ascetic, world-denying ethic. The common exhortation to flee from "worldliness" was defined at times as pride and ostentation but more often the appeal suggested rejection of this world as the place where life is lived and from which escape is desirable.[22] The most common meaning of the term, however, was indulgence in questionable amusements, drinking, and sexual immorality. The same confusion was seen in the concept of "flesh." Thompson defined it as "the animal part, the physical part of man, decayed and sinful, the seat of many disorderly appetites." Concupiscence then became "love for those things which please and satisfy the senses, and . . . of beautiful things, clothes, houses, jewels, and money."[23] If love for things which satisfied the senses was considered wrong there could be little basis for an adequate social ethic. Thus most believers limited their concern to personal morality and looked on the world in which they lived either in negative or, at best, neutral terms.

Included in the rejection of worldliness was abstention from vices, which, in addition to those mentioned, included gambling, smoking, and dancing. At times church members did not live up to the hopes of their pastors, and Aníbal Nora, who opposed the use of all alcoholic beverages because of the danger of drunkenness, admitted that not all of his flock were total abstainers. But he had succeeded in bringing numerous ranchers and businessmen to the point where they no longer made or sold *cachaça*, the common sugar cane rum. They refused to profit from that which brought disgrace to others.[24]

Of special concern to the churches was *Carnaval*. The parties, parades, and general celebration during the last three days before Lent appeared to Protestants and to many Catholics as well to be a travesty of Christian piety. Drunkenness, immorality, and violence usually accompanied the celebration, making it doubly abhorrent, and Presbyterians were prohibited from participation. The attitude of most Protestants was expressed by a writer who said, "The believer who takes any part in this mockery is tramping on and mocking the Lord Jesus and His doctrine."[25] Jerônimo Gueiros found it necessary to use the "keys of the Kingdom of Heaven" against one member who had broken the seventh commandment and two who had taken part in *Carnaval*.[26]

Discipline was taken very seriously. Nora taught that if a member were suspended for a fault he should have the sympathy and prayers of the church, but if he persisted and were eliminated, this would indicate that he had rejected the gospel. In that case believers should have neither personal nor commercial relations with him. However, considering the difference between the standard of conduct expected by the church and that of society in general, discipline was not very frequent. Nora received approximately 320 people on profession of faith from 1908 to 1912 but only eliminated thirty-eight and suspended fourteen more. Of those eliminated, several were members of the first Protestant families in the area. The subsequent restoration of six of them indicated that perhaps family pressures were a factor.[27]

Just as it was in North American Presbyterianism during the

period, the proper observance of the Sabbath was a great concern, and a number of pastoral letters from judicatories treated
the subject.[28] The ideal Sunday, with time set aside only for essential activities, was one given entirely to church attendance,
devotional activities, and visitation of the sick. Recreation, social
events, business, and nonessential travel were to be left for the
other six days. Because stores were normally open seven days a
week this entailed personal sacrifice for some. Nora told of a
young convert who left his business and lost his investment
when his partners refused to close on Sunday.[29] It was a greater
problem in the North where the weekly *feira*, or street market,
was held on Sunday, bringing rural folk to town for the busiest
day of the week. There some believers bought and sold on Sunday
while others refused to do so, and the church adopted a tolerant
attitude.[30]

But many leaders believed that the failure to observe a strict
Sabbath was the beginning of moral decay. Showing that the confusion of cultural norms and Christian morality was not limited
to the United States, Álvaro Reis wrote: "English feminine suf-
frage is the greatest visible indication of the moral and religious
decadence of that nation, and accompanies, step by step, the open
decline in the observance and sanctification of Sunday."[31]

The question provided an example which showed the relative
importance, in the mind of the church, of personal and social
ethics. The church taught that it was the duty of every eligible
believer to take an active and patriotic part in the destiny of the
nation by voting in elections. But the practice of holding them on
Sunday created a difficult dilemma for Presbyterians. After two
unsuccessful requests to the government that they be held on another day, the General Assembly of 1915 voted to recommend
that believers "abstain from participating in elections held on
Sundays."[32]

The political concerns of the church during the period were
limited to sporadic protests against the frequent violations of the
constitutional provision for separation of church and state. Most
common were cases where the crucifix was placed in public buildings, and pupils in public schools were obliged to take part in
religious processions.[33] When Brazil sent an ambassador to the
Vatican Presbyterians criticized the act as an insult to the Italian

government and expressed fear that the next step would be the concession of subsidies to Catholic institutions.[34] The only article in the church press during the period which showed concern for oppressed groups was one by Erasmo Braga, calling on the government to protect the Indians.[35] But the lack of a political ethic was not a result of the concern for personal morality alone. Important also were the conviction that the church and state should remain separate and the fear of the corrupting influence of political activity within the church. Reis expressed it clearly: "Politically speaking the influence of Protestantism is nil, and hopefully the Evangelical churches will never think of mobilizing themselves politically. Every church which becomes involved, directly or indirectly, in politics, becomes even more corrupt than political life itself."[36]

The Calvinistic emphasis on work—with its disdain for worldliness and excessive luxury and its effect on the accumulation of wealth in Europe and North America, both of which have been explored by Max Weber—was also present in Brazilian Presbyterianism. It came as a welcome corrective to a mentality formed by the Iberian aristocracy, which had used slaves to perform all manual labor and considered such work unworthy of anyone with status. Presbyterian leaders repeatedly condemned the aversion to work as the cause of economic stagnation and poverty. Honest labor, they declared, was the will of God and a religious as well as a patriotic duty. They also implied that the adoption of Protestantism would bring economic progress.[37] Aníbal Nora preached that the Christian life was happy and prosperous because the believer abandoned the vices which caused poverty and poor health, began to work harder, and acquired legitimate wealth. "If anyone on earth is equipped to be happy, strong, and rich," he said, "it is the Evangelical believer."[38]

The result of this Calvinistic asceticism could be seen in the life of Manoel de Melo in the Minas Triangle. After his conversion, despite illness, he and his wife worked hard, saved, sold their products, started the first store in their town, and eventually prospered. As they did so they paid their workers a wage that was above average in the area.[39] In the relatively uncomplicated frontier society, where land was available and a rural middle class could develop, this ethic raised the standard of living of its followers in a relatively short time. The "Advice to Believers," writted by Melo and widely circulated, is an excellent example of this rural Calvinistic ethic:

1. The believer cannot be idle, not even one hour a week. If he is, he steals time and will be tempted to rob to support his family.
2. The believer should have a clean habitation, even though it is a shack. He also should be clean. Jesus loves the poor but condemns laziness.
3. He cannot lie. It is condemned.
4. He should not go into debt. Not to pay is to rob.
5. The believer should not be sad. He is the temple of God.
6. The believer should not be fanatical, but with love should call sinners to the feet of Jesus.
7. He should not fail to pay taxes, even though they be heavy.
8. He cannot take arms to worship.[40]

Cleanliness was another important virtue for rural believers. Nora taught his people that to allow their children or houses to be dirty was to deny the spirit of the gospel.[41] Along the river where Willis Banks worked as a lay evangelist for over three decades, a government doctor sent during an epidemic told Banks' son-in-law: "I knew when I had arrived at the port of a Protestant. The canoe dry, the path from the port cleared, flowers planted on both sides, around the house the weeds cut, inside the children good and clean, everything in order. . . . On the table, two books, the Bible, and the Hymnal."[42]

However, the ethics of Brazilian Presbyterianism were not entirely moralistic and individualistic. In 1910 the church established an orphanage which would provide children an Evangelical family atmosphere and education.[43] Support, however, was disappointing and it did not operate long as an institution of the General Assembly. Through the efforts of laymen, it was reopened later. More successful and widespread were efforts to build Evangelical hospitals, led in most cases by Presbyterians. The first was constructed in Rio in 1912, and several were built in other cities. Nursing was a badly neglected profession in Brazil, and the Rio hospital instituted a course in 1914.[44] Evangelical doctors contributed their services to the institution, which was open to those of all creeds and, particularly, to the poor. Members of most Protestant churches supported it, but a large share of the leadership came from Presbyterians.

The Identification of Protestantism with Progress

The predominantly individualistic ethic did not mean that Brazilian Presbyterians had no interest in the progress of the nation. But they firmly believed they could make their most important contribution to its well-being through evangelization. The keystone of their social ethic was the conviction, shared with Rui Barbosa and other nineteenth-century liberals, that a growing Protestant community would inevitably bring social and economic progress as a result of spiritual and moral improvement. Commenting on the motto written on the Brazilian flag, Álvaro Reis proclaimed that without Evangelical faith society was the victim of "disorder and regression," adding that only true religion would bring "order and progress."[45] It was common for Presbyterian churches to give great emphasis to the celebration of November 15, the Day of the Republic, with services of prayer and thanksgiving, sermons relating the progress of the Evangelical faith to that of the nation, and exhortations to evangelize.[46] And to charges that Protestants were not true patriots of the "Land of the Holy Cross" (the original name of Brazil), because they had rejected its faith and were helping to sell the country to North Americans,[47] Presbyterians countered with the affirmation that they were better Brazilians than their rivals because their church was governed by national leaders and owed no allegiance to any foreign head. They also reminded their critics that, unlike the Catholic clergy, Protestants believed in the Constitution and its provision for the separation of church and state.

Thus, acceptance of Protestantism was often linked to the nation's fulfillment of its destiny. Lino da Costa, an ex-priest, preached that God had made the light of the gospel shine in northern Europe just at the time of North America's colonization in order that its most powerful nation could send apostolic messengers to other countries. He concluded that if Brazil wished to become a strong and unified nation it must accept that message.[48] Gammon, one of the most influential missionaries, also related Evangelical Christianity and progress:

We need to make it perfectly clear that when Evangelical
Christianity comes to Latin America with its message, it has
in view the winning of the individual to the acknowledge-
ment of the Lord Jesus Christ as the only Savior of men. We
should also make it perfectly clear that the Gospel is the only
moral dynamic sufficient for the uplift and purification of the
world. Again . . . it should be made clear that Evangelical
Christianity is the sole basis for individual freedom of speech
and for liberty in Church and State.[49]

Erasmo Braga added that without true Christianity, liberty would
lead to corruption and ruin and concluded that if Biblical faith
had flourished in Latin America from the beginning, the area
would have enjoyed more public education, stability, and progress.[50]

The first assumption underlying the belief that Protestantism
contributed to progress was that it brought a higher standard of
personal morality. It was undeniable that drunkenness and other
vices prohibited by the Evangelical churches contributed to poverty and misery. In an address on the Day of the Republic, Álvaro
Reis argued that the believer, whose body and home were clean,
who worked six days a week and provided for his family, who
rested on the seventh day, and was free from vices, was less apt
to fall prey to diseases such as tuberculosis, a scourge in Brazil.
Consequently he would progress more in his personal life and
contribute to the greatness of the nation.[51] Presbyterians also
believed that the higher standard of morality would have its effect in the political sphere as Protestants rose to positions of
responsibility in public life. A pastor in Rio wrote: "If the nation
could always count on Evangelicals in administration in general
and especially in the affairs of the Republic, it is clear, it is undeniable, that morality would always be systematic in the acts of
public functionaries. From this would come progress in every
sense."[52] Apparently no one asked if public responsibility and
power might not prove to be forces of corruption in the lives of
Protestants as they had been in others. Perhaps Brazilian Presbyterians were not sufficiently Calvinistic in their understanding of
sin.

A second assumption, especially important in the young republic whose precarious political institutions were threatened by
growing Roman Catholic clericalism, was the conviction that Prot-

estantism, and particularly Calvinism, was the only spiritual and historical basis for political democracy. Júlio Nogueira put it succinctly: "Presbyterianism is equal to Calvinism, and Calvinism is equal to republicanism."[53] Frequently cited was the thesis of de Laveleye that wherever it had established itself, Protestantism had contributed to economic progress by encouraging the formation of free institutions. Those of Spain and Portugal were often contrasted with their counterparts in England and the United States.[54]

The third major assumption was that progress would come because Protestantism established educational institutions and stimulated much greater interest in learning on the part of its adherents. The impetus given to popular education in the Reformation and the great difference in literacy rates between Protestant and Catholic countries were often cited. The *Puritano* said in 1915 that the illiteracy rate among Catholics in Brazil was between 60 and 80 per cent, while that of Protestants was only a fourth of that.[55] The religious concern which frequently led people into Protestantism was often accompanied by the awakening of interest in study. Maria de Melo wrote that when a friend visited her mother before the family's conversion and learned that her husband was reading to her on Sunday afternoons, the guest immediately became suspicious because ". . . at that time, in that environment, any person who said he was reading a book was suspected of becoming a Protestant. Only the Protestants owned and read books. No one else was concerned with such a thing. . . . Read, study, instruct . . . why? Studying would not put beans on the table."[56]

The Melo family was the first in the area to send its children away to study, in this case to Lavras, and when the oldest returned, she opened the first school in the town. It was only then that the priests began to visit the locality and forced the authorities to open a rival institution.[57] This was not uncommon, and Willems wrote that among the Methodists in Cunha:

The parents feel the obligation to teach their children to read, they themselves teaching them when there are no schools. In the schools maintained by the Methodists the students receive, not only instruction in their first letters, but acquire the habit of reading. They are characterized by greater development in conversation and by the interest which they show for subjects and events completely beyond the horizon of the local culture.[58]

Even the Sunday schools which were formed in nearly all Presbyterian churches and congregations encouraged interest in reading by their stress on Bible study and the lesson. In many cases this provided the stimulus for adults to learn to read, while in the North a number of Sunday schools included special reading classes for illiterates.[59]

The most visible outgrowth of the concern for education was the establishment of schools by missionaries and Brazilian Presbyterians. While the majority were on the primary level, some secondary schools and university faculties were included. The stated goals of the mission institutions were five in number: to aid in propagation of the gospel, especially among the upper classes; to prepare believers for life on a higher economic level which would enable them to support the church and exert greater influence on society; to provide a more spiritual and moral educational environment than that of the public and Catholic schools; to prepare church leaders; and to contribute generally to the culture and progress of the nation by teaching students how to use its resources more efficiently.[60]

The first two and best known of the institutions were Mackenzie and the *Colégio Internacional*, founded in Campinas but moved to Lavras and later known as the *Instituto Gammon*. The Lavras institution pioneered in the study of scientific agriculture in Brazil, beginning in 1908, and also led in stimulating education and introducing modern pedagogy in southern Minas Gerais. An elder from the Lavras church wrote that before establishment of mission schools in that area, 80 per cent of its children did not attend school, but by 1915 the figure had dropped to 20 per cent.[61] Mackenzie's influence was even greater. It introduced emphases on laboratory work, physical education, the study of modern languages and sciences, and silent study instead of rote memory and recitation aloud. In 1890 two of its teachers, a North American and a Brazilian who had studied in the United States, were asked to become consultants to the state of São Paulo as it modernized its educational system. The progress that would make São Paulo the nation's leader in education began when it adopted many of the methods used in Mackenzie, and its president, Horace Lane, was considered such a benefactor that the state legislature closed in mourning on the day of his death.[62] In 1916 it was still no exaggeration to say that "Mackenzie practically sets the pace for higher education of the modern type in Brazil."[63] But while the school in Lavras continued to maintain a strong Christian emphasis and prepared a number of future pastors, the São Paulo institution did not. Partly because of the bitter controversy surrounding it and partly because of Lane's failure to see the difference between the gospel and North American "Christian" culture which Mackenzie attempted to embody, it lost most of its contact with the church and prepared very few of its leaders. On the other hand, by 1923 nineteen ministers, seven seminarians, and a large number of lay leaders had studied at Gammon, with twenty more future seminarians attending the school that year.[64]

Several mission schools, founded in the first two decades of the century, became well known and made great contributions both to the church and the areas they served. The missions of the PCUSA established self-help schools in Castro, Paraná, and Ponte Nova, Bahia, while the North Brazil Mission founded the *Colégio Agnes Erskine* in Recife and the *Colégio Quinze de Novembro* in Garanhuns, Pernambuco. Ponte Nova and the Quinze produced a number of future pastors, while the Agnes, a girls' school, prepared teachers for Evangelical primary schools. The *Instituto Ponte Nova*, established by Waddell in 1906 in a poverty-stricken region 350 kilometers inland from Salvador, developed into a complex which included a farm, a secondary and normal school, a hospital, and a course for practical nurses. In an area where it was traditional for "educated" men to shun manual labor, the school required each student to work on the farm. Much to the amazement of his students, C. E. Bixler taught Greek and Latin in the mornings and worked in the fields with the boys in the afternoons. Under Waddell's leadership, over forty parochial schools were developed in Bahia and Sergipe, frequently staffed by graduates of Ponte Nova, and supported by local churches and communities. By 1916 local governments had taken over nearly all of them, often with the Protestant teachers remaining. Their specifically Evangelical character eventually disappeared, but they made a great contribution to education in the area.[65] As late as 1953 all of the public school teachers in the

prosperous municipalities of Lapão and Irecê in Bahia's interior
were graduates of Ponte Nova, and government statistics showed
the area served by the institution to have a higher literacy rate
than any other region in the interior of the state.[66]

The self-help plan was an attempt to solve the problem of
charging tuition from Protestant families, most of whom were poor.
On the other hand, financial needs and the belief that the schools
would be a vehicle for evangelism led them to admit non-Evangelical students, evoking criticism from many Brazilian pastors.
One of them charged that the schools concealed their religious
purpose in order to attract students from hostile families, then
only to alienate them later with rules for compulsory chapel attendance.[67]

Thus, while most Brazilian pastors and missionaries recognized
the need for schools, they usually disagreed as to the type of institution desired, the constituency to be served, and the purpose
involved. Brazilians were naturally less inclined to confuse North
American culture with the Christian faith, less optimistic about
the evangelistic effect of the schools, and more sectarian in their
wish to restrict admission to children from Protestant families.
They advocated institutions which would educate the children of
the church, remove them from the poor atmosphere of the public
schools, and provide seminary preparation. Juventino Marinho
criticized the mission schools in the North on this basis and pled
for more small parochial schools like those which his wife and
daughter had established in cities where he had been pastor.[68]

An important educational institution maintained by Brazilian
efforts alone was the Atheneu Valenciano. Founded by the ex-
Salesian, Constâncio Omenga, it prepared a number of men for
seminary. However, there were other schools established without
foreign aid which aimed at contributing to the community at
large. Jerônimo Gueiros founded a secondary school in Natal
which he hoped would become a model of pedagogy and a moral
beacon to progress. His church already conducted a night course
for illiterate women.[69] Presbyterians established the only secondary and normal school in Canhotinho, Pernambuco, while Antônio Maciel, a member of one of the leading families of Minas
Gerais, who was converted at Gammon, opened a school in Patos
which later became a state normal school.[70] Other examples were
found in Campo Formoso, Bahia, and eastern Minas Gerais.

Presbyterian ministers often served as teachers and school directors as well as pastors, and a number of them made outstanding contributions to education, especially in philology and grammar. By 1954 Trajano's *Aritmética Elementar* was in its 131st edition and his *Aritmética Progressiva* in its 84th; Pereira's *Gramática Expositiva Elementar* was in its 147th edition and his *Gramática Expositiva Superior* in its 91st. Erasmo Braga's famous series of primers was still in print forty years after it was written and was translated into Japanese to aid in the orientation of immigrants from that country.[71] Otoniel Mota's works on the Portuguese language made him an authority in that field, while T. H. Maurer, Jr., earned recognition as Brazil's leading philologist by mid-century. In most cases these texts were prepared by men of marked ability who, impressed with the dearth of material available, wrote to meet specific needs. Many were professors of Portuguese, and, ironically enough, Pereira prepared his grammars for his classes in Mackenzie. But the Calvinistic concern for the word in preaching must have been an additional factor in stimulating the unusually large proportion of Presbyterian ministers who became outstanding grammarians.

Teaching did have its pragmatic appeal for ministers. Salaries from the churches were usually inadequate, and in most communities the Presbyterian pastor was part of a tiny minority with higher education. As prejudice against Protestants began to wane, invitations often came to teach in public and private schools. The Brazilian tradition which encouraged professional men to add to their income and status by teaching part time was another factor. The concept of the pastor-schoolmaster, well known in the United States in the previous century, was encouraged by missionaries, especially under the increasing pressure to find Evangelical teachers for their schools. The local pastor almost inevitably became part of the administrative or teaching staff of a mission institution. Such was the case of M. G. dos Santos, pastor of the Igreja Unida in São Paulo and director of the Escola Americana, part of Mackenzie Institute. When the South Brazil Mission wanted nationals to assume control of its schools in Castro and Curitiba, local pastors became their directors.

As a consequence, Presbyterians made an impressive contribution to Brazilian education, one greater in proportion to its size than that of any group except possibly the Methodists.[72] At the same time there were complaints that the educational institutions often diverted resources from direct evangelistic work and hindered the growth of the church. Pastors tied down to schools could do little to start new work in outlying areas and at times were unable to develop the full potential of the local congregation.

A number of Presbyterians who prospered through their work and discipline went beyond an individualistic ethic and demonstrated an impressive sense of community awareness. Examples were Joaquim Ribeiro dos Santos, an elder, self-made man, and philanthropist, who established a school and hospital in Rio Claro;[73] Manoel de Melo, who worked to bring a school and railroad to his area;[74] and Antônio Januzzi, a bricklayer who became a building contractor and contributed heavily to medical and educational work in Valença, Rio de Janeiro.[75] Gustavo Ambrust, a physician and elder in First Church, Rio, became one of Brazil's pioneers in literacy work by establishing the National Education Crusade in 1932. In spite of strong opposition from the Catholic clergy,[76] the non-sectarian organization received support from the government and laymen of all creeds. It was credited with stimulating, directly and indirectly, the establishment of 8,000 schools with 600,000 students and the distribution of large quantities of primers and textbooks.[77]

Perhaps the most outstanding example of community service was that set by Willis Banks, the son of North American Confederates, who was converted in Castro, Paraná. Although he had little formal education, he served as administrator of an isolated *fazenda* for over forty years and became one of the most notable evangelists in Brazil. Traveling whenever his work would permit, he established a number of churches and congregations in the depressed and backward south littoral of São Paulo. In order to construct the local church he built the area's first brickyard. Finding the area's illiteracy rate to be nearly 100 per cent, he and his wife brought children to live with them for periods of six months, teaching them and sending them home to teach others. Because the region was devoid of medical help and filled with superstition, he taught himself with a home medical guide and treated infections, tuberculosis, malaria, worms, and malnutrition. He invented a device to make manioc flour, introduced better methods of agriculture and care of livestock, built the first silo in the area, and constructed machinery to cut silage for himself and others. Because almost everyone suffered from internal parasites, he harassed public health officials until they furnished medicine which he distributed widely. After people had taken it he gave them "Banks pills" of his own making, containing extracts of citrus juices, avocado leaves, a local herb, magnesia, and iron.[78]

A striking illustration of the Presbyterian contribution to progress appears in Willems' comparison of two villages in the region twenty years after Banks' death. Both were isolated, situated in virtually identical circumstances, with inhabitants of the same racial and cultural backgrounds. But one was Presbyterian, while the other followed the traditional folk Catholicism. The contrast between them indicates how Presbyterianism has motivated people in some cases to utilize existing human and natural resources and raise their standard of living. Volta Grande, whose people were converts, had brick and wooden houses, used water filters, and in some cases had home-produced electricity. The inhabitants owned canoes and motor launches for travel to a nearby city, cultivated vegetables along with the traditional rice, beans, corn, manioc, and bananas, had two small herds of dairy cattle, and consequently produced and consumed milk, cheese, and butter. They received and read newspapers and some books in addition to the Bible, and all were literate. The community had taken the unusual initiative of pooling its resources to build a school, afterward donating it to the state with the stipulation that a teacher be provided and paid. The result was an excellent primary school, many of whose graduates continued their studies in the city. Religious services were held three times a week, even though the pastor visited only once a month.

On the other hand the inhabitants of Jipovura lived in daub and wattle houses with no furniture, engaged only in marginal agriculture, did not boil or filter their water, had no canoes, used tiny kerosene lamps for light, and were mostly illiterate. During more prosperous days a few Japanese families had lived there, built a school, and donated it to the community. But the people showed no interest in maintaining it and ruined the building by stealing its doors and windows. The institution continued to function in a room donated by one of the two remaining Japanese families but received little cooperation from the villagers.

Leisure time was filled by playing cards and drinking *cachaça*; alcoholism was common, even among children; and there was no organized religious worship except on the rare occasions when the priest visited.[79]

Thus, the villagers rejected the example of the Japanese, even though it would have raised the standard of living in Jipovura substantially. In Volta Grande, on the other hand, Presbyterianism provided a powerful incentive for the acceptance of new values. But the example of Jipovura makes it clear that mere contact with another level of culture was not sufficient stimulus to bring the same results.

It is significant that the communities in which Willems found Protestantism motivating acceptance of new values and leading to higher living standards among its adherents had one characteristic in common. The local farmers were usually small landowners constituting a rural middle class, and in none was there dominance by powerful *fazendeiros*.[80] This pattern is seen in several areas where Protestantism contributed markedly to progress: eastern Minas Gerais, the Minas Triangle, and Lençois, Bahia, for example. There is little evidence of this phenomenon in the regions of the Northeast where a feudal landholding structure dominates or where the land is so poor as to defy rising above a level of extreme poverty. There the drive for improvement which often accompanies Protestantism frequently shows itself in migration to larger centers where there are more opportunities and better educational facilities for the young.

It seems clear that, even though economic and social progress did not inevitably accompany adherence to Presbyterianism, for a substantial number the new faith provided powerful stimulus to education and greater self-discipline in work and personal habits. This in turn brought better health and use of resources, helping families rise from poverty and illiteracy to the middle class and achieve university-level education in one or two generations.[81] Those who proclaimed that progress would inevitably accompany the Evangelical faith often spoke from personal experience. Their error lay in oversimplification, in assuming that the problems of the poor and of the nation as a whole could be solved by education, morality, and the ascetic virtues alone. They also forgot the possibility that once Protestants had risen to a comfortable level of life, they might be as selfish as others. Indeed, as the most recently arrived members of the middle class, they might become pillars of conservatism in a society seeking more radical solutions to its problems. And at times they were easily led into self-righteousness by their ethic, believing that if everybody became Protestants and gave up their "vices," they too would improve their lot.

The Shape of the Ministry

Presbyterianism in Brazil, just as in other frontier environments, created a dilemma by its concept of the ministry and its preparation. Adopting the ideal of their Puritan and Reformed forefathers, Presbyterians decided that each parish should have its own resident pastor and that he should be well prepared in order to expound the word of God faithfully. Administration of the sacraments was kept in his hands for the sake of ecclesiastical order, but this did not imply any inherent right or quality conferred by ordination. The definition of proper preparation was graduation from a university-level seminary, and the 1924 Book of Order required, somewhat unrealistically, that a candidate for licensure present a seminary diploma and be examined ". . . in Latin and the original languages of Holy Scripture, in mental philosophy, logic, rhetoric, and ethics, in the natural and exact sciences, in natural and revealed theology, in church history, and in the sacraments and government of the Church." In addition, he had to present a discussion in Latin of a theological point, an exegesis paper, a homily, and a sermon.[82]

The other side of the problem was the need for more pastors in the rural areas and for a style of ministry which provided closer contact with the poor in the cities. There were never enough schools and money to accommodate the rural youth who wished to study for the ministry, and those who finished the long course often gravitated to urban areas and to secular employment, leaving little time for the pastorate. At the same time they tended to think and speak in terms which often were unintelligible to the urban poor. Their training, allied with other factors, thus helped impose a middle-class pattern on city churches.

A related but frequently neglected aspect of the question was the need to stimulate greater lay participation in leadership. Not only was it inherent in the nature of the church, but the missionary situation in which Brazilian Presbyterianism found itself, with far more organized churches and *congregações* than pastors,[83] made it imperative. Many laymen, with varying degrees of formal education, preached regularly and were largely responsible for the vitality of their congregations. Nor was intensive lay activity confined to the hinterland. The one hundred ten men, who composed the Christian Endeavor Society of First Church, Rio, visited the sick and the jails and established several new *congregações*.[84] But such leadership was not always present, especially in older churches where believers had become too dependent on an ordained leader or in situations where laymen were not encouraged to use their gifts. The pastor of several congregations in Pernambuco wrote that the Palmares church, the oldest in his field, was like a dependent child, opening its doors only when he was present.[85] It seems clear that the emphasis on a well-prepared ministry contributed at times to the development of Protestant clericalism by leading clergy and laity alike to feel that a local congregation could not function properly unless an ordained seminary graduate were present. However, it is also clear that the church showed far more vigor in witness and service to its community where a high level of lay activity existed.

Perhaps the best solution to the three-sided dilemma would have been provision of more than one path to ordination, with the recognition that different levels of formal instruction were needed. While young men would normally complete the full seminary course, older men and even youths who lacked opportunity for all of the necessary formal education could have been licensed for prolonged periods after they had proved themselves through service to local churches, with ordination coming after prescribed reading and study. Such a system, similar to that which the Baptists adopted, would have stimulated a greater degree of lay leadership by encouraging the use of the varied talents available in the church. Quite possibly, too, it would have provided pastors who were more responsive to the varying social needs of the people. It could have supplied a high level of theological education for some as well as a more numerous and broadly based ministry to the masses.

The few men without formal training who became pastors were exceptions. For example, Willis Banks, whose ministry of evangelism and service to the community was outstanding, was never ordained. Believers in his field partook of the sacraments only when a pastor could make the long journey from the state capital. If Banks had been a Baptist or Pentecostal, he would have received ordination after proving himself. The churches he organized would have been more nearly self-sufficient, and others from the area would have been ordained in them eventually.

In 1938, with creation of a new category, *provisionado*, men of proven gifts could be accepted as lay evangelists by presbyteries.[86] They served mainly in East Minas, Espirito Santo, and the fields of the missions. However, there was no plan for eventual ordination, and the 1950 Constitution abandoned the innovation. Although paid lay evangelists often did effective work, they confronted special problems. Pastors of congregations and professional church workers in effect, they had no actual pastoral authority. Nor, as a rule, could they aspire to ordination. This anomaly created tensions at times in their relationships with the local church, the missions, and the presbyteries.

But, after the church had struggled so long to establish its seminary, perhaps it would have been too much to expect it to consider other levels and types of ministerial preparation. And the relatively high level of theological education also brought a number of advantages. It prepared men who would later give service to all of Brazilian Protestantism, especially since Presbyterians contributed the greatest proportion of leadership to Protestant cooperative movements in the nation. It prepared pastors who, in some cases, were able to interpret the Evangelical faith to the better educated minority of the population. It served as a stimulus to a number of pastors who made outstanding contributions to education and cultural life. The seminaries produced men such as Natanael Cortez and A. T. Gueiros, who were members of their state legislatures and gave leadership to their communities without neglecting the building of the church. The emphasis on strong preparation eventually helped Protestantism gain a hearing in the community at large through the contributions of men like Álvaro Reis, Miguel Rizzo, Jr., José Borges dos Santos, Jr., Jerônimo Gueiros, and Benjamin Moraes, who commanded respect in circles beyond the Evangelical Church. And despite deficiencies, the seminaries produced pastors whose preaching had far more theological content than that of most other Brazilian Protestants.

The disadvantages, however, were to have serious implications. The requirement of a long period of formal study before ordination seriously restricted the number of pastors and, eventually, the number of churches. Church papers constantly referred to the need for more workers, to once flourishing fields now fallen into stagnation and decadence, and to opportunities lost for want of pastors. This was the case not only in the Amazon basin, from which appeals came repeatedly, but in growing cities in the South. The SBM had difficulty turning over its work in Paraná to the national church because it was almost impossible to find pastors,[87] while the once rapidly growing fields of Campos in the state of Rio and Sana in Espirito Santo, with three churches and two schools, suffered frequently for the same reason.[88] But while churches, presbyteries, and missions called for more pastors, some felt the number should be limited even more. M. G. dos Santos in São Paulo criticized presbyteries which sent men to seminary with incomplete preparation and complained that too many being ordained were "mediocre intellectually and deficient spiritually."[89] Conversely, a pastor in Espirito Santo argued that it was wrong to require twelve years of study for pastors in a region where 90 per cent of the people were illiterate, adding that although he had only the short seminary course, he was considered too well educated for his people.[90]

The influence of a concept of ministerial preparation and support more suitable for North America or Europe was shown in 1916 when a visitor asked a Campinas Seminary professor if the institution did not want more students. The reply was, "we believe we should graduate students only as fast as there are self-supporting churches ready to receive them as pastors."[91] The contrast between Brazilian Presbyterians and other Evangelicals was much the same as that on the North American frontier. There, as Sweet has shown, the Methodist circuit rider was sent to new settlements almost before the people arrived, the Baptist farmer-preacher went with his flock, and the Presbyterian minister waited to be called by an already established congregation that could pay his salary.[92] Brazilian presbyteries assigned pastors to new areas at times, but usually they had to have local churches to support them, and their outreach was thus limited. On the other hand, Baptist and Pentecostal pastors were usually products of local congregations whose formal consecration took place when they had shown sufficient leadership qualities. In a number of fields abandoned by the Presbyterians for lack of pastors, Baptists began work and grew rapidly.[93]

The scarcity of pastors, the great size of Brazil, economic problems, and the rapid expansion in many rural areas made it impossible for most interior congregations to have a resident pastor. The size of rural fields often forced ministers to travel constantly, visiting their scattered congregations and opening new work in promising areas. The church in Caxambu, Minas, complained that it had not seen its pastor for two months because he was traveling through his field,[94] while a layman in Paraíba visited a group of believers who had not welcomed a pastor in two years.[95] Benjamin Cesar warned that if a pastor made only rapid visits, limiting his activity to preaching, administration of the sacraments, discipline, and the receipt of offerings, without going to the homes of isolated believers, he caused resentment and was judged a mercenary, without love for the gospel or his flock.[96] When the Presbytery of Rio was divided to form that of Niteroi in 1929, the new judicatory was found to be in difficult straits because nearly all the pastors had lived in the city of Rio, making only sporadic visits to the outlying churches. A rule requiring residence within the field brought rapid progress.[97]

If some rural pastors had little time in which to visit their churches they could not be blamed. Most did heroic work in extremely difficult circumstances. The constraint to proclaim their message to those who had not heard and were often spiritually hungry led them into lives of hardship and constant travel. When José Martins de Almeida Leitão died, the *Puritano* said of him:

An evangelist occupied with twelve churches and various congregations . . . writing his sermons and other works by the light of a smoking kerosene lamp, always tired from long journeys, a pastor concerned about the well-being of his numerous sheep, for whom he sacrificed himself; the head of a numerous family (thirteen children, the youngest just born when he died) who spent three hundred days a year away from his home . . . fulfilling the holy task of evangelizing, of pastoring; ruining his health . . . he ended his days in deep poverty.[98]

But, despite examples like Leitão's, the university-level seminary course usually acted in fact as a means of social mobility, almost inevitably transforming the pastor into a member of Brazil's small middle class. This in turn created an economic problem since it was impossible for most churches to support a pastor even on a very low middle-class level.[99] Often three or four churches and *congregações* together paid one salary, but, increasingly, despite the ideal of a full-time ministry, pastors took outside jobs to make ends meet. Antônio Almeida informed the Recife church in 1916 that he had found it necessary to take such a step, even though he regretted that it would prevent his doing much pastoral visitation.[100] Financial needs also drove many pastors from North to South and from rural areas to cities, where, even if their churches could not support them, it was easier to find a second job. While most rural presbyteries had four or five churches and twice as many *congregações* for each pastor, in 1935 Rio had twenty pastors for its sixteen churches and two *congregações*.[101]

Other influences led pastors to adopt a second profession. It was traditional in Brazil for professional men to have two or more jobs and was believed to increase status as well as income. Often the Protestant pastor, living in a society which accorded him little prestige, sought secular employment because he believed it would enhance his witness in the community. Others felt that, because of the frequently criticized mercenary spirit of the Roman Catholic clergy, they could serve the gospel better if they earned a living outside the church.[102] In their polemic against the dominant church they often emphasized the free grace of God and noted that Protestants did not pay for baptism and other religious services. At times this undercut the development of stewardship and church support. Also the common view of the priest as a social parasite was sometimes transferred to the Protestant pastor, even by members of his own flock, if he did not earn at least part of his living from a second job.

The size of the fields, the divided time of many pastors, the constant drive to evangelize new areas, and concentration on the proclaimed word almost to the exclusion of all else in the life of the church, made the minister's role principally that of a preacher-evangelist, in his own thinking and that of his people. The missionary orientation of the church, which encouraged the presence of nonmembers at worship, accentuated the tendency. At the same time the only functions reserved to the pastor were administration of the sacraments and presidency of the session, which involved reception of new members and discipline. Preaching and teaching, the primary tasks for which the minister studied to prepare himself, were often performed by laymen. There was no rationale for this other than the lack of pastors, which made it necessary for laymen to preach on the one hand, and the need to maintain order by keeping the sacraments in the hands of ordained men on the other. Thus, while the Calvinistic tradition taught that the minister should be well prepared primarily in order to expound the Scriptures, circumstances in Brazil necessitated interpreting that tradition to mean that while both ministers and laymen preached, only the former could baptize and serve communion.

Consequently, a large number of rural congregations maintained their own worship and prayer services, Sunday schools, and evangelistic work for long periods with lay leadership alone. They were autonomous churches without a pastor, except that they could not receive baptism or the Lord's Supper; nor could they administer discipline. Local laymen, who held the genuine leadership of the church in their hands, could evangelize their neighbors but could not baptize them. Thus, the Reformation ideal of a local leader, educated in theology so he could preach and teach and designated by the local church to administer the sacraments, was distorted by the Brazilian situation into an implicit denial of the New Testament pattern of ministry. Untrained laymen preached and often gave heroic service in leading rural congregations, but they and their flocks were deprived of baptism and Communion except on the rare occasions when a pastor visited.

This situation, along with three other factors, contributed to the development of clericalism and authoritarianism. First, the two models which a Presbyterian pastor followed, consciously or unconsciously, were the Roman Catholic priest and the North American missionary. The priest, who shaped the concept of a religious leader in society as a whole, was frequently distrusted and considered a social parasite, but he had authority to rule the local church. It was believed that the gifts of the Spirit were concentrated in his hands, and that through him the grace of God came to the faithful. Understandably, this concept of the pastoral role was transferred, at least in part, to Protestant congregations. At the same time, whether or not the missionary desired it, he was also thrust into a paternalistic pattern. In Brazilian society his foreign origin, his financial resources, and, in many cases, his ability and position as spiritual father of most of the churches in which he worked led the uneducated to look to him as a *doutor*, a person of authority. Secondly, the pastor, despite his middle-class education, was the leader of a minority, sometimes despised, religious group. Thus, he had more difficulty than the priest in establishing his position in the community. Any status he might acquire was almost entirely dependent on his authority over his flock. Finally, in most small-town and country churches, the minister was the only man with a university-level education. Thus he was also a *doutor*, one whose counsel was to be sought and followed by believers.

It was obviously necessary and advisable for many pastors to take secular employment in the economic and cultural climate of Brazil. But it was unfortunate that because of its implicit clericalism, the church failed to stimulate sufficient lay activity. Especially in the cities it placed too much authority and leadership in the hands of the minister, even though he often did not have time to exercise it properly. When laymen did preach, some felt it necessary to emphasize the difference between clergy and laity. Use of the title *reverendo* was strongly defended by Álvaro Reis[103] and still receives far more emphasis in Brazilian Presbyterian churches than in sister institutions in North America. A number of pastors in the South advocated the use of pulpit robes, partially to add solemnity to the service but primarily to distinguish ministers from laymen.[104] The most striking example came in a 1907 Synod vote that when the latter preached, they should stand behind a small table instead of the pulpit. The General Assembly of 1910 left the matter to the discretion of each local session.[105] Neither use of the robe, which was considered too "catholic," nor the rule of 1907 ever prevailed in the North.[106]

The rural origins of most pastors had great influence in shaping the church. Davis noted in 1942 that 80 per cent of the students in Campinas Seminary were from rural and lower-class homes, a pattern which has continued.[107] This was not surprising since the church usually grew more rapidly and developed a more vital Christian community in rural areas. For the young believer with ability and a desire to serve, the pastor or missionary was often the only well-educated believer he knew, and a logical example to follow. With financial aid from a presbytery or mission often provided, study for the ministry supplied an avenue of social mobility.[108] Thus, almost without exception, the pastors of large city churches came from small interior towns or rural homes,[109] just as did many of their church members. They were frequently men of ability and dedication, but their backgrounds and those of a substantial number of their people, complicated by the over-simplified individualistic ethic and middle-class status of the clergy, made it difficult for them to understand fully the complexities of city life and sympathize with its problems. An ethic which was meaningful and helpful to new converts in rural Minas often seemed intolerable and irrelevant legalism to young third-generation Presbyterians in Rio, especially when allied with conservatism and dogmatism which overlooked deeper national problems.

As the church expanded and new generations grew up, it became necessary for Brazilian Presbyterians to modify the shape of their piety and the forms of their worship to meet the needs of the youth, especially in urban situations. Brazil's increasingly complex social problems demanded a reevaluation of the individualistic ethic with its essentially liberal faith in progress through evangelization and morality. And the growing urban character of the nation would make it necessary for the church to reexamine its predominantly rural ethos and base and to provide greater flexibility in the roles of ministers and laymen.

Chapter Six

Continued Evangelistic Growth: 1917-1934

After the First World War the future appeared bright with hope to Brazilian Presbyterians. Álvaro Reis wrote in 1919 that partly because of the example of Wilson, the great Protestant statesman, "there never was a year in which Protestant Christianity had such high prestige in Brazil and in the world as the one which has just ended."[1] But, although Presbyterianism continued to grow during the post-war period, it began to lag behind other groups with more flexible structures and forms of ministry. This was especially true in the burgeoning cities, a tendency which became even more clear in subsequent decades. By 1931 the Baptists, who had entered Brazil twenty-two years after Simonton, constituted the largest Protestant church of missionary origin in the nation with 41,190 members, compared to 32,500 in the Presbyterian church. The total of Presbyterians and Independentes combined was 45,550 communicants, with an additional 3500 in the mission fields, but the Baptists would soon surpass even this number.[2]

Along with the pattern of ministerial preparation, a more rigid, centralized structure hindered Presbyterian growth. Presbyterians usually kept newly organized groups in the dependent status of unorganized *congregações* longer than the Baptists, who established autonomous churches with smaller constituencies. In most cases emancipation of these groups put greater responsibility on local leadership and contributed to more rapid growth.[3] Combined with a more flexible pattern of ministry, the practice soon led to creation of a larger number of churches and pastors. Thus in 1931 the Baptists had 485 churches and the Presbyterians only

250, while Baptist pastors numbered 200 in comparison with 120 in the older church.[4] A comparison of these figures with the total membership of each denomination indicates clearly that Baptists organized autonomous churches with fewer members than did Presbyterians.

By sharply limiting the number of pastors and elevating those who completed seminary into the middle class, the Presbyterian pattern of ministerial preparation restricted church growth, especially in the cities. Although most urban churches had a resident pastor, he was frequently isolated culturally, economically, and spatially from the poor, far more than he was in the less complex rural society. There were no Presbyterian pastors who were also shoemakers or industrial workers, living in the poorest sections of the cities among those who had recently arrived from the North or the hinterland. Yet Baptist and Pentecostal preachers were living and working among them. And it was usually in that stratum, the largest segment of Brazil's population, that Protestantism grew most rapidly. Even though Presbyterian ministers delivered a message with better theological content because of their seminary training, the uneducated often found it abstract and difficult to understand. The isolation of many pastors from the humble made it difficult to state the message in terms meaningful to the poor.

Ministerial preparation was not the only factor which molded urban churches into a middle-class structure. Another was the social mobility despite a rigidly structured society which came as the second and third generations grew up in the church and were stimulated by its educational and ethical emphasis. Waddell spoke of this as a conscious goal:

> If society consists of superimposed strata, then the Evangelical Church in Brazil will not be a vertical section but a funnel, widening as it rises. This is due to two causes: (1) the ignorant classes cannot easily understand the full Gospel or study it. If, therefore, pastors and missionaries use great care in receiving members, the resulting church is preponderantly intellectual. (2) Protestants educate their children, hence such families tend to rise gradually higher in the intellectual scale.[5]

The problem was, of course, that the "ignorant classes" comprised about 85 per cent of the population, and if, intentionally or not, they were eliminated as future church members, only a small minority would be potential Presbyterians. Thus, social mobility, combined with the middle-class pattern of ministry, often separated city churches physically, culturally, and socially from the poor. Members who migrated from rural areas to large cities and failed to find a spiritual home in the large downtown church with its well-dressed people often joined a Baptist or Pentecostal congregation or drifted away from the church entirely. Those two groups soon became much more effective among the masses than were Presbyterians.

The strategy of the North American missions which had led them to leave the densely populated littoral and move west also weakened urban work. While the Baptists concentrated a large missionary force in Rio and São Paulo, the Presbyterian missions had no personnel in either city except for those at Mackenzie, and opportunities in the cities surrounding the capitals were frequently lost. When the Presbytery of Niteroi formed in 1929, over half a century after Presbyterian missionaries had entered the area and then abandoned it prematurely, there were churches in only three of the thirty-two cities in the region. The presbytery included a number of rural congregations, but the population was rapidly moving to the cities. This left the country churches weak, while there was little upon which to build in the urban centers. Population shifts and lack of pastoral care had caused the Barra Alegre Church, organized in 1901, to drop from one hundred to twenty members within two decades.[6] During the same interval the Baptists had established churches in most of the region's cities and counted a greater number of rural groups as well. The rapid growth of the Presbytery of Niteroi, even though it had only five active pastors, is indicative of what additional personnel could have done in the growing satellite cities around major urban areas.[7] The same kind of people who were so responsive to Protestantism in eastern Minas were moving into the areas around the southern cities, but there were few Presbyterian pastors to work with them.

Rio and São Paulo

Presbyterianism in the city of Rio de Janeiro depended on the leadership of Álvaro Reis from the time of his arrival there in 1897. His preaching and writing made its First Presbyterian

Church the largest Protestant congregation in Latin America, and a number of daughter churches were also established. When Reis died suddenly in 1925, a struggle over the question of his successor nearly divided the local congregation and caused two pastors to leave the Presbyterian Church. M. G. dos Santos, who was called from São Paulo, finally assumed the pastorate in 1926. New congregations organized and growth continued under his ministry, but at a diminished rate. The Presbytery of Rio was divided into three in 1929, with Niterio comprising that city and the northern part of the state of Rio; Barra do Pirahy covering the rest of the state; and Rio de Janeiro, now limited to the city of Rio, or the Federal District.[8] Thus, statistics began to indicate more clearly where the church was growing most rapidly. In 1930 and 1931, the Presbytery of Rio had twelve churches, six *congregações*, 1898 communicant members, and nine pastors. During the period, it added 205 persons on profession of faith and 260 by transfer.[9] The largely rural Presbytery of Niteroi, in contrast, had twenty churches, nine *congregações*, 2000 communicants, and five pastors, while it received 457 members on profession of faith and maintained a balance between its losses and gains by transfer.[10] Thus, it grew more than twice as rapidly as Rio in proportion to the total number of members, and nearly four times as fast in proportion to the number of pastors. There is no indication that the disappointing Presbyterian growth in Rio was due to lack of interest in the Protestant message. Baptists in Rio, for example, had a Sunday school enrollment of 3166 in 1931, while Presbyterians had less than half that number.[11]

The Presbyterian Church in the city of São Paulo, weakened by the schism of 1903 and neglect of the missions, began to consolidate itself after the arrival of M. G. dos Santos as pastor of the Igreja Unida in 1913. Five years later the three churches in the city totaled 250 communicants, and each congregation had its own pastor. With fewer workers than there were in Rio, and no missionary aid, outreach was not so great as it should have been. But the Lapa Church was organized in 1924, and Unida began to grow rapidly through evangelization and, even more, through the influx of believers from the interior. By the time Santos left for Rio, in 1926, it enrolled 1200 pupils in its nine Sunday schools,[12] some of which later grew into churches.

Santos was succeeded by Miguel Rizzo, Jr., son of the Mason

who had received John Boyle in his home years earlier. Under Rizzo's leadership Unida grew to rival First Church, Rio, in size and influence. But four churches, three of them small and struggling, were hardly enough in a city whose population was approaching one million. While statistics for São Paulo are not so clear as those for Rio during this period, evidence suggests that there too evangelistic growth was slower than in the church as a whole. The Presbytery of São Paulo, which included the city and surrounding area, received 261 people on profession of faith in 1919 and 1920, bringing its total communicant membership to 1674.[13] This was significantly less than the rate of growth in rural Pernambuco, Niteroi, eastern Minas, and Espirito Santo.

Eastern Minas Gerais and Espirito Santo

Rapid expansion continued in eastern Minas and spread into the Valley of the Rio Doce and the state of Espirito Santo. When Aníbal Nora began his ministry in 1908 there were two churches in eastern Minas and one in Espirito Santo; when he accepted another call in 1927 he left two presbyteries with nine pastors, thirty-three churches, 194 unorganized congregations, and 5250 communicant members.[14] Nora himself had received 2103 people on profession of faith during the nineteen years and had organized fifteen churches.[15] In addition he began the first secondary school in Alto Jequitibá, one of a number of Presbyterian institutions to be established in the region.

The area continued to enjoy one of the highest rates of population growth in the nation. New settlers poured in to take advantage of the excellent soil, and towns developed rapidly. But while the church grew by transfer of members from elsewhere, its greatest spurt came through professions of faith, which totaled 512 in the two presbyteries in 1927.[16] Rapid expansion, the need for more workers, and the dynamism of the churches all stimulated a relatively large influx of men into the ministry. In 1927 the Presbytery of East Minas, with only four pastors, had five men in training,[17] while Espirito Santo received two new ministerial candidates.[18] But not all aspirants from the area went to seminary, disrupting the normal Presbyterian pattern.[19] A need for more workers, the difficulty of providing the necessary preseminary training, and impatience with the insistence on the high level of preparation for the rural frontier ministry, led Nora and his colleagues to ordain some men without the regular theological course. The practice led to "storms in the higher councils" of the church, where many denounced the "Seminary of Jequitibá, the factory of crippled ministers."[20] Ordination without a seminary course never became the norm, but it was more common in this area than any other. While the church's rapid growth in eastern Minas no doubt prompted the departure from standard procedure, the innovation in turn contributed to that expansion.

Espirito Santo, whose population growth exceeded that of any other state during the first half of the century, and the Rio Doce Valley in Minas, an area of similar expansion, exhibited many of the same social characteristics as Alto Jequitibá, and in both places the Protestant movement thrived. New settlers poured in, carving out farms, building rude houses, and planting coffee. Many were Evangelicals, and their robust faith led them to organize small, dynamic, rural congregations to witness among their neighbors. Other newcomers were impressed by the quality of community spirit among the rural Protestants, by their high standard of morality, and by the hard work which led them to prosper. Free from the strong family ties and religious pressures of the more traditional communities from which they had come, they often accepted the new message. Thus the Presbytery of Espirito Santo organized nine new churches from 1926 to 1932. Among them was the church in Vitória, the state capital, which was established through a special missionary effort by the rural congregations, in a reversal of the usual pattern. Despite economic problems, the new church prospered and eventually became the parent of several others in the city.[21] Rapid expansion also occurred in the Valley of the Rio Doce, which had six churches by 1932.[22] Each included a central congregation, usually in a small town or city, and a large number of outlying groups. Apolinário Sathler told of visiting the Resplendor Church and its thirteen congregações. "Eight, ten, and twelve leagues away from the central church there are groups of believers. Some of them in humble houses, surrounded by great forests, lacking in comforts, and without any kind of social intercourse."[23] Such groups usually grew rapidly; of the thirty-four people whom Sathler received on two successive visits, thirty were from the congregações.[24]

The North and Northeast

The vast area covered by the Synod of the North, which included half of Brazil's territory, created serious obstacles to the functioning of the Presbyterian system. On a number of occasions the Synod could not meet because its presbyteries could not afford to send delegates.[25] For the same reason the presbyteries of Pernambuco and the North were not represented at the 1930 General Assembly.[26] Thus, distance and poverty fostered isolation of the North and its pastors from the rest of the church.

Compounding the problem was the appalling scarcity of pastors and the numerous transfers to the South. The sons and grandsons of Belmiro Cesar, one of the first *Pernambucanos* to study for the ministry under John R. Smith, contributed significantly to the church as pastors and elders, but all served in the South. In 1919 J. M. de Almeida Leitão, the pastor in Belém, transferred to eastern Minas, while Pernambuco lost a pastor to São Paulo and a ministerial candidiate to Rio.[27] With the exception of Pernambuco, the nine states from Alagoas to Amazonas seldom had more than one Presbyterian pastor in residence, and lack of funds often made it impossible to send candidates to seminary. In 1928 the two northern presbyteries were able to send only one of the five who presented themselves.[28]

The Presbyterian system, which presupposed a number of pastors and laymen working together to plan and supervise the work could not function properly in the situation. Rural congregations were isolated from each other and from their pastors, and they, in turn, from their colleagues. Thus, along with regionalism, something more akin to Congregationalism than Presbyterianism emerged in the area. Individual congregations, which in most cases had no resident pastor, took care of their own lives as well as they could, with varying degrees of success. Some were strong and vital, while others stagnated between pastoral visits. None, of course, could baptize new members or celebrate the Lord's Supper except on the infrequent occasions when the pastor was present. Poverty and isolation also alienated the northern churches from the national body. Struggling to maintain themselves and seeing no benefits from the General Assembly program, they contributed little to its causes.[29]

Drought, intolerance, and persecution, which were worse in the

North, complicated the issue. The strong and growing church in Quebrangulo, in the interior of Alagoas, was crippled by the exodus of most of its families in 1921 because of drought.[30] In 1932 *O Puritano* reported the emigration of believers from Cedro, Crato, Iguatu, and Senador Pompeu, Ceará, "so they would not die of hunger." The church in Cedro alone had lost nine families, comprising fifty-seven people.[31] Clerical persecution, also more prevalent in the area, created problems but sometimes had a positive effect. A. T. Gueiros visited Hebrom, Maranhão, where the local priest had waged a campaign against a local Presbyterian woman. Because of the affection in which she was held by her neighbors, and her perseverance, Gueiros baptized eighteen adults on one visit there. Forty others expressed their intention to be baptized as soon as they could be legally married to their respective spouses.[32]

Nearly all missionary personnel and resources in the North were dedicated to institutional work. Butler, who had been a great evangelist as well as physician, died in 1919, and Henderlite was occupied with theological education. Other missionaries in the North were concentrated in the schools in Recife and Garanhuns,[33] while most of the few national pastors in the area were responsible for evangelism and pastoral care throughout an entire state. The situation motivated an appeal to General Assembly in 1930: "Considering that there is not one Presbyterian missionary directly occupied in the evangelization of the great Brazilian North which stretches from Alagoas to Amazonas . . . the Synod of the North requests that this judicatory look with sympathy on these abandoned fields and send a worker with resources to the North."[34]

The appeal brought a response from the PCUS Board, which in 1931 sent Langdon Henderlite, son of the professor in the Seminary of the North. His arrival stimulated a renewed evangelistic emphasis in the program of the North Brazil Mission.

The original northern judicatory, which included the area from Alagoas to Amazonas, was divided into the presbyteries of Pernambuco and the North in 1920, and the former, into Pernambuco and South Pernambuco in 1927. Statistics after that year made it clear that here, as in the South, the church grew more rapidly in rural areas than in the cities. In 1927 the Presbytery of Pernambuco, which included Natal, João Pessoa, Recife, and some interior towns, had seven pastors, eight churches, and 1466 communicant members. South Pernambuco had nine churches, all in the hinterland except Maceió, eight pastors, and 1546 members.[35] By 1930 South Pernambuco counted 2177 members, having had 244 professions of faith the previous year.[36] Pernambuco had 1786 communicants, having received only ninety-nine new members by transfer and profession of faith in 1929.[37] Thus, the interior churches grew twice as rapidly as the city congregations. Location of the largest church in the North was not a major city but Canhotinho, the small interior town where Butler had worked. The church numbered 542 communicants in 1930.[38]

Organized in 1920 with four pastors, five churches, and sixty-four congregações, the Presbytery of the North included the states of Ceará, Maranhão, Pará, Piauí, Amazonas, and the territory of Acre—an area constituting half of Brazil and containing a population of four million. Eleven years after its founding it had added only two churches, two pastors, and twenty-eight new congregações.[39] Nearly half the members were in Ceará, a result of Natanael Cortez's activity. Presbyterians had been present in Sena Madureira, in the territory of Acre, before 1910, and in 1912 a group of eighty believers and interested persons offered to pay the salary if a pastor would come.[40] It proved impossible to place a worker there for any length of time, and in 1930 the presbytery noted with sorrow that José Duarte, "unable to stand it there," was leaving the long-vacant field again without a pastor.[41] Distances were almost unbelievable. The pastor in Manaus, for example, was theoretically responsible for an area of one million square kilometers, with its population of 450,000, nine tenths of which had never had exposure to the Protestant message. In order to visit the Sena Madureira congregation he had to travel at least twenty days by boat.

Attempts to put more workers into the area failed. General Assembly subsidized the work in Belém for a short time, requesting aid from the North American missions. The Nashville Board replied that it had no one to send,[42] but in 1930 the South Brazil Mission, led by Waddell, outlined an elaborate plan for a joint Amazon mission, in which the two North American boards and both groups of Brazilian Presbyterians would cooperate. It envisioned a plantation, two river boats, a school, and a hospital, served by evangelists and other necessary personnel.[43] Falling victim to the economic depression, the project never materialized.

Statistical comparison between Presbyterians and the other groups in the region is revealing. The Baptists, combining a traditional North American missionary effort with a more flexible pattern of ministry and preparation, employed considerably more missionary personnel and funds in the area. Use of missionaries, allied with a strong program of medical help, characterized the Adventist method, while the Assemblies of God, founded in Belém in 1911, spread rapidly throughout the Amazon region with almost no missionary aid or foreign funds. Utilizing zealous believers as evangelists, the group "consecrated" them as pastors after a period of in-service training and attendance at annual institutes. In Acre, Presbyterians had been the first to begin Evangelical work, but their traditional insistence on a well-trained ministry made it impossible to place a pastor there for any length of time and led to disappearance of the work by 1960. By that year the Assemblies of God had five churches with approximately 2000 members in the territory; the Baptists had four, with 621 members; the Adventists, none. Amazonas numbered six assemblies with 3244 members, fifteen Baptist congregations with 1905 members, two Adventist groups with 1700 members, and one Presbyterian church with 169 on its roll. Pará, later to become the center of a greater Presbyterian effort, counted seventy-five assemblies with 25,102 members, seventeen Baptist churches with 1514 on their rolls, eight Adventist congregations with 1697 members, and five Presbyterian churches with 1355 communicants.[44]

The Portugal Mission as a Voluntary Society

The original mission to Portugal ended when insufficient support forced Mota Sobrinho to return to Brazil in 1923, two years after he had sent his family back because he could not support them. Giving to General Assembly causes never met expectations during the period, but the project's failure also stemmed from a second factor. Some leaders felt that as long as the Brazilian church depended on the North American missions for aid in confronting the overwhelming tasks in its own country, it should not channel any resources into outside ventures. Jerônimo Gueiros argued that both the missionary and the funds sent to Portugal belonged in the impoverished North.[45] Thus, in 1924, General Assembly voted to dissolve the mission and use its funds to help maintain a worker in the Amazon Valley. It also requested, without success, that the New York Board assume responsibility for the work in Portugal.[46]

The moving spirit behind the second phase of the mission was Erasmo Braga, who became convinced of its necessity on visiting Lisbon in 1924. A voluntary organization, the "Missionary Society for the Evangelization of Portugal," began work with the blessing of the church and the support of a number of prominent laymen. Braga's conviction was so great that he persuaded Pascoal Pita, the promising pastor who had moved to dissolve the project in 1924, to become the new missionary to Portugal, despite the opposition of his presbytery.

Pita arrived in Lisbon in 1925 to find that the church had lost its building, was now meeting in a basement, and had dropped from over two hundred members to only fifty-five.[47] His Masonic ties helped overcome opposition from the Catholic clergy and the government, and he succeeded in organizing a presbytery which included a Scottish Presbyterian, David Scott, and the former Congregationalist, Eduardo Moreira. By 1931 the work included two organized churches, fourteen unorganized congregations, and a Bible institute to train evangelists, while a Portuguese candidate for the ministry was studying in Brazil.[48] In keeping with Presbyterianism's concern for education, O Puritano noted that in 1929 only 24 per cent of Portugal's Presbyterians were illiterate, contrasted with a national average of 70 per cent.[49]

The Missions' Thrust into the Interior

The North American missions continued to move west during the period, at times bypassing promising new fields in areas where they had previously worked. The analogy with the frontier experience in the United States still dominated their planning, despite the rapid growth of the coastal cities. A missionary at the Montevideo Conference in 1925 spoke of the Amazon Valley and agricultural regions in Goiás and Mato Grosso and continued: "Much of this territory may be compared with the great prairie and plains states of the United States and Canada in the days when the push of population westward preceded and outdistanced the movement of the churches."[50] At times the migration toward the frontier led the missions to areas such as southwest and central Goiás, where population was growing rapidly, but it also led them to older stagnant regions such as northern Minas Gerais and eastern Goiás where it was either decreasing or growing very slowly.[51]

The Central Brazil Mission had left a presbytery organized in the coastal area of Bahia and Sergipe while it concentrated its resources in the institutions at Ponte Nova and in extensive itineration throughout the interior. It established the Colégio Dois de Julho in Salvador to aid in evangelistic work in that city,[52] but the new institution contributed little to the building of local churches, even though it became one of the finest schools in the state. Evidence indicates that preparation for the formation and maintenance of the presbytery was inadequate. A number of its churches enjoyed initial rapid growth, only to stagnate in the 1920's. By 1929 the church in Cachoeira, one of the oldest in the state, was without a pastor, had closed its school, and had entered a "phase of decadence."[53] The Canavieiras congregation, at the center of the promising southeast Bahia field, had similar problems. In 1930 the entire presbytery, with seventeen churches, eleven pastors, and 1958 communicants, added only eighty-eight members by profession of faith.[54]

As the mission moved farther into the interior, some of its members almost lived on muleback, covering vast areas, but unable to give the necessary pastoral care. The dilemma was complex. Towns where no one had ever preached always awaited, isolated new believers requested more visits, and personnel was scarce. Alexander Reese, who left his family for eight months in 1928, traveled 2600 miles by mule and preached 138 times, opening work in three new areas. H. C. Anderson taught in the Seminary of the North, in Recife, while his wife taught in Ponte Nova.[55]

Franklin Graham moved across the border to eastern Goiás where he baptized his first two converts in Arraias in 1921.[56] He resided in Planaltina, in the future Federal District, where he established a school and evangelized widely. In this vast, stagnant, sparsely settled region, he worked for twenty-five years. In 1942 he rode 900 miles on horseback to baptize one person.[57]

Many of these men were extremely able. Reese, who spent nearly all of his career in the hinterland, became a master of

Portuguese and wrote a serious critical work on Darbyism.[58] Graham was a tireless and capable evangelist who became well-known and beloved among the poor of eastern Goiás. The talents, education, and energy of men like these could probably have been better utilized in the rapidly growing centers. Working within the presbyteries alongside their Brazilian colleagues, establishing new work in the suburbs, they could have entered more completely into Brazilian culture. But both the Brazil Plan and the missionary strategy which gave birth to it continued to push them westward.

The South Brazil Mission, overburdened with work and the same lack of personnel,[59] anticipated the day it would move beyond Paraná and Santa Catarina to the west, even though from 1920 to 1940 these were the two most rapidly growing states in the nation, with population increases of 82 and 77 per cent respectively.[60] Here, as elsewhere, the mission abandoned the most rapidly growing areas, leaving a precariously established church behind.

The strategy of the two PCUSA missions, reflecting Waddell's experience in Ponte Nova, was stated by the Brazil Council in 1922:

> The Kuldee station: Germanic Europe was converted by Irish monks who secured agricultural property and founded civilization centers. In fact, they conserved about all of scientific agriculture that traversed the Middle Ages. They invariably had schools. They equally and invariably had hospitals, and they were centers of evangelistic itineration. We believe that for the interior work in Brazil and for following up the world's last great frontier as it rolls down into the Amazon Valley, we cannot do better than imitate them. . . . Let us create central stations, like Ponte Nova, each with a farmer, a doctor, a traveling evangelist, with their wives, and . . . an American teacher. Let us gather about these nuclei Brazilian helpers, teachers, nurses, drug-mixers, and above all, let us gather to them as many students as we can. Their work would be nearly self-supporting. . . . Such a center evangelizes a region much more rapidly than traveling, and backed up by traveling, extends the Gospel in a comparatively short time to a very wide region.[61]

Eleven such stations were proposed in 1922, but in 1928 the SBM requested personnel and funds to establish only two, to be located in Planaltina, Goiás, and Buriti, near Cuiabá, Mato Grosso. They hoped to move north from those points into the Amazon basin. The final field of the missions was to include the Amazon Valley, the interior of the Northeast down to the lower São Francisco River, Goiás, and Mato Grosso. As envisioned, the Planaltina and Buriti stations would reach much of the population as it moved west and north into the "world's last great, rich, empty space." When the Brazilian Church was ready to take over the work on that last frontier, the general missionary work would be done.[62]

Following the plan, a second evangelistic missionary, A. J. Martin, was sent to join Landes in Mato Grosso in 1918, a self-help school opened on a large farm at Buriti in 1923, and A. C. Salley was sent to southwest Goiás in 1930.[63] These men and their colleagues did impressive work and laid the foundations of two future presbyteries, but they did not have the resources to build the "Kuldee" stations, and the population shift to the west and north was far less than expected.

While the East Brazil Mission of the PCUS concentrated mainly on institutional and evangelistic work in southern Minas Gerais, the West Brazil Mission followed the railroad from the growing city of Ribeirão Preto, São Paulo, into the Minas Triangle and south-central Goiás. Because of the rich coffee land around it, Ribeirão Preto was to become one of the most important cities in the interior of the state, while population growth of the Minas Triangle took impetus from the expanding cotton industry. The area to be occupied by the mission in Goiás included the most rapidly growing section of that state as well, and progress was rapid and steady. From 1925 to 1932 the number of communicants in its fields rose from 1053 to 1977; the number of congregations, from eleven to thirty-two.[64]

But despite progress in some areas, the Brazil Plan hindered over-all planning and cooperation between the missions and the church which would have benefited the work of both. The plan's basic presupposition, that the missions should turn over their churches in more settled regions to national judicatories and continue their march to the west, virtually prohibited their turning back even when the church requested aid in meeting new opportunities in the East. When the Presbytery of Espirito Santo, after making an impressive effort by itself, requested a loan or grant from the SBM to aid the promising Vitória project, no help was forthcoming.[65] The problem of using North American personnel and financial resources to help the national church enter into new opportunities without pauperizing it or robbing it of its self-reliance and independence was always a dilemma for missionary strategists. But it is clear that during the period prior to, and immediately following adoption of the Brazil Plan, the desire for complete self-sufficiency prompted the missions to deny resources for church-sponsored projects of greater potential value than those in the interior mission fields. At the same time, the increasingly middle-class character of its urban churches, caused in part by its pattern of ministry, combined with missionary policy in attenuating the penetration of Presbyterianism among the new city dwellers, the fastest growing segment of Brazil's population.

Chapter Seven

The Struggle Against
Roman Catholic Clericalism:
1917-1934

Established amidst great optimism in 1889, the Brazilian Republic never achieved stability, and the military forces and the land-owning aristocracy soon gained control. After 1910 a series of mutinies in the navy and struggles between state and federal governments further weakened the structure. Suspension of constitutional guarantees became commonplace, and war in Europe aggravated the nation's financial situation.

Since independence, the wealthy and populous states of Minas Gerais and São Paulo had dominated political life, and civilian presidential candidates came almost exclusively from the ranks of their outgoing chief executives. Epitácio Pessôa, an exception, was succeeded in 1923 by Artur Bernardes of Minas, whose administration was disturbed by bitter strife and insurrections. During the most serious uprising army captain Luis Carlos Prestes marched with one thousand men from Rio Grande do Sul to Maranhão, and finally to Mato Grosso and into Bolivia, while fighting off superior forces. Although his political position at the time was not clear, he later became head of Brazil's Communist party.

Washington Luiz, the *Paulista* who succeeded Bernardes, brought a degree of peace and prosperity until 1929 when the world economic crisis, accompanied by a catastrophic drop in coffee prices and the huge national debt, brought the nation to the edge of disaster. The President's insistence that Júlio Prestes, another *Paulista*, succeed him, resentment over the predominance of Minas and São Paulo, and the conviction that it would be impossible to destroy the patriarchal oligarchy by constitutional means made revolt inevitable. Prestes won the election but soon afterwards, in October, 1930, a military coup placed power in the hands of the defeated candidate, Getulio Vargas of Rio Grande do Sul. Vargas promptly suspended constitutional guarantees and appointed new state executives. In 1932, a revolution erupted in São Paulo, the state which furnished one-third of the federal budget but received only 4½ per cent of its funds in return.[1] The rebellion failed, but it showed the intense feeling of *Paulistas* about their rightful place in Brazilian political and economic life.

During the same period the movement of renewal in the Roman Catholic Church, begun by D. Vital of Olinda in the 1870's, manifested itself more pervasively in the life of the nation. The number and quality of priests, a large proportion of whom were foreign, had increased. Positivism and liberalism, viable alternatives to Catholicism at the end of the century, were on the wane, while the influence of Marxism was rising. In opposition to the Marxist alternative, a renaissance of Catholic commitment and thought resurged among a small but influential group of intellectuals. The critic and poet, Jackson de Figueiredo, after violently rejecting religion, returned to the church of his fathers in 1918 as a militant lay apostle. Soon afterwards, with three companions, he founded the *Centro Dom Vital* and *A Ordem*, the latter, an organ for the propagation of Catholic doctrine. The purpose of the *Centro*, which was strongly anti-Protestant, was the study of Catholic thought and the spread of Christian philosophy, mainly by personal sanctification and example. When Figueiredo died in 1928, Alceu Amoroso Lima, soon to become the best known Catholic intellectual in the nation, became his successor.

Renewed interest in Catholicism at a time when social and political institutions seemed to be disintegrating prompted the suggestion that the nation's survival depended on its return to the traditional alliance with the Roman church. Totalitarian tendencies in the government also posed a potential threat to Protestants. In 1932 missionary leaders warned that Communism, Fascism, and Roman Catholic clericalism were all struggling for power in the nation,[2] and the possibility of an alliance between the latter two movements constituted the greatest danger to Protestantism since its arrival in Brazil.

The Catholic Nationalist Movement

While North American Protestants sought cooperation with the Roman church in Latin America, Catholic leaders confirmed the worst suspicions of Brazilian Protestants by unleashing a new offensive. The program was designed to upgrade religious life, restore Catholic dominance in education, reduce Protestant influence, and forge a new alliance between church and state.

With the influx of foreign priests after the establishment of the Republic, the Roman Church seriously attempted to improve its ministry, especially in areas where Protestants were active. The Central Brazil Mission reported in 1918 that:

> The Roman Church continues her active propaganda against the Evangelical religion and her steady and persistent efforts to maintain her hold on the people. When she is forced to she establishes her schools similar to ours and seeks to imitate whatever measures our missionaries have found helpful. Especially is this true in the Cactité field where schools have been established, house to house visitation by Jesuit priests begun, and now a movement is on foot to do something for the sick, all of which is a high compliment to our missionaries.[3]

At the same time the dominant church attempted to maintain and increase its grip on education. Public schools, which were lay in character, were denounced as monstrosities and condemned in a series of pastoral letters.[4] Protestant school buildings were sacked in some places, and priests often ordered parishioners to withdraw their children even from nonsectarian schools directed by Evangelicals.[5] A report at the Montevideo Conference noted with alarm that in Brazil's most populous state nearly half the students preparing to teach in primary schools were under the "direct and positive influence of official representatives of the Church." It added that the hierarchy seemed determined to use education to increase its influence in society.[6]

Sporadic persecution against Protestants continued in the interior and, less openly, in the cities. A priest led a mob to the home of the Reverend Mário Neves in Laginha, Minas Gerais, and ordered him to leave town within eight hours.[7] The Central Synod charged that the Roman church pressured journalists to prohibit publication of Evangelical news and sought the dismissal of Protestants by industry and government agencies.[8] While most authorities upheld the law and protected Protestants and their property, a new campaign, launched in 1919, extended beyond the reach of constitutional guarantees. That year Cardinal Arcoverde, Archbishop of Rio, called the Brazilian clergy to "war without quarter" against Protestantism and outlined a plan for the campaign.[9] Beginning in 1921 a series of pastoral letters from a number of bishops, including a member of the Brazilian Academy of Letters, condemned circulation of the Protestant Bible, and added: "Only that which appears convenient to the proper ecclesiastical authority should circulate among the people."[10] The main thrust of the campaign was an appeal to nationalism and patriotism with the cry that to be truly Brazilian was to be Catholic. Protestant missionaries came under attack as spies and agents of the government of the United States whose purpose was to enslave Brazil as they had purportedly done in Cuba, Puerto Rico, and the Philippines; Evangelical schools were denounced as hotbeds of political subversion.[11]

Fear of North American power had always existed, especially after the Spanish American War. Erasmo Braga wrote that Latin American liberals had always admired American democracy and had welcomed the Monroe Doctrine at first. However, he added: "That which served as a guarantee against the reconquest of Latin America was transformed into a source of concern. And when Pan-Americanism was born in the first Congress of Washington in 1889 . . . there began to circulate in Latin America the fear that the new doctrine brought with it the germ of the predominance of the Eagle of the North."[12] It was no novelty to call Protestant missionaries from the United States and England agents of social, political, and commercial penetration. But the intensity of the charges, now made openly by prelates, soon disseminated them widely throughout the nation. Because Brazil was completely Catholic, they said, the missionaries could not be there to save souls. They came with rivers of money furnished by "Uncle Sam" to denationalize Brazil, hoping to transform it into a province of the United States. Thus, the patriotism of Brazilian Protestants was attacked, and they were termed "children who had turned against their own mother."[13] Priests who had become Evangelicals were called "traitors of the homeland . . . paid by

North America in its egoistic policy of expansion."[14] Even non-religious philanthropic organizations from the United States, engaged in programs to eradicate disease and improve public health, were targets.[15]

The *Centro Dom Vital* became the primary organ of Catholic nationalist propaganda. Jackson de Figueiredo, Alcibíades Delamare, and later, A. A. Lima, sounded the trumpet in lay circles that to be a patriot was to be Catholic. Delamare, journalist and founder of a nationalist organization, called Protestantism the "sewer pipe of Catholicism." It threatened national unity, he said, ". . . because its implantation in Brazil would mean the breaking of the religious bonds of the nation . . . bonds which maintained intact the immense territory which the Jesuits and the *Paulistas* had conquered foot by foot."[16] Concluding with an exhortation to keep Brazil Catholic, he added: "To liberate it from Masonry, from Protestantism, from Spiritism, and from Positivism, it is necessary that we intervene, organized and cohesive, in political struggles, that we reconquer the place which belongs to us, which was snatched away by surprise, insidiously, in an underhanded manner."[17]

Members of the secular press took up the cry, and when Jerônimo Gueiros was appointed Director of the Normal School of Recife, *A Noite* lamented that it would be better to choose an atheist than this "tenacious propagandist of religious Americanism and zealous agent of Yankee propaganda."[18] He lost the position three years later because of clerical pressure even though he had gained the support of the press and his faculty, which included one priest.[19]

Presbyterians retorted that they were more patriotic than the representatives of the dominant church. Presbyterianism, they argued, was completely Brazilian in its government and owed no allegiance to any foreign authority, while half the Catholic clergy was foreign and all received orientation from Rome. Protestants also repeatedly affirmed their whole-hearted support for the republican constitution, contrasting their attitude to that of the hierarchy.[20]

Resurgent Roman Catholic Clericalism

Accompanying the campaign against Protestantism was a drive for increasing clerical influence in government and society as a whole. Even though many Catholic thinkers recognized, in retrospect at least, that the republican constitution had freed the church from an intolerable situation, it had been criticized from its inception by prelates who could not reconcile its religious neutrality with Roman Catholic teaching. Indication of the church's attitude came shortly after establishment of the Republic when the incumbent Bishop of Rio was replaced by a well-known monarchist, and a Catholic congress condemned the secularization of the state.[21] Protestants, who had heard tales of the Inquisition and the massacre of St. Bartholomew's Day, believed their worst fears justified when Júlio Maria, the Redemptorist, wrote in 1911: "Military duty, in the face of national apostasy, is not fulfilled by this passivity. On the contrary, it implies the honor of the sword used in the defense of the Church and the restitution of religion in Brazil."[22]

The hierarchy soon ended its blanket condemnation of the Republic and began to seek change through political action. A *Liga Católica* was formed in São Paulo, bishops warned the faithful to vote only for Catholic candidates, and in 1911 the bishops of southern Brazil called for elimination from the Constitution of the "note of atheistic radicalism which made it an odious example in the whole civilized world."[23] The primary goals of the campaign were recognition of the "Roman Catholic Apostolic religion" as that of the Brazilian people, legal recognition and registry of marriages performed in the church, and religious teaching in the public schools.

The attempt to identify Catholicism with nationalism and the condemnation of Protestantism as foreign and treasonous spawned an attack on religious liberty. After denying that one could be a genuine Brazilian patriot without being Catholic, Figueiredo continued: "Tolerance . . . is an honest synonym for indifference, and indifference is a crime for the Catholic. . . . Intolerance is a FUNDAMENTAL and VITAL law for every individual or collective being. . . . It is a question of life or death."[24] At the same time their open admiration of Italian Fascism showed that the commitment of Catholic intellectuals to democracy was tenuous indeed. Delamare, one of Figueiredo's associates, invoked the specter of anti-Semitism as a weapon against Protestantism by calling it: ". . . the Judaism of decadent Europe filled with hatreds and competitions, it is the Judaism which decreed the war and decided the peace, it is the judaizing spirit of the Old World allied to the ambition, the passion for money, and the thirst for fabulous profits which intends to divide, through religious struggles, the Brazilian family."[25]

He praised Mussolini's redemption of Italy from its past errors and promised, "Nationalism will dominate Brazil just as Fascism has grasped Italy."[26] The Catholic paper, A União, echoed the praise of Catholic governments in Italy, Austria, and Germany and continued: "It is necessary, in a word, to re-establish the decisive influence of God in society. . . . All that I have said indicates the necessity of a reformation of the relationship between the government and the Church, that is, in regard to separation. We need religious teaching and respect for the religion of the Brazilian people, translated into official acts."[27]

Plínio Marques, a congressman from Paraná where clerical influence was strong, took the next step, proposing constitutional amendments which would declare Roman Catholicism to be the "religion of the Brazilian people" and establish religious teaching in the public schools.[28] To protestants and liberals Marques' action seemed certain to lead toward reestablishment of the church, the end of religious liberty, and destruction of the Republic. They understandably feared increasing persecution if the amendment passed. Despite the clauses on religious liberty and separation of church and state in the 1891 Constitution, harassment had never ceased entirely, and even before the vote on Marques' proposal, two incidents inflamed Protestant fears. In Paraná Luis Cesar, pastor of the Presbyterian Church in Curitiba, the leader of the Spiritist Federation, and three other prominent citizens protested to the President against the state government's subsidizing two new dioceses. For this act they came to trial, paid a heavy fine, and were sentenced to a year in jail.[29] Shortly afterwards, members of a mob who destroyed the Presbyterian chapel in Aparecida do Norte, São Paulo, told a bystander: "Now our religion is going to be official and it is necessary to get rid of heretics."[30]

While Catholic groups held street meetings and fought for passage of the amendments, Protestants, Masons, Spiritists, and others sent telegrams to Congress. Most of the secular press opposed the measures, but some law faculties were divided on the issue. To the relief of most, the proposals met defeat when they came to a vote in September of 1925.

But the struggle did not end. After Figueiredo was killed in an accident in 1928, he was succeeded in the leadership of the *Centro Dom Vital* by Alceu Amoroso Lima, Brazil's leading literary critic, recently converted through the influence of Figueiredo and Jacques Maritain. Convinced that only Catholicism could save the nation from Communism, Lima was instrumental in establishing the Catholic Institute for Higher Studies, the Association of Catholic University Students, and the National Confederation of Catholic Workers, all under the aegis of the *Centro*.[31] Lima made it clear that he considered "false" religion worse than atheism and strongly advocated reestablishment of the church by the state. He expressed as well his admiration for Mussolini, Hitler, Dollfuss, and Salazar. Democracy, he affirmed, was decadent.[33]

It was inevitable that when the revolutionary government took power in 1930, the clericalists would again attempt to reestablish the Catholic Church. Even though Vargas had spoken and voted against the Marques amendments, the hierarchy did an immediate about-face. Opposed to the revolution before it was victorious, it now sought an alliance with the new government. Lima formed the *Liga Eleitoral Católica* with strong support from Cardinal Leme, Archbishop of Rio, and when a constituent assembly was called, the Liga petitioned:

That the new constitution should be promulgated in the name of God and thereby cease to be an atheistic document: That the Catholic Religion be officially recognized as the religion of Brazil and that its principles be applied in the formulation and interpretation of the laws of the Republic: That Christian marriage and the indissolubility of the marriage bond be officially recognized by the State so that the family may once more become the solid basis of society: That religious instruction be given in all public primary and secondary schools, and that the seminaries, while remaining under ecclesiastical jurisdiction, be incorporated and affiliated to the state university as graduate schools for advanced study.[34]

Other provisions included a demand for chaplains in the armed forces, hospitals, and jails and a request for the recognition of Catholic labor unions. To the dismay of Protestants, a decree was issued in April, 1931, allowing religious teaching in public schools if at least twenty students desired it. Those who did not could be excused if their parents or guardians so stated in the act of matriculation.[35] The intent of the church was soon made clear by Cardinal Leme when he declared the decree on religious instruction to be only the beginning: "We will make Catholicism the official religion, to be taught in the schools and proclaimed in government offices, we will tolerate other cults, which will be permitted. But the official religion will be Catholicism. The State will not be neutral. We are the majority and we wish it so. We can impose our will."[36]

The appearance of Plinio Salgado's *Intergralista* Party in 1932 brought a new factor to Brazil's political scene. Modeled on Italian and Portuguese Fascism, *Integralismo* had the support of many Catholics, including a number of prelates.[37] Vargas, who was a skilled politician was thus forced to show far more sympathy for the church than most republican governments had done, and this made itself felt at the local level. In a number of towns in Minas pastors were prevented by mobs from entering their churches; in Manhumirim the Presbyterian church was dynamited; in Conceição dos Ouros the Protestant school was closed. The alarming difference now was that police and civil authorities refused to act, sharing the common belief that soon it would be illegal to preach against the "religion of the State."[38]

Presbyterian leaders were the first to protest the renewed clericalist campaign. They sent a memorial to Vargas in November, 1930, requesting that religious liberty, separation of church and state, and the lay character of public schools be maintained.[39] The *Congresso Evangélico Brasileiro*, composed of Presbyterians, Methodists, Episcopalians, Congregationalists, and Independentes, met in May, 1931, and declared its support for all efforts to maintain liberty of conscience. It adopted a manifesto which answered common charges against Protestants, defended the principle of a free church in a free state and stated that Brazilian Evangelicals had no political relationships with any foreign missionary, institution, church, or government. All foreign ties were strictly fraternal.[40] The same year Protestants entered the "National Coalition for the Lay State," with M. G. dos Santos becoming its vice-president.[41]

Many Protestant fears were confirmed with completion of the new constitution in 1933 and its promulgation the following year. Although Catholicism was not recognized as the religion of the nation and religious liberty and separation of church and state were maintained, the document was, in the words of a Catholic writer, "a decisive victory for the Catholics . . . thoroughly Catholic in form."[42] With the exceptions already indicated, almost all the demands of the *Liga Eleitoral Católica* were adopted. Lima himself wrote:

> With the Constitution of 1934, and one can say, with the Revolution of 1930, this legal separation . . . was succeeded by a regime of real collaboration. . . . One can say that we have passed through three stages in the relationship between Church and State—that of union, that of separation, and that of collaboration. . . . Regarding the spirit of Catholicism, among the people and the elites during this third period, one can also note a strikingly new aspect. The state of apathy and division of the second period has been succeeded by a state of dynamism and reorganization.[43]

Among Brazilian Presbyterians effects of the new clericalism were varied. It gave impetus to development of a social and political ethic, mainly as a defensive measure. Along with Protestant ecumenical currents from abroad, it motivated Protestant cooperative efforts. But, paradoxically, the partial Catholic victory in 1934 influenced Presbyterians to assume a more introverted and defensive stance, thus ending or attenuating the promising new movements of the 1920's. It also increased the suspicion of the dominant church which had always existed among Brazilian Protestants, making it even more difficult for them to respond positively to changing attitudes in that institution in the future.

New Ethical Concerns in Presbyterianism

Increasing Roman Catholic clericalism, revolutionary ferment inside the nation, influence from Europe and North America,[44] concern over Communist and Fascist influence,[45] and, perhaps, growing confidence regarding the place of Protestantism in national life fostered new social and political concerns among Presbyterians during the period. While the traditional individualistic ethic continued to receive major emphasis, some Protestants began to participate more actively in political affairs and to advocate social reform. At the same time Presbyterians clung to the belief that increasing Protestant influence in society, more education, and the democratic process would eventually transform the nation peacefully. They urged respect and obedience toward constituted authorities and rejected any hint of violent revolution.

At no point did the new politically oriented ethic clash more openly with the traditional one than on the question of Sunday voting, a practice long prohibited by Protestants, even though it was the usual procedure. Miguel Rizzo, Jr., wrote in 1918 that Protestants should vote in order to defend democracy,[46] but the General Assembly continued to oppose their doing so on the Sabbath.[47] When Couto Esher, a prominent Independente layman, wrote in 1924 that it was essential to vote, regardless of the day of the election, a PCUS missionary replied that because it was not a necessity, voting was still not legitimate on the Sabbath.[48] The 1926 General Assembly modified its rigid position, recommending that each believer adhere to tradition unless his conscience dictated otherwise.[49] With the near-triumph of clericalism after 1930 the shift was almost complete. In 1933 Júlio Nogueira observed that while the Evangelical Church in Brazil had always been primarily concerned with evangelism, it was finally beginning to see its political and social responsibility. Protestants had neglected their obligation to vote, he added, in part because of the general scepticism about politics and in part because their churches had been established by foreign missionaries who properly refrained from political interference. But now, he concluded, the three greatest duties of each believer were to pray, to evangelize, and to vote.[50] The following year Presbyterians were instructed to vote even on Sunday. To do so, the reasoning went, would not dishonor the Lord because it was for the good of the nation.[51]

Anxiety over clericalism also brought Protestants closer together at times in a unified voice against the danger. But the indifference to politics and the strong sectarian antagonism existing among many Evangelical groups prevented much success. The *Conselho Geral das Igrejas Evangélicas da Cidade de São Paulo* protested in the name of the state's 100,000 Protestants against the Governor's request for a legislative grant of Cr$2,000,000 (about US$500,000) for aid in construction of the new cathedral.[52] Couto Esher called for organization of a *Liga Eleitoral Protestante* to counteract the Catholic organization, but received no response.[53] His bid for state deputy in 1924 brought few votes in a number of cities hosting strong Protestant churches, and he met defeat.[54] In 1928, as a major party's candidate for the Senate, he was again unsuccessful, even though the election was not held on Sunday. Apparently, he received no special support from Evangelicals.[55] In contrast, Natanael Cortez, the well-known pastor in Ceará, won a seat in the state legislature in 1929 with the support of the liberal party, despite clerical opposition.[56] Increasing political interest prompted twenty-nine Protestants, including seven Presbyterians (five of them ministers) to run for state or federal deputy in 1934. In a number of areas anti-Protestant sentiment kept aspiring candidates off party slates.[57] When they did run, clerical pressure and continuing Protestant apathy toward politics insured that few were elected.

As political interest increased, a few Presbyterian leaders began to speak out on social issues. One was V. C. de Almeida, a former priest, who called for Protestants to go beyond talk about the gospel as the "answer" and present specifically Christian solutions to the nation's problems. He advocated better salaries and profit sharing for workers, and agrarian reform, attempting to trace a middle way between socialism and Catholic conservatism.[58] Jerônimo Gueiros, speaking to the Institute of Sciences and Letters of Pernambuco, condemned the unjust and dehumanizing exploitation of workers by rich industrialists,[59] while a group of Presbyterian leaders presented a comprehensive social program to Evangelicals in 1932. Along with preservation of the lay state and civil liberties, they recommended establishing cooperatives, in which workers would receive a fair share of profits; free civil marriage with divorce in case of adultery or obstinate abandonment; aid to children, the elderly, and fallen women; compulsory popular education with professional training more accessible to the poor; and pacifism in international relations with military expenditures reduced to a minimum.[60]

Despite the new note of social and political concern, Brazilian Presbyterians did not want their church to become a political party or pressure group. Such a course, they cautioned, would divert the church from its primary purpose, divide, and ultimately corrupt it. Nor did they ever call for the overthrow of the government, even though many supported the Vargas regime after its 1930 revolution. Undergirding Presbyterian political faith, even though scepticism often contradicted it, was an unswerving conviction: if a democratic government with civil liberties and separation of church and state could prevail, if education could be made accessible to more people, and if Protestantism continued to grow, progress was inevitable. Both Gueiros and Almeida, after castigating the rich industrialists and landowners for their treatment of the poor, concluded that only the power of the gospel, working in individual lives, would insure the needed changes. Shortly after an abortive revolution in 1924, *O Puritano* urged that everything ". . . be done within the law and by the law" and published chapters XXIII, 1–4, and XXXI, 4, from the text of the Westminster Confession.[61] Against conservative clericalism and Fascism on one hand and revolutionary socialism on the other, Presbyterians maintained their belief in the nineteenth-century liberal tradition which they admired in North America and which had been instrumental in forming their Republic and bringing religious liberty.[62] If they were naive about the problems of entrenched power, they were probably no more so than Protestants elsewhere who adhered to their faith in liberal political traditions.

The newly awakened interest in politics was primarily a reaction to Roman Catholic clericalism, however. With a few exceptions it did not reflect a serious attempt to understand the role of the church in society. Thus, with consummation of the new relationship between the Roman church and the state, Presbyterians again moved to an introverted position, their political viewpoints on most issues determined more by local and personal factors than by theological principles. When Brazilian Protestants did enter political life they were usually known more for their personal honesty and morality and for opposition to measures favoring the Roman church than for positive programs. Perhaps this was inevitable, given their minority status, but it also indicated a limited concept of Christian ethics. However, even as the church fought, with only partial success, against clericalism, a new and positive movement toward Protestant cooperation promised to bring a deeper concern and more adequate theological understanding of the mission of the church and its role in society.

Chapter Eight

The Partial Failure of Protestant Cooperative Efforts: 1917-1934

During the first sixty years of its existence, Brazilian Presbyterianism had shown greater interest in Protestant unity and cooperation than any other group, although with few specific results. In 1916 the Panama Congress added stimulus to the movement and developed plans for concrete steps toward unity. Dedicated to the establishment of united nonsectarian Protestant churches throughout Latin America, the regional conferences which met after Panama, strongly supported by the Committee on Cooperation in Latin America, planned a host of cooperative projects. Among the most important were union seminaries in Mexico, Peru, Bolivia, Chile, and Brazil.[1] Other areas in which rapid progress of cooperation seemed imminent were literature and journalism, education, and comity agreements.

Thus, at a time when pressures inside Brazil from resurgent Roman Catholicism and government instability urged greater Protestant unity, new impulses were entering from outside. The presence of Erasmo Braga at the center of the cooperative movement was also significant. The most able leader Latin American Protestantism had yet produced, Braga, with his brilliant mind, deep devotion to Christ and His Church, sensitivity to issues, and wide ecumenical contacts after 1916, far transcended the parochialism dominating most Latin American Protestantism.

Despite the positive influences on the development of cooperation, the movement was to meet almost total defeat. Sectionalism, manifested in the São Paulo revolution, and the nationalistic spirit exploited by Catholic clericalism both had their counterparts in Brazilian Protestantism. Regionalism and personal rivalries within the churches, denominational pride, nationalistic suspicion of programs which seemed to be imposed from North America—especially in the crucial area of theological education —antagonisms resulting from past controversies, and the defensive stance of Brazilian Protestants, even against other Evangelicals, combined to destroy or seriously weaken promising steps toward unity. Crucial to the failure was the strong denominational spirit which dominated the Presbyterian Church and led it to reject any significant degree of cooperation by the end of the period. Despite frustration in most areas, the *Comissão Brasileira de Cooperação*, which was a direct product of these efforts, continued in existence to become the foundation of the Evangelical Confederation of Brazil in 1934.

Erasmo Braga and the Comissão Brasileira de Cooperação

Erasmo Braga, born in Rio Claro in 1877, was the son of a Portuguese immigrant, J. C. Braga, who was converted to Protestantism through reading a page from the Bible which had been used to wrap a package. Aided by Blackford, the elder Braga had studied and become a bookkeeper and pastor. After attending a primary school established by his mother, young Erasmo continued his course in Mackenzie with the help of Chamberlain. Abandoning his original intention to study law, the youth entered the *Instituto Teológico* in 1893, graduating four years later. Ordained early the following year, he became the pastor of the church in Niteroi, across the bay from Rio. He soon began to write for the secular and church press, his published articles showing an impressive catholicity of interests: history, geography, botany, education, and religion.

When the controversy between Pereira, the church, and the New York Board left John R. Smith as the only professor in the seminary, the young pastor was called to help in 1901. The following year he published an elementary Hebrew grammar and glossary. When the institution moved to Campinas he competed for the chair of English in the prestigious state *ginásio*, winning over nine other candidates. Braga supported himself from the salary which it brought, relieving the church of that burden. At the same time he carried a heavy teaching and administrative load in the seminary.

Commitment to the gospel and the church were always foremost in Braga's thought and action, but his ability and concern for

Christian witness in society involved him in other areas as well. He joined Rondon in founding a society for protection of the nation's Indians[2] and later encouraged the establishment of a mission to one of the nation's largest tribes. As an educator he became especially well known outside the church. At the request of a group of teachers he wrote primers for each of the four years of primary school, which were widely used and eventually published in over one hundred editions.[3] Both Calvinistic and North American influence were revealed in his analysis of the need for new directions in Brazilian education. He criticized the rigid university system which, he said, prepared an elite for the bureaucracy but alienated students from work and productive activity. And he called for education which was more socially oriented, pupil centered, flexible, and pragmatic. Turning to the secondary level, he wrote: "The remodeling of secondary education in Brazil, with the purpose of educating all adolescents for life, in function of the vocations both of those who are educated and of society, is equal to the fight against illiteracy as a condition essential to the economic and moral independence of the nation."[4] His pragmatism and nationalism were demonstrated in response to an inquiry from the Brazilian Educational Association. The function of a university, he said, was not to create mere exponents of erudition, but to help youth develop "the spirit of initiative, independence, and self-confidence which would make them capable of resisting foreign economic colonization" and contributing to the greatness of the nation.[5]

Articles published before 1916 indicate that Braga was already interested in the church beyond Brazil, but the Panama Congress initiated a new and even more productive period in his life. Chosen to interpret the movement for Christian unity to Latin Americans, he wrote *Panamericanismo, Aspecto Religioso*,[6] which was published in Spanish as well as Portuguese. In 1917 Presbyterians, Methodists, Congregationalists, Episcopalians, and Independentes established the *Comissão Brasileira de Cooperação* to coordinate cooperative Protestant efforts and act as a liaison between the Brazilian churches and the CCLA in New York. Projects were to include the production of literature in Portuguese, a press and bookstore in Rio, a family magazine, a Protestant university, and an orphanage. With the encouragement of S. C. Inman, Secretary of the CCLA, funds in excess of one million dollars were requested from participating churches in the United States.[7]

Although Inman suggested assigning a missionary the production of literature, Gammon and Waddell insisted that the appointee be Brazilian.[8] In 1918 Braga was elected Secretary for Publications and, two years later, full-time Secretary of the *Comissão Brasileira de Cooperação*. This necessitated his leaving the seminary to establish the Commission office in Rio. Two years later he resigned from his chair in Campinas, requesting that the General Assembly withdraw his name from its committees in order that his work in cooperative efforts might not be prejudiced.[9] Despite the subsequent loosening of ties with the internal structure and various currents of thought within the Presbyterian Church, he was elected its Moderator in 1924.

Under Braga's leadership the newly formed office became a center for the publication of literature, promotion of cooperative efforts and interdenominational contacts within Brazil, and a bridge to the worldwide church and the developing ecumenical movement. The publishing program did not live up to expectations, mainly because of insufficient funds, but a Bible dictionary, commentaries on the gospels, and the *Revista de Cultura Religiosa* were published. More important was the contribution to Sunday school literature made through the *Conselho Evangélico de Educação Religiosa*. From 1922 to 1929 Braga edited and did most of the writing for a series of quarterlies for children, youth, and adults, based on the International Lessons. His goals were to create literature specifically for Brazilians and to build up a group of collaborators who would help permanently in preparing material.

Braga's concern for Brazil's Indians led to a cooperative venture of evangelism and social service among the ten thousand members of the Caiuá tribe in southern Mato Grosso. General Assembly had already expressed interest in such a project,[10] and additional stimulus came when General Rondon, Brazil's best-known Indian specialist, expressed disillusionment with Roman Catholic efforts and asked Protestant help for the group.[11] A. S. Maxwell of the EBM, showed great enthusiasm for the plan and made three exploratory trips with it in mind.

The result was the establishment of the Caiuá Mission in 1929, when a team including the Maxwells, Dr. Nelson Araujo, a Methodist physician, Dr. Eston Marques, an Independente dentist, and João José da Silva, a Presbyterian agriculturist, set up residence on the edge of the reservation, not far from Dourados, Mato Grosso. They learned Guarani, the language of the Caiuás, became friendly with them, and started a farm, an orphanage, a church, and a clinic. Funds promised by the churches often failed to arrive; sickness was a frequent problem; and bad health forced the Maxwells to leave in 1941. But by 1940 about one thousand Indians were receiving aid.[12] In 1943 the EBM sent Orlando Andrade and his gifted wife, Loide, to replace the Maxwells, and the dynamic couple became the soul of the work.

Most of the original workers eventually left, and the Methodists ended their cooperation in 1950, but Dr. Araujo practiced medicine in Dourados and continued to aid the mission. By 1959 the work included an active church with a number of outlying congregations, a vocational school which taught carpentry, bricklaying, farming, sewing, and animal husbandry; a farm, a sawmill, a number of primary schools, a brickyard, a clinic, an isolation ward for tuberculosis patients, and a hospital under construction. The orphanage, which had grown to house over one hundred children, was closed on the discovery that the young wards experienced difficulty adapting themselves to Brazilian society and were often victims of exploitation. As an alternative, they began living in Indian foster homes and studying in mission schools.[13]

Earlier organizations, designed to bring Brazil's Evangelicals into closer association, had never been nationwide in scope. But the combination of Roman Catholic pressure and new ecumenical currents fired Braga's enthusiasm for a permanent national organization of Brazilian churches. It was to operate alongside the *Comissão Brasileira de Cooperação*, which included mission boards and the CCLA in its membership. Thus in 1925, at the height of the controversy over the Plínio Marques amendments, the *União de Obreiros Evangélicos* of Rio nominated a group with Braga as chairman, to formulate plans for a federation of churches. The principal object of the body would be to defend liberty of conscience and speak for Brazil's Protestants on matters of common concern.[14] Not until 1930 did the Presbyterian Church appoint a committee with power to enter such an organization.[15] But finally, in 1931, under the renewed threat of clericalism, the *Federação das Igrejas Evangélicas do Brasil* came into being. Braga considered it one of his major achievements; after the constitution was adopted, he turned to a friend and asked if he could not now say his *nunc dimittis*.[16]

The *Federação*, the *Comissão*, and the *Conselho Evangélico de Educação Religiosa* merged in 1934 to become the *Confederação Evangélica do Brasil*. The organization, which included in its membership Brazilian churches, foreign missions, and groups such as the Bible societies, proposed to "express and stimulate the substantial unity of Protestantism, coordinate its forces in joint action, and maintain relations with the Church of Christ in all the world."[17] Its three divisions corresponded to the founding agencies. The *Conselho de Igrejas Evangélicas do Brasil*, composed only of Brazilian churches, was to represent Protestantism before the government and the public. The *Conselho de Educação Religiosa* would promote cooperation in religious education, and the *Conselho de Cooperação* was to bring churches and other Christian organizations together and coordinate their joint action in evangelism, publications, education, and social work.

A fifth cooperative venture with which Braga was associated, although not its moving spirit, was the Evangelical University Federation. It too was organized in 1916 as a result of the Panama Congress, even though the original suggestion had come from Gammon several years earlier.[18] The purpose was to strengthen and expand Evangelical education in Brazil by establishing a degree of standardization and preparing suitable textbooks. While the federation hoped to include and orient Protestant schools at all levels, its central goal was to create a university by combining the *faculdades*, or professional schools, already existing in Protestant institutions, upgrading and coordinating their programs, and possibly adding others. Mackenzie already offered engineering and commercial courses; Lavras had agricultural and normal schools; Granbery, a Methodist institution, included schools of theology, dentistry, and pharmacy. Law, medicine, and pedagogy, added possibly in Rio, would complete the university. Since each *faculdade* in Brazil was traditionally a separate institution, the new venture would have become the first coordinated university in the nation. With uniform courses and examinations in affiliated secondary schools leading into the institution, it would have wielded great progressive influence on Brazilian education.

Waddell, who, with Gammon, was the moving force behind the plan, was elected Chancellor of the Federation in 1916 and later succeeded by Braga. Grants totaling one million dollars were requested from North American churches through the CCLA, and government approval sought. Although the idea was excellent and might have enabled Protestantism to continue its creative contribution to Brazilian education, it did not become a reality. Giving in the United States fell far short of expectations, not only for the university but for the other cooperative ventures as well. Still more important were the pressures within the nation which caused the government to withhold its approval.[19]

In that period of resurgent clericalism the Catholic Church opposed the idea because of the prestige it would bring Protestantism. Further, at a time of increasing nationalism, many saw a threat of cultural imperialism in the project, which would have made North American owned and oriented *faculdades* into the most advanced educational institution in the nation. Waddell, despite his great ability and vision in some areas, may have fed the suspicion. Noticeably uninterested in Brazilian culture, he appeared to feel that the solution to Brazil's educational problems lay in the implantation of North American methods.[20] The scope of the problem became obvious in the struggle Braga faced in securing accreditation for Mackenzie's engineering course. Clerical pressures created great obstacles despite the prestige which both Braga and Mackenzie enjoyed in educational and government circles.[21]

Because of his position and ability Braga became a catalyst to various groups and activities which envisioned greater Christian unity. He played an important role in the formation of the United Seminary, visited judicatories of various denominations to encourage cooperation, and helped organize local councils of churches, weeks of prayer for Christian unity, congresses for pastors and laymen, and a retreat center. His office acted as a clearing house for Brazilian Protestantism and represented it before the government and the press, especially when the Plínio Marques amendments were under discussion.

Braga also became a bridge to the worldwide church and those movements working to express its unity. His office, housed in the same building as the Bible Society, became the Brazilian representative of a number of North American and European based ecumenical and philanthropic organizations, including the Federal Council of Churches in the USA, the Commission on Faith and Order, and the Conference on Life and Work, as well as the CCLA and the International Missionary Council (IMC). He took an active role in a number of gatherings: the World Sunday School Convention in 1924; the Congress on Christian Work in South America in 1925, at which he presided; and the Jerusalem meeting of the IMC in 1928, becoming a member of the Executive Committee of the latter.

Even more important was Braga's constant effort to interpret ecumenical currents in world Christianity to his own nation and church. In 1923 he published a series of articles which outlined the history of the ecumenical movement and explained the function of the IMC.[22] He encouraged Andre Jensen, a Brazilian Presbyterian, to attend the Conference on Life and Work in 1925, where he was the only delegate from South America.[23] Braga also urged Brazilian churches to send a delegate to Jerusalem in 1928, not only to be represented at that gathering, but to stimulate awareness of the universal dimension of the church. He warned that:

> To abstain from such movements is to isolate ourselves, it is to lose contacts, it is to limit ourselves consciously to a small circle in which pessimism increases and the shadows of insurmountable difficulties grow. To answer these calls is certainly to commit ourselves to sacrifices and to invite responsibilities, but it will mean the opening of new spiritual horizons before us.[24]

Going beyond the unique role which he played in interpreting Latin American Protestantism and the world church to each other, Braga became a valuable contributor to the whole ecumenical movement through his participation in the IMC and other organizations. The importance of his leadership was recognized nine years after his death when John R. Mott listed thirteen men "to whom the ecumenical movement will be eternally indebted." Along with Brent, Soderbloom, Oldham, and others, he named "Erasmo Braga of Brazil."[25]

With his brilliant mind and worldwide contacts, Braga became the leading thinker in Brazilian Protestantism, especially about the nature of the church and its relationship to the world. Even though he remained orthodox enough to satisfy his most conservative colleagues,[26] he moved beyond traditional thought in a, number of areas. Recognizing the contribution of European theology, he published an article on Karl Barth in 1929, the first mention of that thinker in Brazil's Protestant press.[27] Rejecting scholastic theology, Braga returned to a concept of faith closer to that of the Reformers than of traditional Brazilian orthodoxy and laid the foundation for an ecumenical theology. Citing the words of the Jerusalem Conference of the IMC, "Our Message is Jesus Christ," he continued: "Belief corresponds to dogma and answers the question, 'What should I believe?' Faith corresponds to personal fidelity, affective union, and the commitment of one's self to another, and answers the question, 'In whom should I believe?' And the answer is, 'In Christ.' "[28] Thus he saw ecumenism as a call to thought and action which was at once Christocentric, social, and missionary.

The most important characteristic of the contemporary church, Braga wrote, "is the concentration around the risen Christ and His intensive and universal action in the social sphere."[29] Christ and His sacrifice, he continued, constitute an appeal to the believer to go beyond the concern with personal salvation alone and work for the regeneration of society. Braga demonstrated his missionary vision in a proposal for the federation of Iberian American Evangelical churches to aid in evangelization not only of Latin America but of Spain, Portugal, and the Portuguese African colonies. Strong Evangelical churches, he was convinced, would help them escape the tragic results of the counter-Reformation and realize their true destinies as nations.[30] He also urged Latin American Protestants to proclaim the gospel more positively and recover the religious values they had lost in their extreme rejection of everything Roman.[31]

But Braga recognized forces at work in his own church which undermined his influence. Optimistic in evaluating trends in world Christianity, he was aware of special problems in Latin American Protestantism. In 1916 he wrote that the individualism and personalism characteristic of his society had produced a sectarian spirit and a type of Protestantism both violently anti-Roman and strongly denominational.[32] He hoped for the development of a new mentality which would combine confessional loyalty and deep interest in the local ministry with a concern for broader movements.[33] At the same time he admitted to a friend that he received his greatest support from the missionaries and boards and feared that the increasing myopia of his own church, especially in regard to Campinas Seminary, was leading it toward isolation.[34]

The resurgence of denominationalism in the mid-1920's indicated just how superficial the commitment to Christian unity had been on the part of most Brazilian Presbyterians. The test came in the struggle over the United Seminary. In 1924 a writer affirmed:

> It is a fact that Providence has permitted these branches within the Church. If it were better not to have them, I think the Lord Jesus would not permit them. . . . Today the cry which goes from city to city is this, "Awaken the denominational Presbyterian spirit." It asks that each Presbyterian be truly Presbyterian, but Christian above all. Who will remain deaf to this sound of the horn of Gideon?[35]

The following year a missionary of the WBM, which strongly supported Campinas Seminary, defended the rivalries between the various churches in North America and concluded, "We ought to be proud of denominationalism."[36] Braga soon saw that his greatest problem was the centripetal movement within denominations,[37] and he noted that unlike the Methodists and Independentes, Presbyterians did not even contribute regularly to the budget of the *Comissão Brasileira de Cooperação*.[38] A year later he confessed to the World Reformed Alliance that Latin American Presbyterians had been slow to assume leadership in cooperative work and that in some areas they had reacted against it.[39]

Admittedly disappointed over his church's increasing rejection of cooperative efforts, Braga refused to become embittered, and attempted to help the world Reformed community understand the reasons involved. First, he wrote, converts from paganism in Asia or Africa will have a quite different attitude toward the Roman Catholic Church than those from nominal Catholicism in Latin America, even though missionaries sent by the same board were the instruments of their conversion. Latin American Protestants feel that Romanism and Christianity are mutually exclusive, and advanced ideas of union are considered apostasy,[40] he said. In addition, loyalty to their fathers in the faith, group consciousness, doctrinal differences, missionary and church administration, and feuds caused by proselytizing were only some of the barriers dividing the indigenous churches. At times, he charged, selfish plans masquerade as attempts to keep the church free from those of dubious orthodoxy. Braga observed also that hasty efforts to promote union had been harmful, especially when the mergers involved old denominational favorites which had cost years of sacrifice to build. This he considered to be a special cause of the recrudescence of denominationalism. Finally, he concluded:

> The Evangelical churches in Latin America are growing up with an inferiority complex. Small struggling communities, attacked on all sides, they are pointed out as negligible minorities. Paradoxical as it may seem, they are developing however, a superiority complex, as guardians of the faith and the holy group among a great mass of sinners. They have become provincial. Controversy has been the ordinary method of propaganda. As the majority of the church members have been converts from Roman Catholicism, they have, in regard to their old church, a most radical attitude of rejection.[41]

The effect of this inferiority-superiority complex was to heighten suspicion even of other Protestants. Brazilian Presbyterianism soon rejected any deep commitment to church unity, even though it had contributed its most able son to the movement. Even before Braga's premature death in 1932, it was clear that his own church had repudiated his vision. Whether he could have exerted greater influence within it if he had remained in Campinas Seminary is a matter for speculation. Had he done so, he could not have given his leadership as effectively to Protestantism in all Brazil and beyond its borders. Such is the dilemma of a gifted individual.

The Presbyterian Church was willing to participate in the co-operative movement as long as no great sacrifice was required. But in the controversy over the United Seminary, whose support would have involved its merger with Campinas and a fundamental reorientation of denominational attitudes, Brazilian Presbyterianism, which had once taken the lead in seeking Protestant unity, turned its back on any profound commitment to ecumenical involvement and determined its course for future decades.

The Failure of Interdenominational Theological Education

The most important cooperative projects, promising more complete unity in the future, were in theological education. A recommendation made in Panama, which appeared to generate enthusiastic support among Presbyterians, envisioned the creation of a union seminary in Rio and possibly another in the north of Brazil. Methodists and Presbyterians had already begun to talk of combining their seminaries; there was hope that Presbyterians and Independentes would soon unite; and many thought that an interdenominational institution would be a powerful influence on the establishment of a united Protestant church. But the United Seminary, founded amidst great optimism, became a source of controversy and threatened another schism. At the same time the Seminary of the North, reorganized with the cooperation of two other denominations, was soon left again as a Presbyterian institution, fighting for survival.

The Seminary of the North

The struggles of the Seminary of the North reflected the conflict between a missiology which insisted on the rapid formation of an independent, self-supporting church on the one hand and the Calvinistic tradition of a well-trained ministry on the other. Neither indicated how a newly formed church was to build and support its seminaries without substantial help from outside. The problem became especially acute in the North where the church was small and very poor. The Central and North Brazil missions felt that its maintenance was primarily the responsibility of the church and devoted few resources to the institution, despite its precarious situation. They invested considerably more money and personnel in their schools in Ponte Nova, Salvador, Garanhuns, and Recife. At the same time, most of the churches in the North —poor, isolated, and surviving with difficulty—failed to accept their responsibility to the seminary, leaving it with constant deficits.

At the request of the Presbytery of Pernambuco, the NBM had assumed responsibility for the institution in 1913 but returned it to the national judicatory in 1919.[42] The following year it ended its existence in Garanhuns and began a promising experiment in Recife as the Instituto Ebenezer. The plan was to provide theological training for laymen as well as future pastors, and most of the students lived, worked, and studied together in rented quarters.[43] Presbyterians, an Independente, and a Congregationalist made up the faculty, and by 1922 the student body numbered twenty-two.[44] Motivation for the new interdenominational character of the seminary apparently was convenience and economy rather than the ideals envisioned at Panama. Nevertheless, in 1923 operations appeared to be proceeding smoothly, and the name was changed to the Seminário Evangélico do Norte. Restructuring called for the three presbyteries and two missions in the North to cooperate with the institution, along with the Congregationalists and Independentes.[45] In 1924 the NBM purchased property for a permanent campus, furnishing most of the necessary funds in lieu of contributing to the seminary budget over a period of years.[46] Shortly afterwards, Robert Smith of the NBM and Harold Anderson of the CBM joined the faculty,[47] which now included Antônio Almeida and Jerônimo Gueiros, pastors of the two Presbyterian churches of the city, and J. Haldane, of the Evangelical Union of South America, which worked with the Congregationalist churches. The future seemed assured as the 1926 budget showed the Presbyterian Church of Brazil contributing the equivalent of US$1,150, the CBM, $720, and the Independente and Congregationalist churches, $180 each.[48] It was a paper optimism. The churches failed to send their offerings, the professors received less than half their salaries, and the Congregationalists, even more concerned about correct doctrine than the Presbyterians, left to establish their own Bible institute in 1927. A year later the seminary had only eight students.[49]

Smith soon left Brazil and was replaced by Almeida, who gave up his pastorate to work full time for the seminary, receiving his salary from the NBM.[50] Instead of supporting the institution at this critical juncture, the CBM noted the drop in enrollment, withdrew Anderson, and cut its financial contribution by two-thirds.[51] To help in the emergency, two local pastors, Israel Gueiros and Samuel Falcão, began to teach on a parttime basis. Even though the northern presbyteries had nine seminary candidates, financial resources permitted acceptance of only three.

They and four others who did not plan to be ordained made up the enrollment in 1932.[52] When the Independentes withdrew their cooperation a year later, the interdenominational character of the institution disappeared.

Cooperation in the Seminary of the North failed because of the excessive denominational spirit of the Congregationalists, fear of identity loss among the Independentes, and financial problems. Apparently, one reason why Presbyterian churches did not support the new seminary structure was dissatisfaction with its interdenominational character.[53] The situation was much like the one in the South, where Presbyterian churches contributed far more to Campinas than to the United Seminary in Rio. Nor did the missions accept their full responsibility, never furnishing enough funds and personnel. The seminary was caught between the short-sightedness of the missions, which felt that the church should maintain it, and the poverty and indifference of the churches, which did not contribute, even in proportion to their meager resources. By 1934 the missions provided no help other than Almeida's salary, and at times the institution had scarcely enough money to pay for light and water. It had few students, functioned on a very low academic level, and included only one full-time professor on its faculty. Isolated from the missions and the wider church, it fed on its own traditional conservatism. Its suspicion of outsiders and innovations thus augmented, the institution was unprepared to help the church in the North meet the new challenges to emerge in the following decades.

The United Seminary

Controversy surrounding theological education, which had been the basic cause of schism in 1903, edged the church close to another split in 1928, and once again the New York Board played a role. An excellent idea failed because of the strong denominational spirit of Brazilian Presbyterianism, nationalistic apprehension over foreign control of theological education, the depth of the scars left from 1903, and the rivalry between São Paulo and Rio.

Just as the 1903 breach marked a shift in the leadership of the church from São Paulo to Rio, the new conflict indicated that the center of power had moved back to the coffee capital. Competition had never ceased between the two cities. The *Puritano* was published in Rio and reflected the powerful personality of Álvaro Reis, and the *Revista das Missões Nacionaes* was published by *Paulistas* during most of its existence.[54] While Rio lost its most able leaders in the 1920's, the Igreja Unida in São Paulo and strong churches in other cities in that state were growing in influence. And because the economic center of the nation had shifted to the coffee state, the southern synod soon surpassed its counterparts in financial resources.

Less than ten years had elapsed since the seminary had moved to Campinas and begun its difficult program of consolidation when the delegates returned from Panama with plans for the United Seminary. The insecurity of the denominational institution became obvious when the 1917 General Assembly accepted an offer of property in Valença, near Rio, with the stipulation that the seminary move there.[55] The *Paulistas*, who were afraid this would be the first step toward absorption into the proposed United Seminary, blocked the plan.[56] But sentiment that the seminary's days in Campinas were numbered must have been widespread, since it ended the following year with only five students.[57] Established only after half a century of struggle caused in part by the New York Board, the institution now faced extinction because of another plan promoted by the same body.

The Secretary of the CCLA wrote that while "denominationalism had produced many obstacles for thousands of sinners, Christian unity will conquer dozens of thousands."[58] Thus, for that organization the United Seminary took highest priority; hopefully, it would be the first step in formation of a united Protestant church.[59] Other arguments in its favor were economy, efficiency, and the desire to raise the academic level of ministerial preparation. Braga, for one, felt strongly that Rio, the cultural center of the nation, should be the major locus of theological education.

The first planning meeting convened at Mackenzie in 1917 with Methodist, Congregationalist, and Independente delegates present, in addition to Reis and Braga of the Presbyterian Church and Gammon and Waddell representing their boards. The group recommended establishment of the seminary with four full-time professors and requested $100,000 from the North American and Brazilian churches for the purpose. Two years of "philosophical" or general studies after *ginásio* would be necessary for acceptance in the theological course.[60] By a one-vote margin Rio won over São Paulo as the location, with Pereira, the Independente delegate, voting with the minority.[61] Braga and Pereira, who were professors in their respective denominational seminaries, declared that once the new institution became a reality, they would resign from their chairs to help remove obstacles to full cooperation. The Brazil missions of the New York Board requested that Porter do the same and included a substantial subsidy in their budgets for the project.[62]

Eveything seemed to move ahead smoothly. At the 1918 General Assembly Braga pled for full participation in the venture, even though the church would have to raise special funds and face a delay in receiving pastors because of the additional preparation requirements.[63] The assembly agreed, electing Reis, who had just resigned the presidency of the Campinas Board of Directors, to be its representative on the United Seminary Board. The key phrase of the motion, later subjected to various interpretations, was: "The seminary of this assembly will not cease to function under its present administration as long as the United Seminary is not completely consolidated."[64] Donald MacLaren, invited to direct the institution, arrived at the end of the year, and in April, 1919, classes began, meeting temporarily in the First Presbyterian Church of Rio. In addition to auditors, six regular students, five of them Presbyterians, enrolled.[65]

Unwilling to accept the demise of Campinas, the *Paulistas* began a campaign to save it during the 1918 General Assembly which soon gathered momentum. When a parliamentary maneuver against the new proposal failed, Herculano Gouvêa protested, sounding the keynote in the battle against the United Seminary. He denied that the different denominations should be extinguished and added, "Our seminary, which cost the sweat of blood, is the best in South America, say the *Panamistas*. After the long struggle to build it, we cannot abandon it."[66]

The prominence of certain missionaries in the venture aroused distrust. Waddell, now President of Mackenzie and one of the moving spirits behind the idea, had long been considered a foe of Campinas. MacLaren had originally come to Brazil to direct the ill-fated theological department of Mackenzie, returning in 1913 to serve as president of the school. Although he was personally acceptable to the church, his association with Mackenzie did not inspire confidence, while the fact that a North American was invited to head the new institution sparked resentment and fears that the missions wished to take theological education out of Brazilian hands.

Suspicion of the Independente Church was also strong. It had rebuffed the recent Presbyterian attempt at union, while its synod had just repudiated a plan for cooperative education supported by most of its pastors and acceptable to Campinas Seminary.[67] The Independents' annual celebration of the schism of 1903 offended Presbyterians, and uneasiness over Pereira's dominant personality had been a significant reason for keeping the new institution out of São Paulo.

Opponents of the United Seminary soon hinted that its orthodoxy was suspect. Coriolano de Assunção, the able pastor in Botucatu, criticized the missionaries' failure to understand the needs of the church and called the new faculty a Babel. But he emphasized a still more important point when he called Campinas Seminary the "mother cell of the life of the Presbyterian Church."[68] Gouvêa put it most dramatically:

> This is the Seminary of the Presbyterian Church . . . which God gave us for the highest ends. . . . No, Presbyterian Church, you cannot deny this institution! If it should fall, you would weep bitterly alongside its ruins. . . . Chained to the corpse of the seminary, you too would die, Presbyterian Church, overwhelmed by the indescribable crucifying pain of your unspeakable bitterness.[69]

It was clear that many Presbyterians were not willing to sacrifice their seminary or their denominational pride to the hoped-for unity. And since their church was the largest one involved, its attitude would determine the project's success or failure.

In the ensuing battle the lines of division were soon apparent. The New York Board and its missions strongly favored the proposal, and Speer wrote that the board would eventually withdraw its man from Campinas.[70] The Nashville Board supported the project, paying half of MacLaren's salary, but its missions were divided. The EBM, led by Gammon, was in favor, but the WBM, closely linked to Campinas, stood rigidly opposed. Brazilian synod positions were predictable. The Synod of the South, centered in São Paulo, fought the plan, saying it had been imposed by North Americans. To the *Paulistas* the scheme looked like a replay of New York's heavy-handed actions before 1903. Central Synod, which included Rio, naturally gave its support, while the Synod of the North remained aloof from the arguments. But opposed to church union, it ultimately endorsed continuation of the denominational institution.

In 1919 Central Synod met at the request of the Campinas faculty to state its position, and concluded: "The United Seminary does not have as an immediate goal the dissolution of the present seminaries. As the General Assembly has determined, these will naturally dissolve themselves when the Faculty of Theology of Rio de Janeiro is functioning properly." In a tone guaranteed to arouse the hostility of the *Paulistas*, the statement compared the older institutions unfavorably with the new one, which, it said, would be located in the "capital, . . . the greatest intellectual, literary, and scientific center of Brazil." Central Synod also requested removal of the denominational seminary to Rio and permission for its professors to cooperate in the new endeavor.[71]

In reply the Synod of the South declared the hope that "our seminary" never close, that it remain in Campinas, and that the boards continue to permit missionary professors to serve on its faculty.[72] But at the year's end the United Seminary Board of Directors, which had already requested the services of Gouvêa,[73] fed the flames by asking for Porter and Smith as well.[74] Since Braga, the only other professor in Campinas, was soon to leave for cooperative work in Rio, the denominational seminary would have had no staff. But the 1920 General Assembly left both the Campinas faculty and the 1918 resolution unaltered, while electing A. C. de Menezes to teach in the united institution.

Cooperation of other groups became a matter of mounting concern. The Congregationalists happily participated as long as the seminary remained in Rio, the site of most of their churches. They furnished a professor and sent students but gave almost no funds. The Methodist Board in the United States voted to contribute $25,000 to the project, but only after the Brazilian churches had raised their quota. However, while the Methodists spoke of moving their theological course to Rio, they established a Bible school, which some called a seminary, in Juiz de Fora[75] and waited to observe the attitude of the other churches before committing themselves completely to the United Seminary. Noting that Presbyterians and Methodists continued denominational theological education, the Independentes also held back. They had never accepted Rio as the location for the institution since most of their churches were in and around São Paulo. And when Pereira's proposal that it move to Campinas and be reorganized as a federation of seminaries was narrowly defeated, they lost interest.[76] Again they explored the possibility of cooperation with Campinas, but once more bitterness over the past frustrated the initiative.

Consequently the new institution made little progress toward stability. Supported by only one synod of the Presbyterian Church it met bitter antagonism from another. The Congregationalists furnished a professor and a few students, while the Methodists provided a professor and temporary quarters after 1920, but almost no students. Except for small amounts contributed by Presbyterian and Congregationalist churches in Rio, the budget came from the New York Board.

By the end of 1920 the institution was on the defensive, and its trustees affirmed that they had never envisioned closing Campinas.[77] Even First Church, Rio, took special offerings for Campinas as well as the new seminary.[78] When the United Seminary initiated a night course for men who were employed, making it possible for a number of professional people to study for the ministry, it was accused of lowering instead of raising academic standards.[79]

The 1922 General Assembly brought victory to Campinas and, in the long run, implied defeat for the united faculty. After two presbyteries had requested immediate withdrawal from the cooperative institution,[80] the assembly declared that it would never close Campinas, adding that if it became necessary to choose between the two, the denominational seminary would receive its support. To raise money to pay the salary of a substitute for Braga, who now presented his resignation, the church initiated a drive for Cr$100,000 (US$25,000) to endow a chair in Campinas. It indicated its priorities by authorizing a campaign of Cr$25,000 for the United Seminary, to begin only after the funds for Campinas were raised.[81] The goal for Campinas was oversubscribed, but the campaign for the other never materialized. Now aware of the situation, the Brazil Council of the New York Board attempted to allay fears that it was advocating any particular plan.

It assured the church that it had no preference as to location or structure of the institution, its only desire being the participation of the greatest possible number of churches.[82]

Despite formidable opposition and problems the United Seminary grew. It offered courses of three and five years and by 1924 had seventeen students, including seven Presbyterians. At the end of the year seven candidates received degrees (B.Th.), and three, diplomas.[83] But the deaths of Francisco de Souza in 1924 and A. C. de Menezes in 1925 robbed the faculty of two respected professors, while that of Álvaro Reis removed its most powerful advocate within the Presbyterian church.

Striving to avoid controversy, the New York Board informed its missions in 1925 that it would continue to cede Porter to Campinas, pay annual subsidies of Cr$6,000 to the Seminary of the North and Cr$10,000 to the United Seminary for two more years. After that the grants would be made directly to the church for use as it saw fit in the field of theological education.[84] Although the same board contributed funds for a classroom building in 1929, it was clear that it would not continue the subsidy indefinitely.

Growth of the United Seminary inflamed existing rivalries. By 1927 Campinas had ten Presbyterian students, while of the twenty-three in Rio, eighteen were Presbyterians.[85] At this point, hints of theological differences were implied. Lysanius C. Leite, an engineer and graduate of the new seminary, and now one of its professors, contradicted the spirit of Presbyterian orthodoxy when he affirmed that while religion is immutable, theology must modernize itself with the evolution of humanity.[86] Guilherme Kerr, newly elected to Braga's former chair in Campinas, spoke for most of the church when he linked the defense of orthodoxy to denominationalism. The great modern danger, he wrote, is not denominational division or even atheism; it is the rationalism which is born at times within the church. Presbyterianism which is strong and cohesive will offer indestructible resistance to rationalistic negations, he added, and its survival depends primarily on a strong denominational seminary.[87]

Animosities intensified, and the Synod of the South, with Kerr as moderator, took the offensive in 1927. Hinting that heresy was taught in the United Seminary, it denied that the venture had ever represented the desires of the national church. Instead, a

few missionaries and the Panama Congress were its sponsors. The
venture was premature, it charged, while acceptance of students
without full preparation and establishment of courses on two
levels reflected a distortion of the institution's purposes. Most important, Synod accused the plan of destroying the initiative and
autonomy of the Presbyterian Church in theological education,
thus breeding disharmony in that body. Since it was impossible to
support two seminaries in the South, the statement concluded,
General Assembly should immediately withdraw support from
the newer institution and transfer its Presbyterian students to
Campinas.[88] The resolution burst like a bombshell in the church.
Braga, known for his patience, called it "the most shameful document in the history of our Presbyterianism."[89] Compromise
seemed impossible, and fear of schism at the 1928 General Assembly became widespread.

General Assembly avoided the issue by assigning one seminary
to each synod,[90] but the world financial crisis and the New York
Board's inability to continue supporting the United Seminary
insured its demise. In 1931 O Puritano emphasized the necessity
of reconstruction. The church was exhausted and disillusioned, it
said, and now must be realistic about rebuilding. The time had
come for concentrating its efforts in Campinas.[91] Methodists and
Congregationalists were no longer cooperating, and the Independentes, who had finally entered the venture, now decided to
withdraw. Thus the 1932 General Assembly bowed to the inevitable and retreated also.[92] Campinas once more became the seminary of the two southern synods.

But the idea of cooperation was not quite dead. Plans were
under way, with the support of the Paulistas,[93] to move the Presbyterian Seminary to São Paulo and form a federated faculty with
the Independentes. The project, which would have benefited both
churches, proved noticeably shortlived. Funds from the sale of
part of the Campinas property which were destined for a building in São Paulo, dwindled away in bad investments.[94]

Although the United Seminary never secured a full-time faculty
and student body, it produced a number of able pastors and took
creative steps toward innovation and flexibility in theological
education and ministry. Because it functioned mostly at night
and on more than one level, enrolling some students as auditors
who did not seek ordination, it aroused criticism from exponents

of the traditional pattern of theological education. But it was precisely these features which enabled a number of men to study while they worked or prepared themselves for other professions as well. Among the students were engineers, doctors, lawyers, and dentists, many of whom later became ordained, active ministers. The majority could not have left Rio to study elsewhere, as witnessed by the fact that Campinas, which had twenty students in 1928,[95] only had twenty-two in 1934, after the dissolution of the United Seminary.[96] If the new faculty had continued, it might have evolved into a multi-level institution. By preparing pastors of varying cultural backgrounds to serve in the urban centers, it could have aided Protestantism in general and Presbyterianism in particular to transcend the rather narrow social spectrum in which they operated.

The Instituto José Manoel da Conceição (JMC), was an indirect contribution of the United Seminary. Founded by Waddell in 1928 near São Paulo, it was a cooperative venture sponsored by Mackenzie, the SBM, the Independentes, Episcopalians, and Presbyterians.[97] Its purpose was to provide the additional years of study beyond *ginásio* required for students in the new seminary. Presbyterian graduates began to attend Campinas only after 1932, but during succeeding decades JMC sent several hundred men to the various denominational institutions, even though for a time the Synod of the South refused to cooperate.

Braga believed it to be the last hope for theological education which would offer a broader outlook and encourage higher standards. In May, 1932, he wrote to Lennington, voicing deep disappointment over his church's rejection of the United Seminary and his own faith in the Instituto JMC. He concluded, "If the Board holds on, we may expect to see a ministry in the near future. Otherwise God will surely pass to others the responsibility for the evangelization of Brazil. Israel was put aside when she proved to be useless."[98] Nine days later Braga died, at the age of fifty-five. It was tragically ironic that his death came the same year as that of the cooperative institution whose survival he considered so crucial.

Although the *Confederação Evangélica do Brasil* began work two years later and continued to function with Presbyterian leadership, it never showed the creativity or dynamism which Braga had supplied the cooperative movement. On the other hand, the rejection of the United Seminary exposed the extent of

denominational pride in the Presbyterian Church and strengthened that spirit within it. The period of greater isolation and
relative stagnation which was to follow in turn left the church unprepared for the new challenges of the postwar world. Rejection
of the ecumenical ideal by the Presbyterian Church became obvious on the twenty-fifth anniversary of Braga's death. While
Cristianismo, an ecumenical Evangelical paper, dedicated an
entire issue to his life and contribution,[99] *O Puritano* ignored the
date.

Chapter Nine

Increasing Isolation and Stagnation: 1934-1946

With the 1930 Revolution came hope for new social legislation and an amplification of the democratic process in Brazil. And although the new constitution favored Roman Catholicism, most Protestants supported it because of guarantees of religious liberty and separation of church and state. But the new structure of government weakened the presidency just at a time when the extremism on both right and left threatened the nation while the center found itself fragmented and ineffectual.

The Communist Party, founded in 1922, was active and growing in power and was instrumental in forming the *Aliança Nacional Libertadora* in 1934. Honorary chairman was Luiz Carlos Prestes, the revolutionary leader of the famous march in the 1920's who had slipped back into Brazil in April of 1934 after a period of orientation in Russia. The *Aliança*, which advocated agrarian reform and the nationalization of foreign-owned business, attracted many non-Communist supporters. But when Prestes called for the masses to prepare themselves for an assault on the government, the organization was immediately proscribed. Retaliation came in November, 1935, with a series of strikes followed by open rebellion and temporary establishment of a Popular National Revolutionary Government in Natal; an attack on the state police in Recife, and the subjugation of an infantry regiment in Rio. After the uprising met defeat the party was outlawed, and it ceased to be openly active for a decade. That its strength survived was apparent when it received about 10 per cent of the votes cast in the 1945 presidential election and placed forty-six of its candidates in the various state legislatures in 1946. The following year it was outlawed once more.[1]

A more serious threat came from the Fascist *Integralistas*, who received support among Italian and German immigrants, military officers, including the army Chief of Staff,[2] and industrialists. Plínio Salgado, the group's leader, had been influenced by Figueiredo's Catholic nationalism, and the movement, which was violently anti-Communist and anti-Semitic, identified Protestantism with both. One *Integralista* leader called Protestantism "a form of disintegrating, communistic Judaism which should be eliminated from Brazil" and advocated the prohibition of Evangelical worship.[3] The cause elicited the sympathy of A. A. Lima and the endorsement of over twenty Catholic bishops, even though it never succeeded in gaining official approval by the hierarchy.[4] At times Vargas himself gave the impression that he favored its goals.

The group controlled a number of newspapers and radio stations which were used to promote Salgado's candidacy for the presidency in 1937. But in September, amidst rumors of an impending military coup, a clumsy forgery fabricated by *integralistas* and purporting to be a Communist plan for revolution gave Vargas an excuse to suspend civil liberties and declare a state of war. A number of Spiritist centers were closed and Masonry was outlawed as "inherently Bolshevist." Because several Roman Catholic leaders had accused Protestantism of preparing the way for Communism, serious consideration was given to a decree closing Evangelical churches.[5]

The President of the Evangelical Confederation, M. G. dos Santos, immediately declared that:

> The Evangelical churches consider that as a matter of faith and order, they owe all loyalty and obedience within the law, to the legitimately constituted public powers. . . . They believe that by their very nature they are compelled to combat Communism. They are ready to collaborate with the government in the urgent task of eliminating this great evil from Brazil.[6]

The statement was consistent with the Presbyterian belief in liberal democracy over against fascism on the right and revolutionary socialism on the left. But the insecurity of Protestantism, allied with its traditional respect for authority, fostered an un-critical attitude toward the government, and when a coup in November perpetuated Vargas in power, Presbyterians were silent. In 1942 a writer noted with approval that one of the char-acteristics of Brazilian Protestantism was "its inflexible acknowl-edgement of the autonomy of the civil powers."[7]

After the coup, which inaugurated the "New State," all political parties, including *Integralismo*, were dissolved. Vargas remained in office until 1945, when he was persuaded to resign in order that elections might be held.

The entrance of the United States into World War II brought a new danger to Brazilian Protestants. Catholic leaders charged that Protestant missionary efforts caused resentment among Brazilians and made cooperation between the two nations more difficult. The Archbishop of Belo Horizonte suggested that the American ambassador, a Catholic, take up the matter with Presi-dent Roosevelt,[8] while the Roman hierarchy in the United States asked the government to restrict travel by Protestant missionaries to Latin America.[9] The efforts failed, but they confirmed Brazilian Protestants' worst suspicions regarding the Roman Catholic atti-tude toward religious liberty.

During the period under consideration the nation's industrial development began, and the cities grew even more rapidly than before. In most cases the population of the capitals increased at a rate two or three times that of other areas in their states.[10] The new Brazil presented a major challenge to Presbyterians, who had been less successful in urban centers than in rural areas. Al-though many rural congregations were strong Christian communi-ties and a stimulus to progress, this was often not the case in the cities. There the traditional message and rural ethos were not adequate for the complexities of modern urban life.

During the 1930's Brazilian Protestantism moved further away from the cause to which Erasmo Braga had dedicated his efforts, rejecting all attempts at union. In its new constitution, adopted in 1937, the Presbyterian Church changed its name to the Igreja Cristã Presbiteriana do Brasil, in order to suggest its unity with the one church.[11] But the word Cristã was dropped in 1950 and the traditional name adopted once more. At the same time the desire of a few for a more open theological stance was firmly repudiated, and the church as a whole reaffirmed its traditional conservatism.

Decreased Evangelistic Growth

Presbyterians had been dominant in Brazilian missionary Protestantism almost since its inception. Arriving shortly after Kalley, Simonton and his colleagues used their greater personnel and financial resources and a more serious program of ministerial preparation to move ahead of the Congregationalists. The Baptists, who began work in 1881, and the Pentecostals, who arrived in 1910, lagged behind the Presbyterians for a time but soon began to grow more rapidly and, in the period under study, surpassed the older church in size.

Although both younger groups benefited in some areas from earlier Presbyterian penetration and the good will toward Protestantism which they had won, there were more important reasons for their rapid growth. The first was a flexible structure of government which facilitated forming new congregations. Another was a pattern of ministry and pastoral training designed to produce leadership in close contact with the poor and uneducated. Both factors combined to stimulate lay activity. Proselytizing zeal, often directed against other Protestants, coupled with a message and ethic which, if overly simplistic, were easily understood by the poor, also exerted influence. Still another advantage lay in the newer groups' concentration on the large urban centers, while almost all Presbyterian foreign missionary effort, and much of that of the national church, focused on the sparsely populated hinterland. A final plus, especially in the case of the Pentecostals, was their style of worship—strong emphasis on music, often of indigenous origin, testimonies, and emotional expression. Unlike the more formal Presbyterian service, these gatherings encouraged greater participation for all and a more authentic expression of the Brazilian spirit.

One result of Pentecostal growth was the beginning of a new attitude toward the group on the part of Presbyterians. In 1939, *O Puritano* published an article which criticized many aspects of Pentecostal life and worship but admitted for the first time that some members "worked with zeal in the cause of Christ" and merited respect.[12] Others, however, still denied that the Pente-

costal churches were Christian and refused any thought of cooperation with them.[13]

Statistics for the most important missionary churches from 1910
to 1948 show that while the newer groups were accelerating
their growth, that of the Presbyterians fell sharply.[14]

Year	Presb. Church	Indep. Presb. Church	Presb. Missions	Baptist Church	Cong. Cristã	Assembly of God
1910	10,000	5,000	0	7,004	0	0
1917	15,198	—	—	—	—	—
1921	18,493	—	—	—	—	—
1923	21,129	—	—	—	—	—
1925	—	—	—	30,000	—	—
1929	29,503	—	—	—	—	—
1930	—	—	3,000	—	—	14,000
1931	32,500	13,000	—	—	—	—
1935	—	—	—	43,306	36,645	—
1940	—	—	4,500	—	50,223	—
1941	43,976	—	—	—	—	—
1943	47,725	—	6,000	—	—	60,000
1945	50,193	—	—	—	69,667	—
1946	52,191	—	—	—	—	—
1947	55,018	—	—	84,512	—	—
1948	59,404	19,000	8,000	—	87,000	104,836

According to available data the Presbyterian Church grew 310
per cent in the two decades after 1910, or 78 per cent per decade.
Then, in a dramatic drop, expansion reached only 35 per cent
from 1931 to 1941, or 3 per cent per year. This rate, which continued until 1946, only slightly exceeded the population growth
of the nation from 1910 to 1940.[15] While it is impossible to discover with precision what proportion of the children of church
members were drifting away, an estimate is revealing. In 1944
when the total communicant membership of the church was
49,331, there were 2771 professions of faith,[16] but at least 2,500
baptized youth must have reached maturity during that year.
Evidence indicates that at least half of those who professed their
faith had not undergone infant baptism. So it is clear that, at
best, only half the children of the church became communicant
members. Obviously, the traditional evangelistic message with its
accompanying moralism was not winning the allegiance of many
of the youth of the church.

On the other hand, during this period when Brazil was laying the foundation of industrialization, and masses of country people were pouring into the coastal cities, Presbyterians did not achieve significant penetration into the new urban groups. They lagged even further behind the Pentecostals and Baptists in the large cities than they did in the nation as a whole. This was especially true in Rio where Presbyterians had once been the dominant group. The seventeen churches of the Presbytery of Rio, with nearly 3,000 communicants served by twenty pastors, received only 363 people on profession of faith from 1935 to 1938, an average of 5.4 per church annually. The churches enrolled 439 members by transfer during the same period, indicating that they were growing at the expense of interior congregations.[17]

The pattern of city life alienated the middle-class pastor from recent arrivals and the poor, the groups usually most interested in his message. The problem of part-time ministers continued to mount, and every Presbyterian pastor in Rio fell into that category in 1943.[18] One writer noted that while the Presbytery of Rio had more pastors than any other, it had fewer conversions than most. He recognized the justifications for secular employment but lamented the result: "The churches of the Presbytery of Rio de Janeiro are almost completely different from the . . . others. Days, months, and even years go by in which the ministers do not make even one visit to the homes of the believers who live far from the center . . . especially the poor."[19] Thus, the sense of Christian community which was often strong in rural and small-town churches seemed elusive in the urban centers. The believer from the interior usually found few fellow members in his neighborhood and saw his brethren only on Sundays. With little or no pastoral guidance, he found it difficult to maintain loyalty to his congregation and even harder to evangelize his friends.

Baptist and Pentecostal pastors also held outside jobs, but their ministry, as stated previously, was more democratic in structure. They usually lived closer to their people and were of the same social class. Lay activity and aspiration toward the ministry also received encouragement. Boasting a larger number of churches in most cities than the Presbyterians, those groups were more easily accessible. By 1945 the Presbyterians had only seventeen churches in Rio, while the Baptists, who had arrived twenty-two years later, had fifty.[20]

The entire picture was not so bleak. Presbyterianism in Rio had lapsed into lethargy, but the Church in São Paulo was thriving. To some extent its development paralleled that of Rio two decades earlier. Building on the foundation laid by M. G. dos Santos in the Igreja Unida, was Miguel Rizzo, Jr., an effective preacher who dedicated all of his time and effort to the ministry. By 1938 the São Paulo church included industrialists and professional men among its 1080 communicants. It maintained sixteen Sunday schools and fifteen congregações, many of which were later organized into churches.[21] The Brás Church, under the leadership of Kerr and others, established six congregações from 1934 to 1942 which later became churches.[22] Thus by 1943 the Presbytery of São Paulo included eight churches and two congregações, with 2766 communicants and fourteen ministers. It had counted 266 professions of faith during the year.[23] Unfortunately by 1946 the latter figure had dropped to 138.[24] The typical urban pattern seemed to be repeating itself.

In eastern Minas Gerais and Espirito Santo growth spiraled at a rate twice that of the church as a whole, and in 1939 the four pastors in the latter state received 347 new members on profession of faith.[25] In 1942 the church in the small town of Alto Jequitibá, Minas, had 998 communicants and enrolled 362 students in its school.[26] But in the North there were indications that a number of rural churches, which had been the backbone of Presbyterianism in the area, were in decline. At the same time few city churches showed the vitality which many rural congregations had once enjoyed. New patterns were needed but few recognized it.

Among the North American missions the WBM seemed to be most concerned to follow new population movements. In 1940 J. R. Woodson established work in Goiânia, the new capital of Goiás, and five years later the church in that city and its eighteen scattered congregações numbered 600 communicants.[27]

An important feature of church life in many rural areas was intensive activity by laymen, whose spontaneous witness contributed immeasurably to evangelism. To help them, annual conventions, similar to the camp meetings on the North American frontier, met in a number of areas, and believers came long distances for inspiration, fellowship, and instruction. One of the largest was in Morrinhos in Willis Banks' former field, where five hundred people came each year, constructed rude huts, and cooked over open fires for several days. Others convened in Espirito Santo, Minas, and the fields of the missions. For many isolated rural folk, these meetings were the high point of the year. Pastors of some city churches also attempted to prepare their members for evangelism. Benjamin Cesar, who remained in Campos over forty years and organized a number of churches in the city and surrounding area, wrote in 1934 that several men, women, and youth in his church were studying homiletics. After completing a brief course they preached in outlying *congregações* and visited *fazendas* to evangelize.[28]

But the traditional style of direct evangelistic activity which was natural and effective in rural areas often disappeared in city churches. Such patterns of witness apparently seemed artificial to the middle-class constituency of urban Presbyterian congregations. It might indeed have proved ineffective among the urban middle class, but too often no viable alternatives were developed. Either patterns which had brought results at other times and places were repeated, or serious attempts at evangelism were dropped. If the churches in Rio were harbingers of the future, Brazilian Presbyterianism was in serious trouble. In 1945 a writer complained that Evangelicals exhibited many of the faults of Roman Catholics. Few were really zealous, he charged, and the leaders who were most concerned and enthusiastic often became disillusioned at the apathy of their audiences. "Those who remain in the ministry," he concluded, "with rare exceptions, are the least capable and most apathetic."[29] The urgency of revitalizing the church would soon become paramount.

The Beginning of Closer Church-Mission Cooperation

The Modus Operandi Committee, theoretically established by the Brazil Plan of 1917, was almost nonexistent for twenty-five years afterward.[30] Although the missions employed a few Brazilian pastors and lay evangelists in their fields, continued to cooperate in Campinas Seminary and helped sporadically in Recife, they were almost totally isolated geographically and organizationally from the national church.

As a result both church and missions at times exhibited a lack of understanding for the other's problems. In addition the church resented the necessity of first subjecting to the scrutiny of the missions any requests it wished to present to the boards, especially when the missionaries had little knowledge of the challenges and problems which it faced. As a result of a request of the 1938 *Supremo Concílio*, as the General Assembly was now called, the newly united mission of the PCUSA recommended that official petitions of the church no longer come through it but go directly to New York.[31] The board went further in requiring that grants for certain missionary programs, including some already initiated, receive approval from the Modus Operandi Committee before being released. Tension rose in the committee when the Brazilian members, unfamiliar with much of the mission program, approved two projects which the missionaries felt were not important, while strongly opposing a third which the mission supported.[32] It was clear that the insistence that the two bodies, isolated from each other's work, participate in decisions regarding the use of funds destined for the other could only cause turmoil.

The Junta de Missões Nacionais

The desire for closer contact and cooperation between the church and missions, combined with the need for workers on several new frontiers, led to a more promising step in 1940. The 1938 Supremo Concílio had asked for one hundred missionaries and substantial grants from the United States to aid in an evangelistic advance. Although the request could not be met it provided the occasion for a meeting of L. K. Anderson and other representatives from New York with the Executive Committee of the Supremo Concílio and representatives of the Central and East Brazil missions. The group decided that each of the boards would aid the national church in forming the *Junta de Missões Nacionais*, which would consist of an equal number of Brazilians and missionaries.[33] The organization was to contract competent seminary graduates for work in areas unoccupied by any Evangelical church, with one-third of their salaries provided by the adjacent presbyteries and the rest by the *junta*. Financing would come primarily through special offerings raised by the church, while the New York Board promised to match the Brazilian contribution up to US$1,250. After some hesitation, the Nashville Board agreed to do the same.[34] But, in keeping with the traditional mission strategy of Brazilian Presbyterianism, the *junta* looked only toward the geographical frontiers and failed to see the burning need in the urban centers.

Response was enthusiastic, and offerings usually exceeded expectations, making it possible for the *junta* to expand its work rapidly. In 1941 the church raised Cr$37.141 (US$1,850) for the project, and by 1945 the amount had risen to Cr$145.603.[35] Contributions from the missions, originally expected for only five years, were later raised, although not to the level of those of the church, and continued throughout the period.

In 1941 the first national missionary, Camilo F. Costa, went to Tanabi, in the growing northwest of São Paulo, and soon was holding worship services in four locations.[36] By 1946 the *junta* supported a full-time executive secretary who supervised the work of nine Brazilian pastors, one North American missionary, two lay evangelists, and four colporteurs. The majority served in western São Paulo and northern Paraná, where new cities were growing rapidly. But the fields also included towns in Pará, Minas Gerais, Espirito Santo, and Santa Catarina. The general attitude toward the Evangelical church became apparent in Votuporanga, São Paulo, where the pastor and his wife had opened a free night school for illiterates. During a land auction, the townspeople stopped bidding on a well-located lot where he hoped to build a church so he could buy it for less.[37] In 1957 the *junta* employed fifteen pastors and four evangelists, had occupied fourteen fields, and counted 1588 communicants worshipping in twenty-seven church buildings.[38]

In 1942 the organization made an exception to its policy of support to new work only and accepted the veteran pastor, José Duarte, as its missionary in Pará. Two years later it was seeking a second worker for the region.[39] Hope for a cooperative effort in the area approached realization in 1945 when J. C. Nogueira, Executive Secretary of the *junta*, and representatives of the missions and boards, presented plans for formation of the long-awaited Amazon Mission.[40] It finally came into being in 1950 as a branch of the *junta*, financed by the church and the two boards. By 1959 workers included three pastors and six laymen.[41]

The Portugal Mission

Pascoal Pita, the church's most effective missionary to Portugal, ended his work there in 1940, leaving behind three churches and two unorganized congregations, with three Portuguese pastors serving 350 communicants.[42] The struggle had been arduous, and funds from the Missionary Society for the Evangelization of Portugal were scarce. After Natanael Emerique arrived in 1944 to continue the work, the church officially recognized the responsibility it had accepted in 1910 and organized its *Junta de Missões Estrangeiras*, inviting the existing Portuguese mission to come under its aegis. That same year the Portuguese church grew stronger with the adherence of a few Congregational churches.[43]

The following year saw another step taken toward closer cooperation between the two boards and the church when the three formed the Presbyterian Committee on Cooperation in Portugal. Each entity was to contribute one couple to the work, with the New York Board paying two-thirds of the salary of the Brazilian workers.[44] Beginning in 1947 the PCUSA sent a number of workers to Lisbon. Among them was Michael Testa who remained sixteen years. The PCUS sent its first worker, Herbert Meza, in 1953. Cooperation from the North Americans made it possible to establish a seminary and brought additional resources and stability to the Portuguese church. In 1952, it was organized as the Igreja Evangélica Presbiteriana de Portugal.

The Instituto José Manoel da Conceição

While closer relationships were developing between the church and the missions at some points, the continuing suspicion and sensitivity of the church concerning theological education showed up in its attitude toward the Instituto JMC. Founded in 1928 by Waddell to give the pre-theological course to students destined for the United Seminary, it sent Presbyterian students to Campinas Seminary only after the other institution closed. But the 1934 General Assembly, fearful of any missionary initiative in theological education, increased the Campinas course from four to five years, making the first two years parallel to the last two of the JMC course.[45] The following year the Executive Committee of the church recommended fusing the two pre-theological courses in JMC, along with that of the Independente Church, anticipating transfer of the denominational seminary to São Paulo.[46] General Assembly refused, recommending that candidates with the full five-year *ginásio* preparation take their pre-theological work in Campinas. It suggested that only older men with incomplete training attend JMC, where they could do their pre-seminary work concurrently with *ginásio*. But to maintain harmony with the Central Brazil Mission, the church declared the institution "necessary to the Presbyterian Church of Brazil" and voted to contribute Cr$200,00 (US$17.00) per month to its budget.[47]

The church had made it clear once more that it intended to retain jurisdiction over all theological education. Only after 1940, when the Brazilian educational system was reorganized and JMC eliminated its pre-theological course to offer only the regular seven years of secondary school, did the institution enjoy cordial relations with the church.[48] In 1948 seven of the ten graduates of Campinas Seminary were alumni of the school.

But despite a few small steps toward closer mission-church relationships, the various Presbyterian groups in Brazil continued to work in almost complete isolation from each other. Reexamination of their relationship and the attempt to discover new structures for their work would soon become a new source of tension.

E. M. do Amaral and the Final Defeat of Church Union

The stated purpose of the Evangelical Confederation of Brazil, formed in 1934, was to stimulate and express the unity of Protestantism, coordinate its forces in joint action, and maintain relations with the Church of Christ in all the world.[49] It was successful in its desire to represent Protestantism before the government, serving in World War II as the channel through which two Protestant chaplains were accepted into the Brazilian army.[50] The Confederation published Sunday school quarterlies which, despite their uneven quality, were useful, especially in isolated congregations with little trained leadership. It also published the *Hinário Evangélico* in 1946, improving the quality of music in the churches which used it.

A more fundamental question as to the purpose of the organization was soon raised. Despite the failure of the United Seminary, the hope of the Panama Congress still prevailed among a few, who saw the body as the first step toward organic union of Brazil's Protestant churches. The most important spokesman for the cause after the death of Erasmo Braga was his collaborator, Epaminondas Melo do Amaral, an Independente, who in 1934 became a secretary of the Evangelical Confederation. That year he wrote *O Magno Problema*, the first serious examination by a Brazilian Protestant of the question of church unity and Protestant fragmentation. His basic thesis was that division neither conformed to the Christian ideal nor was a necessary feature of Protestantism. Expounding the Biblical basis of unity, he accused denominationalism of hindering evangelism and social action, as well as causing expensive duplication of effort in theological education, publishing, and pastoral work.

Amaral placed the blame for denominational division on zealous but misguided missionaries who had imported differences and disputes of no relevance to Brazil.[51] Because, he continued, the national spirit had been shaped by Roman Catholicism's emphasis on unity, Protestant fragmentation accentuated the foreign nature of the Evangelical churches. Thus, he believed, perhaps naively at some points, that a united church would be more genuinely Brazilian:

> We have copied North American divisions which are fabulous in number, we have translated their creeds, we have put into our language, and this is shocking, their codes of ecclesiastical government . . . we have perpetuated, not rarely, practices and tendencies which do not speak so much to our own soul, and of these the form of worship is especially important. If the Brazilian soul, sentimental, vibrant, friendly, and brotherly, had given to the new church in the country an ethos all its own, the ecclesiastical situation today would be very different.[52]

Amaral urged the formation of a united church with great flexibility in government, liturgy, and doctrine.[53] Envisioning immediate goals, he published a separate article calling for renewed forms of worship, greater concentration on work with youth and preparation for the ministry, and coordination of Protestant forces for the evangelization of the nation.[54]

Although it left a number of difficult problems unsolved, the book made an honest and bold effort to treat one of the central problems in Protestant ecclesiology. But it was either rejected or ignored by the leadership of the Presbyterian Church. One prominent layman praised the attempt, expressing hope that a new generation would make unity a reality[55] but Campinas Seminary took no notice of O Magno Problema. Unable to conceive of Christian unity without uniformity, Gouvêa wrote that any plan which allowed differences of government and doctrine would produce a caricature of a church.[56] Apparently the concept of adiaphora was alien to Brazilian Presbyterianism.

But despite indifference or opposition from most, attempts to unite the Presbyterian Church with other bodies still continued. In 1934 a group of Methodists, Presbyterians, and Independentes submitted plans for unity to their respective judicatories. The Methodist General Council showed interest and nominated a commission to study the matter. Presbyterians, who had once sought unity with the Methodists, also authorized further study but dashed cold water on the proposal by adding, "Even though it is a beautiful ideal the present facts indicate that any step in that direction is premature."[57]

A more significant advance toward uniting the two Presbyterian churches came in a new concession by the General Assembly of the Presbyterian Church of Brazil.

> Considering that Masonry, in spite of the good service it has rendered in social and political spheres, is dispensable for the believer and much less desirable than . . . union with the *Independente* brethren; Considering . . . that the *Independente* Presbyterian Church cannot give up the attitude which it took regarding the question without offense to its conscience; It is resolved: a) to renew the recommendation that believers who are Masons refrain from attending lodge meetings; b) to recommend that the sessions of churches, beginning now, receive no more Masons on profession of faith and that minister and officers not be Masons.[58]

Disavowing commitment to a position, the motion ended with an ambiguous statement that it only reflected the desire to begin discussions which would lead to union.

Unfortunately, the discussion which followed was mostly negative. Amaral, who was now the Moderator of his church, and a few other leaders favored union,[59] but most Independentes remained suspicious because the resolution stopped short of a complete condemnation of Masonry. The reaction was no better in the Presbyterian Church. Complaints abounded that General Assembly's action implied complete capitulation to the Independentes and absorption of the larger church into the smaller; thus, Gouvêa called the proposed union fictitious. Benjamin Cesar, who strongly favored the move, cut through the arguments to the basic problem when he observed that self-love was the greatest obstacle. No one was willing to admit he had been in error.[60] As the second serious attempt to repair the breach of 1903 failed, each church was locked more solidly than ever into a position alienating it from the other, despite their common theology, system of government, and historical roots.

It is clear that the movement toward Protestant unity, which had seemed so promising shortly after Panama, had steadily lost momentum. Although Amaral was correct in assigning initial responsibility to the missionaries, the national leaders now seemed more determined to perpetuate the divisions than their North American colleagues. Nor were Presbyterians the only ones who set denominational interests above cooperation and unity. In 1934 the first Brazilian Methodist bishop, Cesar Dacorso Filho, "condemned interdenominational agreements which limit the frontiers of Methodism and advocated complete liberty of action within the limits of mutual respect between the churches."[61] Despite efforts by the South Brazil Mission, the Methodists repudiated previous comity agreements and refused to enter into new ones.[62]

Participation in international ecumenical gatherings lagged after Braga's death. Pita, the missionary to Portugal, attended the Faith and Order meeting in Edinburgh in 1937, as did Wilson Fernandes, Secretary of the Student Christian movement for Brazil,[63] but church papers devoted little attention to the event. Brazilian Presbyterians sent no delegate to the 1938 meeting of the IMC.

Further proof of the attitude of Brazilian Protestantism toward unity presented itself in 1938 when the financially pressed Evangelical Confederation asked for Amaral's resignation, thus losing his creative voice. Retained as General Secretary of the organization was Rodolfo Anders, whose responsibility had been the Conselho de Educação Religiosa.[64] In 1942, eight years after he had served as its Moderator, Amaral, with seven others, was forced by the Independente Church to leave its ranks. The central issue was the fideism of the group which led it to affirm the preeminence of spiritual and ethical life over the traditional symbols of the church. For the liberals, such an emphasis laid the basis for an ecumenical theology, but for the majority it implied an antidenominational stance which was unacceptable. "We were generally considered," the group wrote, "worthy of the Christian ministry but undesirable in the Independente ministry."[65]

Insistence on denominational loyalty was no less fervid in the Presbyterian Church nor, indeed, in all of Brazilian Protestantism.

The demands of institutionalism and the emphasis on orthodoxy, both important in the United Seminary struggle, became even stronger. In 1941 the Presbytery of the South echoed the thought of most of the church in its warning to Campinas Seminary: "This judicatory has suffered harm because of a certain loosening in the principle of denominational fidelity on the part of some workers. This judicatory upholds the sound principle of fraternal coopera- tion between the various Evangelical denominations . . . but re- jects the 'UNIONISMO' defended by a few elements."[66] Even though it is quite certain that students were not hearing unionist ideas in Campinas, the statement concluded with an exhortation to correct the error and clarify the thinking of the seminarians.

While the drive for Protestant union within Brazil was dead, another aspect of the ecumenical question would soon convulse the church. In 1945 *O Puritano* noted that eighty-six churches from twenty-nine countries had approved the constitution of a world council of churches in formation. In Brazil, only the Meth- odists had shown interest, but hopes were high that others would "not delay in accepting the invitation to inscribe themselves as members."[67] The issue soon triggered, in an unsuspecting church, a controversy which touched it at two of its most sensitive points and again threatened its unity.

The Beginning of the Conflict Between Modernity and Traditionalism

Along with the dangers it faced from political extremists allied with the Roman Catholic Church, Presbyterianism in the period found itself besieged by internal problems. Early converts had found the Protestant message to be both a liberation from empty religious tradition and vices and a stimulus to an austere piety and moralism, but frequently their children did not repeat that experience. More often than not they felt the prohibitions of the church to be a heavy and, in some cases, meaningless burden. A pastoral letter from the Synod of the North estimated that the church was losing 70 per cent of its youth, while some said the church was bankrupt and rotten, filled with "modernism, heresy, indiscipline, and disorder."[69] A more careful evaluation came from a congress in 1937 which concluded that:

1. Brazilian Protestantism does not possess a clear collective conscience of its mission. . . .

2. The interpretation of Christianity given by the Evangelical churches is not entirely adequate, either in satisfying the interest and education of its youth, or that of those who are outside. . . .

3. The progress in evangelization is generally encouraging. . . .

4. The activities of the churches are taking the place of piety in some cases.[70]

One of the few voices which went beyond the usual cry for rejection of "innovations," "worldliness," and "modernism" was that of the Independente pastor, Eduardo Pereira de Magalhães, grandson of the church's founder. The recent graduate of the United Seminary warned: "Now the Church finds itself in a crucial situation. It will either orient and direct its youth and thus be strengthened in its action, or the Church will suffer the consequence of its neglect. . . . Youth today does not believe that which it heard from its parents and teachers. . . . It has lost its traditional faith."[71] Soon afterward Magalhães was elected youth Secretary for his church.

Complicating the dilemma were the authoritarianism of many pastors and the rigid traditionalism of most churches, which tended to equate change with modernism, as well as the messianic attitude of a few youth leaders. A strident voice which was not always helpful was that of Wilson Fernandes, the Presbyterian pastor who was the first Secretary of the *União de Estudantes para o Trabalho de Cristo*, forerunner of the *União Cristã de Estudantes do Brasil*. Fernandes attended the 1937 meetings in Oxford and Edinburgh before going to study in Switzerland. While in Europe he wrote a series of articles urging the Brazilian church to follow the pattern of theological development on the continent, which, he said, was modern without being modernist. Accusing Latin American theology of stagnation, he urged Brazilian Protestants to discover the biblical message for the specific needs of their own people.[72] Subsequent articles recommended a more open stance toward biblical criticism, receiving as little appreciation as the first series.[73] Upon returning to Brazil Fernandes openly expressed his disillusionment. "Evangelical youth is tired of being despised. . . . It hoped to be led but has not found a guide . . . it asked for help but was not heard."[74] Unfortunately, as sometimes happens with impatient young leaders who consider themselves prophets, Fernandes left the ministry shortly after coming back to Brazil. In 1944 he was succeeded in the leadership of the student movement by Jorge Cesar Mota, son of the pioneer missionary to Portugal.

In attempting to answer criticisms the Presbyterian Church moved in two directions. Benjamin Moraes, another United Seminary graduate, recommended organization of a department "to keep youth linked to the Church until their Christian character can be completely formed."[75] General Assembly acted on his suggestion and nominated Moraes as the group's first secretary.[76]

Changes made in the government of the church at various levels were even more important. In 1937 the Book of Order was replaced by a constitution which centralized the structure of the institution and delegated greater control over activities of local congregations to pastors and elders. In keeping with the Brazilian concept of authority the presiding officer of a judicatory was now called a *presidente* instead of a *moderador*. The *Assembléia Geral* became the *Supremo Concílio*, and the local *Sessão* was now the *Conselho*. The latter had authority to "orient and superintend all spiritual, social, and administrative activities of the church,"[77] but the pastor could veto a resolution by the church assembly, session, or any internal organization "when he judged it to be unconstitutional or contrary to the interests of the Kingdom of God."[78] Divine sanction for the Presbyterian form of government was also a provision of the constitution. Where ordinands had formerly vowed that they approved and sustained the government of the Presbyterian Church of Brazil, now they were to swear to receive not only the Confession of Faith and catechisms but the Constitution of the Church as the "system of doctrine, government, and ecclesiastical discipline revealed in the Word of God."[79] In the future, the strengthened government would facilitate the use of authority against groups thought to be too avant-garde. The Synod of the North expressed a common apprehension when it warned that the increased liberty desired by the young could easily lead to heresy, doubt, incredulity, and revolt against legitimate authority.[80]

The defensive stance against winds of "modernist" change, real or imagined, became undeniable after *O Puritano* published a sermon by Charles C. Morrison in 1936. Criticizing the exclusive concern of many Christians with individual salvation even while the church compromised itself by supporting an unjust social order, Morrison concluded that true Christianity was social and that the Kingdom of God must be understood in such terms.[81] Among the protests was one from the Synod of the North which expressed fear that Brazilian Presbyterianism was being invaded by theological modernism through its official paper.[82] The following year Campinas Seminary assured the church that it had no tolerance for rationalism or modernism and that its professors maintained "Presbyterian orthodoxy upright."[83]

But so-called modernism soon became an issue, not in the Presbyterian Church, but among the Independentes. The fact that it resulted in two divisions in a church which had no foreign missionaries working within it indicated that neither new theological currents nor schism were the result of missionary influence alone. The great irony lay in the fact that it was an honest attempt to formulate a more ecumenical theology which precipitated the new division. Among those accused of liberalism were Amaral, soon to be dismissed from his position in the Evangelical Confederation; Magalhães, Secretary for Youth Work in his church; and Otoniel Mota, one of Brazil's outstanding grammarians. In their common concern for the younger generation and Protestant unity they sought a theology which would be more ecumenical as well as more meaningful to intellectuals and youth. Magalhães complained that Brazilian churches had published nothing which could satisfactorily explain Protestantism to a cultured person, and he charged that suspicion of new ideas and fear of heresy were the primary reasons.[84] A second source of friction was the urban orientation of the liberals over against the traditionally rural ethos of their church. Reaction came not only from the rural presbyteries but from two of Pereira's oldest collaborators, pastors Augusto Pereira and Bento Ferraz, and the son-in-law of the latter, Dr. Flamínio Fávero, a layman who was widely respected in educational circles in São Paulo.

At the Synod of 1938, a recent seminary graduate admitted he had no firm opinion about eternal punishment but was inclined to accept the theory of annihilation. His remark ignited concern about the teaching in the Independente Seminary, where four of the liberals were professors. Synod resolved that no one who denied eternal punishment could be ordained but nominated a committee to study possible revision of the symbols of faith. The conservatives, dissatisfied with the latter decision, formed the *Liga Conservadora* to fight any revision in the confessional position of the church. At a special synod meeting later that year the liberals presented their Declaration of Faith which was orthodox enough for most but concluded: "We believe in the preeminence of spiritual and ethical life over the symbols of faith which, although necessary and based on the Scriptures, are fallible and should be accepted with a spirit of free examination."[85]

Synod responded in a curiously contradictory manner, expressly prohibiting reservations regarding the Westminster Symbols, while nominating a committee to write a new confession of faith. Two years later it reaffirmed its loyalty to its traditional symbols and gave up plans for revision, but recognized the right of pastors and laymen to maintain reservations. This was enough to cause the conservatives, numbering five pastors, eleven churches, and 741 members, to withdraw and form the *Igreja Presbiteriana Conservadora*. The group received words of support from the Presbyterian Church, and only the Masonic question hindered its joining the larger body. The new church did decide to send its ministerial candidates to Campinas Seminary, which evidently was sufficiently orthodox.[86]

But the division failed to bring peace to the remaining factions. While most Independentes now felt the need to demonstrate their fidelity to the Westminster Symbols and disprove the accusations of the Igreja Presbiteriana Conservadora, the liberals expounded their position in the *Questão Doutrinária* in 1942. After reavowing in a few lines their adherence without reservation "to the fundamental doctrines of Christianity and the orientation of the Reformation," the liberals filled three pages with an examination of those points from the Westminster Symbols which they no longer accepted:

> . . . the divine right of Presbyterianism . . . the untouchable nature of its forms . . . such as a confession of faith and catechisms written three centuries earlier by different mentalities in a religious situation which was entirely different; and finally, the denominationalism which unjustifiably made antimasonry the basis of a religious organization.[87]

The document also violated the traditional anti-Romanism of Brazilian Protestantism by affirming the validity of Roman Catholic baptism.

Asked to leave the Independente Church, the group formed the *Igreja Cristã*, which it hoped would be ecumenical in character. The stated purpose was to spread Christianity in the framework of greater tolerance and liberty, to cultivate and propagate an ecumenical spirit as a model for the union of churches with greater liberty in doctrine and government, and to form a free organization for those who felt constricted by the limitations of existing churches.[88] Despite its hopes, the movement never advanced beyond a single congregation in São Paulo.

Overcome with horror at the controversy in their sister church, Presbyterians became even more convinced that a strong denominational spirit was necessary to protect orthodoxy. The church insisted that two distinguished professors at the Instituto JMC, who had joined the Igreja Cristã, be dismissed if it were to continue cooperating with the institution.[89] At the same time, the Synod of the South declared that no letters of transfer to the new body could be issued "since it was clearly heretical."[90] When the Supremo Concílio met that year it resolved that:

> Even though, by the mercy of God, our Presbyterian family has maintained its laudable and healthy loyalty to the doctrines of the Word of God according to our Symbols of Faith, it seemed good . . . to reinforce fully the position of our church regarding its doctrinal points of view in the face of certain evils, vices, and liberalism which are subtly attempting to invade.[91]

Perhaps the strongest statement of all came from a writer who boasted that a characteristic of Brazilian Presbyterianism was "its energetic, absolute, and almost violent attitude of intransigence against rationalistic and modern doctrinal novelties."[92]

Pernambuco was the focus of a strange question which also disturbed the church's equilibrium during the period. The curious controversy over ordination of women as deaconesses, which seemed unimportant to some, threatened to split the church again and indicated the rigidity of attitudes in the North. It also showed the confusion of certain aspects of the traditional patriarchal culture with theological orthodoxy. The Presbyterian Church had never elected women to any office for which ordination was necessary, and the 1930 General Assembly restated that position.[93] But opinion was changing. After the Independentes pro-

vided for the election of deaconesses, the Constituent General Assembly, which met in Rio in 1937 without the presence of any
northern representatives, inserted an article in the constitution
which read: "For the office of the diaconate there is no distinc-
tion of sexes."[94] The change nearly incited rebellion in the North,
which had boycotted the assembly in protest against what it considered its illegal convocation.

In a conciliatory move, the Supremo Concílio of 1938 met in
Fortaleza, Ceará, and elected Kerr, the South's strongest defender
of orthodoxy, as its president. It also declared unanimously that
no women should be ordained while the presbyteries were voting
on a proposal to amend the offending article. When the decision
was delayed, the Synod of the North, under the presidency of
Israel Gueiros, warned that if the article were not removed from
the constitution by 1946, that body would renounce the jurisdiction of the church. At the same time it issued a pastoral letter
denouncing "feminist modernism" and linking the question to the
defense of orthodoxy.[95]

No one in the South wanted schism over the issue and it was
resolved to the satisfaction of the North. But, as trivial as it was,
the question glaringly illuminated both the intransigence of
Northern leaders on any matter involving their concept of orthodoxy and the precarious nature of Brazilian Presbyterian unity.
That unity would soon be put to a far more severe test over a
much more important issue.

The threats from right and left which the church faced in the
political sphere during the 1930's heightened its sense of insecurity, which in turn strengthened its uncritical attitude toward
the government, maintained as long as the institutional liberties
of Protestants were respected. At the same time the desire on the
part of a minority for a more open theological stance and greater
interest in the questions being raised by youth looked to many
like a threat from within. Two repercussions were greater cen-
tralization of church structures and an increasing determination
to protect denominationalism and orthodoxy. At the same time
the decreased evangelistic growth, which left Presbyterianism
trailing Baptists and Pentecostals in outreach, made clear the
necessity of renewal. But the meaning of renewal and the form it
should take would be subject to various definitions in the period
to follow.

Chapter Ten

A Church in Need of Renewal: 1946-1959

After fifteen years in power Getulio Vargas was forced to resign in 1945 but returned to political life five years later and again was elected President. Mass internal migration, increased industrialization, and an exploding population brought rapid social change during the period, while Vargas appealed to the urban proletariat and the rural poor with nationalistic themes and promises of new economic policies, far-reaching social legislation, and a march to the West. The rising nationalism inspired new hope and, in some cases, constructive new directions for the nation, but it also aroused excessive optimism and, at times, xenophobia.

Foreign investment, responsible for much of the nation's industrial expansion, was often exploitative and was opposed by many Brazilians who bitterly resented their status as an economic colony of the more developed nations. It was understandable that the United States, the largest investor in the country and ally of the most conservative forces in the nation, became the major target of Brazilian economic and political reformers. Nationalism took on anti-American overtones even in the Protestant church, adding fuel to the suspicion of missionaries and their boards which past differences had kindled.

Vargas soon found himself in grave trouble because of increasingly complex social and economic problems and his own inability to govern within a democratic framework. Widely criticized, he committed suicide when the army demanded his resignation. His legacy was a "political testament" which described "years of domination and looting by international economic and financial groups."[1] His successor was Vice-President João Café Filho who although not a professed Protestant was the son of a Presbyterian elder. It was symbolic for Brazilian Presbyterianism that five years before its Centennial, such a man arrived at the presidency. The dream that Evangelicals would rise to important positions in government was coming true long before anyone had expected. But although Café Filho was honest, it soon became clear that solution of the nation's problems would require far more than personal morality on the part of men in public office. The administration of Juscelino Kubitschek, who became president in 1956, saw an even greater spurt of industrial progress, accompanied by spiraling inflation. Brazil was moving rapidly into what one of its greatest economists called a pre-revolutionary stage.[2]

At the same time important developments taking place outside Brazil would soon affect the nation and its churches. Communism, no longer just a revolutionary political party, now had the support of a strengthened Russia, and the right and center became increasingly fearful. During the Kubitschek era the left took over leadership of the nationalist movement, exposing its sympathizers to accusations of Communism, while leading them to analyze Brazil's problems almost entirely in Marxist categories.

Three movements in the world church, all concerned to take the unity of the Body of Christ more seriously, had repercussions in Brazil during the period. The first was the formation of the World Council of Churches (WCC) in 1948, a result of forces put in motion by the modern missionary movement and, more specifically, the Edinburgh Conference of 1910. The postwar meetings of the International Missionary Council and its attempts to define the proper relationship between mission boards, missionaries, and the younger churches also had an impact. Again, just as in 1903 and 1928, concepts of the nature and mission of the church which had originated outside of Brazil aroused serious controversy among its Presbyterians. The third movement, which would make it necessary for Latin American Protestantism to rethink its message and purpose more completely than at any time since its inception, was the new orientation given the Roman Catholic Church after the election of John XXIII to the papacy in 1958.

Thus, as it ended its first century, the Presbyterian Church of Brazil was challenged to think more deeply than ever before about its nature, mission and relationship to the Body of Christ throughout the world. But during this era of ferment in social, economic, political, and religious life, it was emerging from a period of insecurity, relative stagnation, and almost complete isolation from the world church. Emphasizing denominationalism, theological orthodoxy, and an individualistic ethic, it was ill prepared to deal with the rapidly changing society. As it moved toward its centennial celebration its greatest task was to renew itself by discovering what it meant to be genuinely Evangelical and Brazilian in the emerging new nation. At the same time it faced the danger that traditionalism, authoritarianism, and zeal for orthodoxy would lead it to reject significant attempts to do so.

The Church and the Ecumenical Movement

Their tentative affiliation with the newly organized World Council of Churches brought controversy to Brazilian Presbyterians and found most of them unprepared to understand fully or discuss rationally the implications of the step. Complicating the problem was the failure of most ecumenical leaders to understand the position of Latin American Protestantism vis-à-vis Roman Catholicism. Even more distressing was the intrusion of the "fundamentalist-modernist" conflict in the person of Carl McIntire. The struggle over membership in the WCC cannot be understood apart from two factors. One was Brazilian Presbyterianism's position as a part of a Protestant minority in a predominantly Roman Catholic nation and the strongly held attitudes created by this situation. The second was the traditional conservatism of the Presbyterian Church of Brazil, which led to a strong fear of modernism and innovations. Both attitudes, general throughout Brazil, were especially strong, almost to the point of fanaticism, in the North.

Traditional antagonism between the nation's Protestant and Catholic churches had diminished little through the years. Movements toward Catholic renewal, rare in Brazil, were unknown to Protestants, while Protestant-Catholic friendships did not extend beyond the personal level. But the sporadic outbreaks of harassment and violence and attempts by the hierarchy to win greater power and governmental support continued to receive attention in the Protestant press. A number of reports described the public burning of Bibles by priests and monks engaged in "holy missions."[3] Mobs led by priests destroyed Protestant church buildings in two cities in Paraíba in 1946 and 1958 and, in the latter case, forced the Baptist and Presbyterian pastors to take their families and flee for their lives.[4]

Other religious groups sporadically felt the effects of Roman Catholic political activity, which did not abate. In 1949, at the request of the Archbishop of Rio, the Supreme Court voted nine to one to uphold a government action which had closed the Brazilian Apostolic Catholic Church, a nationalist schismatic group. The lawyer defending the rights of the new church was Benjamin Moraes, a Presbyterian pastor.[5] At the same time the hierarchy solicited and received large government grants for its institutions in violation of the Constitution,[6] while an unofficial religious establishment existed in many public schools. Protestants were especially critical when the federal government helped finance the Eucharistic Congress in 1955, the central act of which was formal dedication of the nation to the "Sacred Heart of Jesus." The event attracted a number of prominent government officials, but President Café Filho was absent, apparently because of a strong protest from the Evangelical Confederation.[7]

Accompanying Catholic political pressures were attacks designed to link Protestantism with Communism and stir up repression. Msgr. Agnelo Rossi, the future Archbishop of São Paulo, published an article in Rio's *Correio de Manhã* in 1953, based on declarations of J. B. Matthews, Executive Director of Senator Joseph McCarthy's Senate subcommittee, which accused American Protestant leaders of Communist sympathies.[8] The incumbent Cardinal Archbishop of São Paulo declared that "Protestantism supported by the United States was as dangerous an imperialism as Communism."[9] The following year a paper in Jaú, São Paulo, called Protestantism a poison which killed the soul and concluded, "It is up to the temporal power to prevent Protestant proselytism by imposing legal penalties."[10]

Presbyterian reaction, especially in the light of published reports of Protestant martyrs in Colombia, was predictable. When the Pope called for Catholics and Protestants to draw closer to each other, the pastor of Rio's First Church spoke of past persecutions and responded: "Rome is always the same, it never changes. . . . We do not want alliances or agreements which will take us from our task of announcing the Gospel."[11] After reporting the burning of Bibles in a Catholic *festa*, *O Puritano* concluded:

> Those pastors and believers who trust in the attitude of the Roman Catholic Church (which is sympathetic at times), even to the point of forseeing ecumenical collaboration with the figure of the woman of the Apocalypse, the Church of the Pope, deceive themselves. . . . Ecumenism, collaboration, union, with those who believe in the inspiration of the Bible, but not with those who burn it in public squares. Against those, struggle to the death.[12]

Only among the younger generation was there any indication of the development of a new attitude. At a youth conference in 1952, Adauto Dourado, a young pastor, advised his audience to seek understanding of the Roman Church and discover the good in it, resorting to polemics only in exceptional cases.[13] But an article by a seminarian which called Catholicism a "sister religion" and referred to "our Catholic brethren," elicited a number of indignant letters violently rejecting his viewpoint.[14] After the election of John XXIII to the papacy and his call for an ecumenical council, an article in *O Brasil Presbiteriano*, the new official paper of the church, expressed the sentiment of the overwhelming majority of pastors and church members:

> When we hear that the Pope will soon convoke an ecumenical council, immediately some naive persons within Evangelical circles breathe a sigh of relief, full of hope that . . . the Pontiff will sweep from his church all the paganism disguised as Christian and effect . . . the reformation begun by Luther in the sixteenth century. Such naiveté on their part makes me want to laugh. But the fact is that we should weep in the face of such a tragedy. Rome, gentlemen, will never leave her path of apostasy.[15]

Except for suspicion aroused by rumors of modernism in the North American and European churches, the theological position of most pastors had not been affected by currents outside of Brazil, and the most influential leaders were staunchly orthodox. The position of Jerônimo Gueiros, the most able leader in the North, satisfied even *O Fundamentalista*: "Very few in our land have known how to forge arms against the enemy as well and forcefully as this tireless servant of Jesus."[16] Conservatism in the North was augmented by its traditionalism and the dispensationalism of many of its pastors, who were quick to discover signs of the "final apostasy" in new movements. The Synod of the North even insisted on dropping the word *Cristã*, adopted in the 1937 Constitution, from the official name of the church.

> Why disfigure it now with the adding of the adjective Christian, favorite word of the most anti-Christian sects, including the one which arose in São Paulo, extending its hand, by ecumenism, to the Roman Church. . . . We repel this tendency toward change, this tendency toward novelties. . . . Let us not allow the giant devil of the modernisms of the century to enter the door of the Church.[17]

Although attitudes were more moderate in the South, those who shaped the thought of the church were no less conservative. Kerr, who inspired great respect for his dedication and ability, told his students in Campinas Seminary: "The Presbyterian Church of Brazil will only be truly great and worthy of its traditions if it continues intransigent in its faithfulness to the doctrine of the Apostles and repels the doctrinal innovations of incongruous modernism. . . . The price of true doctrinal orthodoxy is eternal intransigence."[18] Other professors in Campinas held the same position, and in 1951 the new rector, J. A. Ferreira, affirmed that the entire faculty was conservative.[19] The following year the student orator of the graduating class reassured his hearers: "In these dangerous times, with modernist philosophies and religious thoughts invading many churches of the old continent and the new . . . it is comforting to know that we do not hold any liberal or advanced theological idea."[20]

After the death of Erasmo Braga, Brazilian Presbyterianism maintained only a tenuous relationship with the organizations which contributed to the Protestant ecumenical movement. Nevertheless, when an invitation came to participate in the formation of a world council of churches, the Supremo Concílio of 1946 elected Samuel Rizzo, a Brazilian pastor residing in the United States, as its representative to the Amsterdam assembly.[21] The understanding on the part of some was that this implied membership in the council. Indeed Rizzo participated fully in the meeting as only a representative of a member church could.[22] His report implied that the WCC represented the most significant movement in Protestantism since the Reformation. He made it clear, however, that it did not mean to be a super church or even a federation of churches but, rather, sought to witness to unity in Christ.[23] Lack of comment in the church press left no doubt that even after the Presbyterian Church of Brazil became a founding member, most of its leaders had little knowledge of, or interest in, the World Council. On the other hand, *O Conservador*, organ of the Conservative Presbyterian Church, sharply criticized the ecumenical movement. Consequently, when Rizzo's report went to the Executive Committee of the church in February, 1949, it refused to recognize its affiliation with the WCC and referred the question to the next meeting of the Supremo Concílio because of "the implications of a doctrinal nature and others which the step implied."[24]

A further indication of the attitude of some sectors of the church came when Marc Boegner, one of the presidents of the WCC, visited Brazil in 1949 after attending the Latin American Evangelical Conference in Buenos Aires. His visit, sponsored by the Evangelical Confederation, was scheduled to include Porto Alegre, Rio, São Paulo, and Recife, but the invitation to the latter city was cancelled unilaterally by Israel Gueiros, pastor of its First Presbyterian Church.

A visit which was to have far greater effect, in the North at least, was that of Carl McIntire, who also came from the Buenos Aires conference where he had been an uninvited observer. The North American fundamentalist exploited three points on which Latin American Protestants were especially susceptible. The first concerned the desire of the WCC that the Roman Catholic Church become a member and the fact that some orthodox bodies, which Brazilians considered almost identical to the Roman church, had already done so. Quoting W. S. Rycroft, Chairman of the Committee on Cooperation in Latin America, regarding the efforts of the Catholic hierarchy to consolidate its power and work against Protestantism, he continued: "How, then, can Latin American Protestants be interested in the World Council of Churches, with its Greek Catholic bodies and its open arms to Rome? It is here that Latin America is open to the testimony and fellowship of the ICCC (International Council of Christian Churches)."[25] He appealed to nationalistic sentiment in emphasizing that the Committee on Cooperation, which, according to Rycroft, had done more to promote the work in Latin America than any similar group, was totally North American in composition. Finally, he concluded: "If Protestantism is to present a united front to the Roman Catholics . . . one thing must be done—one thing. The churches must remain truly Protestant. Modernism, which kills and divides, must be removed from the churches and the churches must stand solidly against Rome and for the Christianity of the Bible."[26]

After speaking in São Paulo, McIntire addressed the students and faculty of Campinas Seminary, despite objections by the missionary professors. His assessment was that "the modernism they have here is mild and everybody is a Fundamentalist."[27] In Recife he delivered a three-hour talk in the seminary and, on the following Sunday, preached in Israel Gueiros' pulpit, where he gained an important ally. The previous year Gueiros had affirmed that modernism was "attempting to corrupt our church and succeeded at a frightening speed."[28] Now he publicly adhered to the ICCC. McIntire's final salvo in the North included the news that the Presbyterian Church of Brazil was already a member of the WCC, a fact hotly denied by the pastors, who had not understood the Supremo Concílio's 1946 resolution in that sense.

While the North American fundamentalist's attacks on respected Christian leaders were causing controversy, Goulart, the irenic professor in Campinas, spoke for much of the church in evaluating him. In Goulart's opinion, while the North American churches as a whole maintained the principles of the Reformation and had leaders who exhibited genuine piety and orthodoxy, several of their pastors were excessively liberal. Some spokesmen for the Federal Council of Churches, he added, were simply unbelievers. The article rejected the methods of the fundamentalists but accepted their cause. One may disagree with McIntire's intolerant spirit and forced exegesis at times, Goulart wrote, but the man is neither ignorant nor a liar. He exaggerates, but the cause is noble, and the Brazilian church must calmly maintain its doctrinal fidelity without falling into extremes of bigotry.[29] The only articles in the Presbyterian press which were sharply critical of McIntire appeared in *Mocidade*, the paper published by the youth of the church. They obviously represented a minority opinion.[30]

It is not surprising that the pastors of the Presbytery of Pernambuco joined with elders from each of its churches in a unanimous protest:

> . . . against the inclusion of the name of the Presbyterian
> Church of Brazil as a member of the WCC, which already
> has as a member, the Greek Orthodox Church, and which invited the Roman Catholic Church to participate as one of its
> members. . . and especially because it is a movement led by
> men who are known as liberals. We . . . protest before the
> Church and the world against the inclusion of the Presbyterian Church of Brazil among the infidels of the WCC.[31]

The presbyteries of Sorocaba and Vale do Rio Doce soon added their voices to the chorus.[32]

Sentiment in the North manifested itself again in May, 1950, when Israel Gueiros was elected Vice-President of the Synod and Ageu Vieira, his brother-in-law and an ardent fundamentalist, was made President.[33] It was clear that even if there existed enough support in the South, any attempt at affiliation with the WCC would trigger a new schism.

Natanael Cortez, President of the Supremo Concílio, and an irenic conservative, outlined the position he believed the church should take. He denied that it was presently a member, citing the action taken by the Executive Committee in February, 1949. Then he spoke of the agitation caused by McIntire among a number of ministers, especially Gueiros, who believed that the WCC was a focus of modernism which would be transplanted in Brazil. Cortez had entered into personal contact with a number of those who were most concerned, and, he reported, they wanted neither the alleged modernism of the WCC nor the quarrels stirred up by McIntire and his International Council. Love for the church and common sense dictated a position midway between the two councils, he concluded.[34]

Thus the Supremo Concílio later that year took the only position which could maintain unity. A number of northerners had arrived, their travel financed by McIntire, hoping to lead the church into the ICCC,[35] while a few others still advocated membership in the WCC. But most Presbyterians feared affiliation with the World Council, while they also rejected McIntire's fanaticism and character assassination. Thus, after declaring that true

unity consisted in submission to Christ and acceptance of the
scriptures as the word of God and only rule of faith and practice,
the church voted neither to ratify its membership in the WCC nor
to join the International Council, but to "maintain itself equidis-
tant" from both. It also expressed a desire to remain uninvolved
in polemics which might be carried on among other ecclesiastical
entities inside or outside Brazil. Reflecting concern over personal
attacks generated by the fundamentalist movement the assembly
also stated that if ministers attacked the church or their colleagues, their presbyteries should take the proper disciplinary
measures.[36]

The attitude toward Roman Catholicism was the most important reason for the decision. If the Edinburgh Conference of 1910
marked the beginning of modern Protestant ecumenism, it also
motivated suspicion of the movement on the part of Latin American Protestants when their area of the world was excluded because
it was nominally Catholic and, therefore, "Christian." Not even
the Panama Congress assuaged Latin American fears on the matter since it held out hope for eventual cooperation with the Catholic Church. Brazilians believed the World Council had gone
even further by inviting the Roman church to become a member.
There was widespread apprehension that its ultimate goal was
organic union of the Protestant churches with each other and,
finally, with Rome. The conviction was intensified when various
orthodox churches, considered by Brazilian Protestants almost
equal to Rome, became members of the Council. The invocation
to the Virgin Mary used by an orthodox worship leader in the
Amsterdam assembly had shocked many and confirmed their
worst suspicions.[37]

Brazilian Presbyterians who had always seen the Roman church
as the greatest obstacle to the propagation of the Protestant message, could not accept it as a sister institution. Because they considered Roman Catholicism apostate and even pagan, a fraternal
attitude toward it seemed to betray the faith they proclaimed.
Both in their theology and experience, conversion to Christ had
always implied leaving the ancient church. Goulart wrote: "The
Protestants, principally of Latin America, ask, with reason, what
does our missionary effort, directed toward reaching the Catholic
masses, the renewal of the mentality and life of our countrymen,

and the bringing of men to repentance, mean if the Roman Church can be considered Christian?"[38]

To make matters worse, the WCC's invitation to Rome seemed to imply a reiteration of Edinburgh's position in refusing to recognize Latin America as a mission field, thus calling into question the legitimacy of its Protestant churches. There was fear that a relationship between the World Council and Rome would eventually end Protestant missionary efforts in Catholic countries or at least bring pressure against proselytizing Catholics. Ageu Vieira charged that in response to orthodox complaints about proselytism, WCC leaders had conceded the necessity of rules of courtesy regarding evangelistic efforts and spheres of influence. "What will they do when the Roman Catholic Church is a member?" he asked. Referring to the attempt by the Archbishop of Belo Horizonte to prevent Protestant missionaries from entering Brazil, he charged that eventually the hierarchy would compel WCC related mission boards to refrain from sending workers and ask Brazilian pastors to preach only to Protestants. "Our evangelistic efforts will no longer be determined by the spiritual needs of sinners but by the rules of courtesy and urbanity established by the World Council,"[39] he concluded.

A second significant issue was the alleged theological modernism of some WCC leaders. This was the result not only of the traditional conservatism of Brazilian Presbyterians but also of their status as a minority group in a predominantly Catholic society. Any compromise in the doctrine of Biblical authority, the conservatives warned, would inevitably lead to a weakening of the church and the disappearance of the reason for its existence. A minor point was the belief that the great divergence in viewpoint toward political institutions indicated in a meeting which included John Foster Dulles and Joseph Hromadka showed loyalty to neither a specific position nor to Christ.[40]

It is obvious that McIntire's activity did not create these fears. While he did exploit them skillfully, he could not have done so had they not already been deeply rooted in the history of Brazilian Presbyterianism. Leonard's observation that nineteenth-century Brazil was religiously similar to sixteenth-century Europe illuminates the problem. The Protestant ecumenism, which had developed in twentieth-century Europe and North America, would not find a ready reception in Brazil where the historical context was more akin in some respects to that of seventeenth-century Europe.

Another factor was the denominational self-protection which had been so important in the struggle over the United Seminary. The common belief in Brazil that the ultimate purpose of the WCC was organic union of the churches rekindled the spirit of isolation. The Executive Committee of the church made it clear in 1956 that its definition of true ecumenism involved safeguarding "the autonomy and characteristics of the denomination and understood that ecumenical mission was not in order to unite ecclesiastical bodies . . . but to promote closer relationships and cooperation between clearly Evangelical denominations."[41]

Finally, there was a pragmatic reason for the decision. The Presbyterian Church of Brazil did not want to repeat the agony of another schism, especially over a question thrust upon it from outside. Division had taken place in 1903 and had become a strong possibility in 1928. It is not surprising that the church was sensitive on this point in 1950.

The position of the church regarding the WCC did not change, and interest in ecumenical activities was limited to a small minority of pastors and youth leaders. The sensitivity of the CBM to the problem showed in a request that its personnel be careful to maintain a position of "equidistance."[42] Professor Waldyr Luz of Campinas Seminary spoke for a significant minority if not a majority of the church in 1955, when he affirmed his support of equidistance. Because both councils sinned against the integrity of the Christian faith, he believed there was danger of being forced toward one or the other. In that case, what would be the choice?

> The ICCC would become a threat to the Presbyterian Church of Brazil only if the latter abandoned its orthodox position. And there is no doubt that if it lost its doctrinal firmness, either it would no longer be the noble and respectable Presbyterian Church of its basic creed and confessions, or it would have to subject itself to serious, radical, energetic, and rigorous treatment which would restore it to its orthodox norms.[43]

On the other hand, Luz concluded, because the WCC represented a potential influence, if not a direct action, which could dissolve the church, it constituted a present danger. There was no question where his sympathies would lie if it ever became necessary to choose between the two councils. It was also clear that for Luz and others any movement of renewal within Brazilian Presbyterianism would necessarily imply not ecumenism but a return to orthodoxy by any who might have strayed, and the strengthening of denominational walls, especially against Roman Catholicism.

The Israel Gueiros Case

An episode which loomed large in Pernambuco but had little importance elsewhere centered around the attempt of Israel Gueiros to take the northern wing of the church into McIntire's International Council of Churches. A member of the most prominent Presbyterian family in the North and pastor of Recife's First Church, Gueiros also taught in the seminary. But his rivalry with fellow professors, frequent absences from class, and his mania to dominate the institution led to increasing tensions. In 1946 Jerônimo Gueiros, his uncle, insisted on his withdrawal from the faculty because of incompetence and resigned from the Board of Directors of the institution when his nephew remained. No theological question was at issue; both men were rigidly orthodox.[44]

That same year the Supremo Concílio, attempting to atone for the years in which the Seminary of the North had suffered neglect, assumed responsibility for the institution, requesting aid from the missions in building it up to the level of Campinas. This involved calling a missionary from each board and another full-time Brazilian professor to the faculty, while Gueiros continued on a part-time basis.

As the 1950 meeting of the Supremo Concílio approached, Gueiros became more violent in his attacks. Hoping to lead either the whole church or a separated North into the McIntire camp, he accused the Presbyterian Church of Brazil of being an "adulterer" and called a faculty colleague a "man of iniquity."[45] Alexander Reese, serving temporarily in the seminary before retirement after forty years of service as a pastor and evangelist, wrote of him: "The methods and attitudes of the fundamentalists . . . have been responsible for more lies, injustices, and slander in only one year than I have seen in a whole generation in Brazil."[46]

Opposing the stipulation by the Board of Directors that professors give full time to the seminary, Gueiros resigned from the faculty, but his presbytery immediately elected him to the institution's board. At the same time he became increasingly active in the International Council, despite the 1950 decision regarding equidistance. It was abundantly clear that he still hoped to lead a separated northern church into the McIntire camp and was seeking the proper occasion for such a move.

It came when the Central Brazil Mission ceded the services of Hershey Julien to the seminary in 1955. Julien, who was well liked and competent, raised a storm of controversy by teaching that there were errors of history although not of theology in the Bible and by casting doubt on the descent of the entire human race from one man.[47] He became the target of accusations and, at the end of the year, on the recommendation of the faculty and Board of Directors, with the agreement of the latter's missionary representatives, he left the institution and returned to the United States.[48]

In January, 1956, after reporting to his presbytery, as he had during the previous five years, that all was well in the seminary, Gueiros refused reelection to its board and asked that the privilege be given to another.[49] Shortly afterward he left for the United States and began raising funds for a fundamentalist seminary to be established in Recife. He had the support of the *Christian Beacon*, which published his allegations based on the Julien case. The existing institution was modernistic, he charged, was undermining the faith of its students, and had lost the confidence of the church. He added that he had been forced to leave its faculty in 1950 because of missionary pressures aroused by his fight against modernism.[50]

Returning to Brazil he began to promote his cause throughout the North, but members of the Presbytery of Pernambuco responded by calling a special meeting on June 14 to treat the matter. Prompt action was necessary, they believed, to avoid a major North-South schism. After attempts at peaceful solution failed, the judicatory took the only possible action and initiated a disciplinary process against Gueiros. After further abortive attempts at persuasion they declared him guilty of making false accusations against colleagues, working against the unity of the church, and calling openly for schism. Specifically, he had used the names of judicatories and ministers of the Presbyterian Church of Brazil to raise money for a new seminary in Recife, making grave and false accusations against the Seminary of the North to justify its establishment, and blaming his forced resignation from his chair in the seminary on retaliation against his fight against modernism.[51] He was suspended from his office on August 1 and deposed from the ministry two weeks later, but he had already renounced the jurisdiction of the presbytery.

Gueiros took with him over half the members of First Church, Recife, along with its valuable property, which the PCUS Board had originally funded. The question never reached the civil courts because of the desire to avoid the spectacle a church fight would involve. Three other congregations and four pastors, two of them related to Gueiros, accompanied him in organizing the *Igreja Presbiteriana Fundamentalista*.[52] Two of the pastors soon became disillusioned, however, and left the movement. Gueiros continued to fester as a thorn in the flesh of the seminary, the church, and the mission in the North, hurling accusations from the pulpit or over the radio at people he called modernists or Communists. Perhaps the best commentary on the case came from Dr. L. Nelson Bell, a well-known conservative layman of the PCUS. After visiting Brazil to investigate the matter, he called it "the most flagrant case of untrue and unjust accusations against Christian brethren and Christian institutions" he had ever encountered.[53]

The controversy and division further weakened Presbyterian forces in the North. Gueiros' constant public criticism of his colleagues led many to become even more defensive against positions which might evoke charges of *ecumenismo, modernismo,* or *communismo.* Just when there was an increasing need for the church in the North to reexamine its interpretation of the gospel, its ethical emphasis, and its relationship to other churches, the atmosphere of suspicion paralyzed its efforts.

The Church and Youth in a Changing Society

In the postwar period, a new awareness of Brazil's social problems, especially among students and intellectuals, stirred renewed cries for reform. The spurt of industrialization combined with population growth and chronic problems in many interior areas to bring thousands of the poor into the cities. This influx not only caused widespread suffering but also made it more apparent. Along with the impressive new skyscrapers rising in Rio, São

Paulo, and other cities, wretched slums proliferated. These festering sores of human misery and despair, sometimes perched on hills overlooking chic apartment houses, insistently called attention to the inequities of Brazilian society.

At the same time urban youth, including those in the church, enjoyed much more freedom of movement than before, and traditional values and customs were increasingly questioned. Idealism and impatience, accentuated in some cases by Christian faith, inspired criticism of the imperfect society in which they lived. The Christian young people, with their heightened ethical concern, felt keenly the contradiction between profession of faith in the gospel as the power of God and the imperfections and indifference of many who professed that faith.

Thus, it is not surprising that the second major issue during the period revolved around the desire of youth leaders, seminarians, and a few young pastors for theological and ethical renewal. The theology of conversion and salvation, accompanied by the acceptance of a moralistic ethic, had brought a liberating experience to many, especially in the small towns and rural areas of the nation. Now, a relatively large and more sophisticated generation of urban youth was appearing in the church. Encouraged by their parents as well as their faith to seek higher education, they became dissatisfied with traditional answers. When they did not abandon organized religion, they sought a deeper understanding of the relationship between the church and the world and its implications for the problems facing Brazil. A substantial proportion of them began to seek church renewal in terms of a new theological and ethical orientation and greater openness to ecumenical relationships.

With few exceptions the church and its leaders were ill-prepared to deal seriously with their concerns. Most pastors were overworked, holding one or more jobs outside the ministry, and had little time to devote to contacts with their youth. At the same time a rigidly moralistic ethical orientation and the lack of any theological basis for a new approach prevented their responding positively to issues raised by the new generation. The easiest reaction was a retreat into authoritarian clericalism. The church program focused on adults living in a simpler society, and most preaching and Christian education was designed either to lead the non-

Evangelical to a decision or to supply moral exhortation. Often forced to seek satisfaction for their intellectual and social needs outside the church, many young people did not return to hear its religious message.

The difference between the intellectual level which Protestant students found in their classes in the university and the Sunday school was usually great. One encouraged them to think scientifically, use literary criticism on the classics, and discuss and challenge accepted ideas. The other often substituted for serious Bible study a moral homily given in dogmatic fashion, which neither considered the circumstances in which the Bible was written nor related it to modern problems.[54] Suggestions by youth leaders that, wherever possible, a class for university students be created in Sunday schools were seldom received favorably.[55] On the other hand, young people were often impatient and at times condescending in their attitude toward the church. At times they formed extra-ecclesiastical groups which, for some, replaced the larger Christian community. Tensions and resentments were inevitable.

Fundamentally, the controversy over the youth question was a struggle over the nature of the church. Was it primarily a clerically operated and oriented institution whose main function was to lead people to salvation and to service within its own walls, or was it first of all a flexible community in which laymen and pastors of diverse callings and gifts would attempt to serve God and witness to the new life in Christ both in the church and in the world? It is clear that the latter definition implied a greater variety of structures and concepts of mission than had been traditional in Brazilian Presbyterianism. As long as it was allowed to do so, the youth organization operated, precariously at times, on the basis of the latter definition, and it helped many capable young people find meaningful orientation for their lives and service. But it was foreign to the rigid traditionalism both of Brazilian society and of the church, which finally asserted its authority and seriously limited the autonomy of its youth.

The Department of Youth of the Church had been organized in 1938, but the same period saw the ecclesiastical structure centralized and the authority of the local session and pastor strengthened. In 1944, the youth established their own monthly paper,

Mocidade, which provided a relatively independent organ for their ideas. Another advance came in 1946 when, at the request of the Supremo Concílio, the East Brazil Mission ceded Miss Billy Gammon, daughter of S. R. Gammon, to be full-time Secretary for Youth.[56] This was not only a breakthrough in youth work but a creative new step in the use of North American missionary personnel by the church. The missions also aided in financing the program. The fact that Miss Gammon was very competent, well-trained, and thoroughly Brazilian brought special advantages. In February of that year the first national convention met, and a national confederation organized. It is symbolic and significant that the most important leaders were all third-generation Presbyterians. Two cousins, Paulo and Waldo Cesar, were grandsons of Belmiro Cesar, a pioneer pastor in the North, while Paulo Rizzo and Tércio Emerique were grandsons of Miguel Rizzo. Older churchmen soon expressed fears that the youth were moving too rapidly and creating too much "machinery" with their own paper and national confederation. One writer indicated his concern about Miss Gammon's leadership and hinted that a stronger hand, probably that of a pastor, should be at the helm.[57]

But the movement grew rapidly. National congresses convened every four years, and the total number of local societies grew from 150 to 600, with approximately 17,000 members by 1958.[58] More important than statistics was the active role taken in local churches by many of the youth and the substantial number of able young men who entered seminary as a result of the program.[59]

Tensions which had been inherent from the start in the relationship between the Department of Youth and the older leadership of the church soon began to appear. Conflict came from the natural desire of competent and exuberant youth in a rapidly changing society not only to run their own organization, but to move considerably beyond the traditional positions of the church and, at times, in directions quite different from those followed in the past. Another irritant was the lack of tact which often characterized criticisms of the church, its institutions, and its leadership. Understandably this prompted controversy and repercussions in a church which emphasized orthodoxy and respect for authority, and often equated the two.

Ecumenism was the first issue on which the position of the

youth conflicted with that of the church as a whole. The new generation often became impatient with ecclesiastical divisions in which they saw little meaning, and their ecumenical interest increased with contacts made by their leaders through the WSCF, the Evangelical Confederation, and the *União Cristã de Estudantes do Brasil*. The latter, established in 1926, was the Brazilian branch of the Student Christian Movement and became affiliated with the WSCF in 1942. Most of its leadership was Presbyterian and included J. C. Mota, M. R. Shaull, Paulina Steffen, and Esdras Costa. An integral part of the organization's mission, expressed at Whitby in 1949, was "to make possible an ecumenical experience in the university. . . to encourage the unity of the churches in its missionary work."[60] Through the WSCF, youth leaders attended a number of world gatherings, and several became enthusiastic supporters of the various ecumenical organizations. Of the six Brazilians present at the 1954 assembly of the WCC, at least five had been closely associated with the Presbyterian youth organization.[61]

With the founding of the WCC and the resulting controversy the youth became intensely interested in unity. The theme of their 1949 national congress was "That all might be one," and one of the editors of *Mocidade* called attention to "ecumenism, this marvelous movement which has arisen in the churches."[62] It was significant that the youth paper published an interview with Marc Boegner in 1949,[63] while *O Puritano* did not. Presbyterian youth also took the initiative in moving into closer contact with other Protestant groups, suggesting in 1949 that Presbyterian and Congregational youth papers merge[64] and holding a joint congress with the Independentes in 1959.

Apparently the ecumenical enthusiasm of the young people made older leaders uneasy. The Synod of the North asked the Supremo Concílio to remind the Youth Confederation that:

1. It did not have authority beyond that given to it by the judicatories of the Church;
2. It was not an organ of interecclesiastical relations either inside or outside of Brazil . . . and
3. The spirit of discipline and representative government of Presbyterianism recommends that these principles, which have contributed to the order and progress of the Kingdom of God in our midst, be observed.[65]

The youth aroused suspicion, too, when their awakening concern for Brazil's social problems led many to take an ideological position somewhat to the left of traditional Presbyterianism and denounce the government for its lethargy. This was quite foreign to the defensive stance the church had always maintained toward the state and, for some, implied a lack of respect for properly constituted authority. But in the late 1940's and early 1950's it was *Mocidade*, rather than the official church papers, which called attention to social problems and Christian responsibility in that sector. The report on a congress of Protestant youth held in Havana in 1946 affirmed:

> In the Bible we should find the inspiration for an effective work of social reconstruction. . . . The Christian Church is an institution which should bring about a reformation in human relations, and youth has the capacity and vision to participate in this social struggle. We protest against the present capitalist system. . . . Economic imperialism is the penetration and absorption of an exploited people by capitalist forces . . . in order to subjugate them economically.[66]

Such statements evoked protests, the first coming from the Synod of the North, which asked the church to "prohibit articles in *Mocidade* which combat the United States and spread Communist propaganda."[67] In 1951 the observation that "the vast *fazenda* called Brazil is again being governed by Sr. Getulio Vargas" prompted an accusation that the paper was systematically opposing the government.[68]

To many Presbyterians, respect for the authorities was a tenet of faith. They complained, and the Stated Clerk of the Church reported in 1952 that he was receiving protests from all sides. He added that he had asked Miss Gammon to "eliminate at once, the criticism and malicious insinuations against governmental and ecclesiastical authorities," insisting that *Mocidade* return to its religious mission. Miss Gammon replied that while she believed freedom of the press to be sacred, she was attempting to have the editors observe certain limits.[69] Shortly afterward the paper accused the church of being afraid to accept responsibility. "It does not want to interfere too much," the writer said, "fearing that it might become bothersome to the State and expect too much from its members."[70] One editor explained that while young people were concerned about the salvation of the soul, they did not want to forget the body and were seeking solutions for the problems afflicting man in society. "However," he concluded, "there are many in the Presbyterian community who do not accept the aspirations of the young."[71]

In his 1952 address to the graduates of Campinas Seminary, Kerr expressed fear that the youth were falling away from orthodoxy. Denouncing those who were bringing a different gospel into the church with the support of the young people and even some pastors, he continued:

> The youth, without even minimal knowledge, but with great presumption of wisdom, edit their papers, and in the use and abuse of privileges which the Church gives them, insult ministers and even churches, while they exalt false teachers and reveal a revolting ignorance of the facts and of the true doctrines in which they should believe. . . . Confusion and more confusion. . . . We are called to a battle without quarter for the good and for the truth in its doctrinal and practical aspects in moral life.[72]

The most crucial reason for reaction against the movement was its criticism of the church, its leadership, and some of its cherished institutions. The apparent indifference of a few local youth leaders to the traditional church organization and program, and their tendency to constitute a church within the church, aggravated the problem and widened the gulf between generations. Commenting on the problems of both the church and the world in 1951, *Mocidade* complained:

> This silence of the Church is continuing longer than it should. Why does it not speak about the disconcerting situation of the world today? Political and social doctrines take charge of us in daily doses. But the pulpit either says nothing or merely repeats superficial phrases of condemnation. . . . And there is also the great and recent silence over an ideal of the young who wish for renewal . . . the ecumenical movement. The Church closes in upon itself calling the new movement dangerous, avant-garde, and modernist. . . . This is the strange and absurd silence which, if it continues, will cause others to speak in place of the Church.[73]

Despite protests from a number of judicatories,[74] the Executive Committee of the church temporarily defended youth's right to express its ideas, even though it denounced language which implied disrespect for ministers and ecclesiastical institutions.[75] Soon, however, the impression that pastors were not always welcome in the organization's planning sessions led to the tightening of control over the group. Adauto Dourado, President of the Synod of the West, called for new directions in the movement, specifying three criticisms. First, he said, "there was a lack of integration of the activities of the youth organizations into the work of the local church," with a tendency toward separatism. Second, "in some places one observed a revolt against the moderating authority of the church session." Finally, there were not enough pastors orienting the youth on a national level. "We contemplate, amazed, youth who do not participate in the activities of their churches, who do not feel any responsibility to sustain the church, who are always absent from meetings for prayer and evangelization, occupying posts of leadership."[76] The Executive Committee determined that the youth should carefully study Presbyterian administration and the authority of the local session, that pastors must have a stronger voice in the movement, and that certain restrictions be put on the selection of speakers for its congresses. The Committee also requested the presbyteries to study a possible restructuring of the entire program.[77]

Although asked to remain as Youth Secretary in 1956, Miss Gammon resigned in 1958 and was replaced by Teófilo Carnier, a young pastor. Finally, the 1962 Supremo Concílio, upon the motion of Boanerges Ribeiro, a São Paulo pastor, stripped the youth organization of its independence,[78] and it soon lost the vitality it had shown previously. The imprudence and impatience of the young people and their attempts to move in ecumenical, social, and theological directions different from those of the church as a whole were reasons. But primarily to blame was the inflexibility and resistance to criticism on the part of older church leaders who feared and distrusted the independence of the youth. The action implied continued definition of the church as a clerically dominated organization, based on the traditional structures and activities, with no place for effective nonclerical leadership or new forms of community and activity. Going further, Waldyr Luz responded to charges against Campinas Seminary, admitting its deficiences, but added:

> There is, however, one aspect in which the Seminary of Campinas is insuperable. . . . It is its traditional doctrinal firmness, its unrestricted fidelity to the Scriptures, its unshakeable orthodoxy, its inflexible loyalty to the Evangelical Faith. This is . . . the true criterion by which to evaluate the greatness, the superiority . . . of the Seminary of the Church.[79]

It was apparently more important to affirm one's orthodoxy and acceptance of the scriptures than to wrestle with them in the attempt to discover their meaning for one's own historical situation. Thus the church was defined not only as a clerically dominated ecclesiastical institution but as the guardian of orthodox faith. It is not surprising that the youth, more concerned with the church's ministry and witness to society, found themselves in conflict with this definition.

Having already repelled efforts to achieve a closer relationship with world Christianity, in the debate over its youth movement the Presbyterian Church of Brazil reasserted its traditions of clerical authority, theological orthodoxy, and moralistic ethics. It rejected any serious questioning of their adequacy for the new situation in which it found itself and thus ended a promising step toward renewal.

M. Richard Shaull and the New Concept of Mission

Closely associated with the conflict surrounding the youth movement was M. Richard Shaull, who came to Brazil in 1952 as member of the Central Brazil Mission after a period of service in Colombia. Originally requested for work with university students,[80] he succeeded Philip Landes as professor in Campinas Seminary in 1953, with the approval of the church.[81] That same year he began to cooperate with the SCM and the Church's Department of Youth.

Teaching in Campinas, appearing often before church groups, and writing for youth conferences and publications, Shaull was soon acknowledged to be one of the most effective and controversial voices speaking to the church. While most young people he encountered, especially seminary and university students, considered him a prophet, older leaders came to regard him with mounting suspicion. The reasons were not hard to find. Shaull's message about the church and its action in the world went far beyond that of traditional Brazilian Protestantism. It fulfilled the longings of the youth by making explicit the new theological and ethical ideas for which they were groping. Church leaders, already suspicious of both the Presbyterian youth organization and the student movement, were quick to discover in his thought and in his wide ecumenical contacts positions which were foreign to them and therefore threatening.

Any North American, especially one of unusual ability, who achieved a wide following in the church would have risked becoming the target of envy. This was true in the seminary as well, where a number of professors were nearing retirement and dissatisfaction with the teaching and curriculum had been expressed. Imprudent students who lauded Shaull while attacking other professors and pastors often exaggerated the issue. The basic seeds of contention, however, lay in Shaull's theology of the church and its mission, quite different from the ideas most Brazilian Presbyterians were striving to defend against enemies they saw coming in the guise of modernism, ecumenism, and communism.

In studies published for youth, Shaull emphasized the dynamic nature of God revealed in Christ and discovered through the Bible.[83] Because God was supremely a being of action, working to establish his kingdom in the world, the purpose of Bible study and worship was not merely to bring intellectual knowledge but to insure the worshipper's personal encounter with God and prepare him for a call to service. "The Bible does not contain any doctrine of God in Himself, nor of man in himself," he wrote, "but of God as the One who comes to encounter man and of man as a person who comes from God."[84] Theology was not primarily a list of doctrines but an attempt to relate God's activity to man's situation. The church was not simply a community of those who had been saved from the world; on the contrary, as the Body of Christ, its only reason for existence was to enter into the life of man and his world as its Lord had done. Clearly this diverged from the position of Brazilian Presbyterianism which defined the church as the deposit of the true faith. In that tradition the main difference between Catholicism and Protestantism lay in the truth of the latter's doctrines rather than the concept of theology in itself. Em-

phasis on the activity of God in place of the doctrine of God was
also foreign to many and ran counter to the customary attitude
toward the world. Instead of a sphere from which Evangelicals
were to isolate themselves, except for evangelistic forays into it,
it was the place where God was active and, therefore, the area
where the Christian was to find his most important place of testimony and service. "Isolation from other men," Shaull wrote, "con-
stitutes a great sin."[85]

A new and more flexible concept of the ministry and laity and
the relationship between them was also implied. Since every believer was to fulfill his mission in the world, a diversity of gifts
and functions was presupposed which in turn suggested more
flexible structures and relationships within the church. The pastor
was not to be primarily the religious authority and leader of an
ecclesiastical institution but one who inspired his people to discover areas of witness and service on the frontier between the
gospel and the world. Obviously this sharply contradicted the
traditional role of the minister as one who preached, served the
sacraments, and made dogmatic pronouncements on questions of
faith and morals.

Shaull's theology presupposed an ecumenical concern which
also challenged the thought of Brazilian Presbyterians. The fact
that we belong to Jesus Christ, he wrote, signifies that we also belong to other members of His body.[86] While no one denied this
theoretically, Brazilian Protestants usually set much narrower limits in defining the Body of Christ than did Shaull. He denied that
he saw his mission as an attempt to move the Brazilian church
toward international ecumenical organizations, but he added that
it was necessary to "enter into live relationships with other
churches and learn what God had done in them, and at the same
time, to contribute to their development."[87] Here also he expressed a point of view popular with most of the youth but contrary to the direction of the church as a whole. The Rector of
Campinas Seminary admitted to the institution's Board of Directors in 1957 that the missionary professor had evidenced a certain
militance in regard to ecumenism.[88]

While Shaull called on the church to take evangelism more seriously and challenged the youth to discover new methods of sharing their faith with others, it was in the application of his concept
of mission to Brazil's social problems that he attracted the great-

est attention, both favorable and unfavorable. The traditional ethic of the church spoke mainly of personal morality, and to the extent that it concerned itself with political and social problems it assumed that the conversion of enough people would solve them. It also put great faith in liberal democracy, believing that as more and more people became literate and took part in the political process, progress would inevitably result. But by the 1950's poverty and suffering seemed to be worse or, at least, more apparent. A number of thinkers, especially those in university circles, now felt that foreign and national economic and political forces active in Brazil made it impossible for the nation to lift itself out of the morass of underdevelopment through normal political processes. Shaull countered a tendency toward cynicism and despair by encouraging political action by Evangelicals. "Political power can control all parts of the Republic. . . . If the Church of Christ is concerned about the grave problems of our world, it must see that it has a great responsibility in this field."[89] He also urged university and seminary students to work in factories and reflect on their Christian mission in the light of their experience,[90] the first experiments of this type among Protestants in Brazil.

His definition of theology, so different from that common to Brazilian Protestantism, and the emphasis on social and political action which grew out of his concept of the church and its mission soon raised an outcry that he was a "modernist" who preached a "social gospel." He was even called a Communist, despite his published studies criticizing that ideology.[91] In defense, Shaull argued that his social concern was a direct outgrowth of Biblical theology and that concern for one's neighbor was an essential part of the faith. He added that the terms "modernism" and "fundamentalism" belonged to a period which was fortunately in the past. He condemned both, one for losing essential elements of the faith as it expressed concern for modern problems, the other for defining Christianity in abstract scholastic terms which were unrelated to modern man.[92] While he realized that fundamentalism existed in the Brazilian church, perhaps his greatest error was the failure to understand its strength. If the fundamentalist-modernist struggle was a thing of the past elsewhere, it was far from over in Brazil. Indeed, his definition of a fundamentalist perfectly described many pastors and elders in Brazilian Presbyterianism, especially in the North.

Shaull was frequently accused of subverting seminary students and youth from their traditional faith and theology. However, if he upset some, he made the faith and its relationship to the world meaningful for others, satisfying the quest of some of the most able young people in the church. Indeed, it was not he who introduced the concern for social problems into the seminary. In 1945, after Mário Licio, a Presbyterian pastor, published a number of articles in favor of the Communist Party,[93] the seminary's Board of Directors denied that the institution was a "redoubt of Communism" but added that a number of students were concerned about "so-called social justice."[94] Thus Shaull achieved his following among students because he related the faith to problems with which they were already struggling, something the church as a whole was unwilling or unable to do. The critical attitude toward the church on the part of youth, which he was accused of stimulating, had prevailed before his arrival. It is true that in recognizing the lack of orientation among the young people and addressing himself to their concerns, he provided a contrast which indirectly heightened their antagonism toward church leaders. However, it is hard to see how he could have done otherwise without failing to fulfill his own ministry.

In part because his situation in Campinas was becoming untenable, and partly because of a new call, Shaull left that institution at the end of 1959 to join the faculty of the Centennial Seminary. Established that year in Alto Jequitibá, it was intended to be a creative new experiment in theological education in the area where Presbyterianism had grown most rapidly. In 1962 he left Brazil to accept a chair in Princeton Theological Seminary.

Two basic problems were involved in the crisis surrounding Shaull and the youth. The first was the concept of the church and its mission. Here he provided the orientation, sought by the young people, which moved in a direction different from that which the church had traditionally followed. The other issue was the attitude with which church leaders met the youth's criticism. Although not always fair or prudent, and often disdainful of the struggles and accomplishments of the past as well as the vitality still present, they did express valid concerns and deserved a hearing. Too many pastors, seeing the changes as a personal threat, were unable to accept them and thus had to rid themselves of their imagined source. Waldyr Luz, responding to comments made by students of Campinas Seminary, wrote: "If the presbyteries will send to the seminary only youths of proven faith, firm character, genuine piety, and incontestable vocation, all of the negative expressions which are prejudicing the institution, will disappear."[95]

The implication that men with a sure vocation would raise no serious theological or ethical questions, and that genuine piety in the modern world consisted only of subscribing to doctrines formulated in the past was tragic and constituted an ominous sign for the future. Many leaders hid behind a façade of orthodoxy and refused to treat difficult questions. They showed themselves incapable of accepting criticism and thus followed the path toward greater rigidity and authoritarianism.

The Establishment of the Department of Church and Society of the Evangelical Confederation

While the concern for personal ethics remained strong in Brazilian Protestantism, the Department of Church and Society of the Evangelical Confederation promised to move beyond it into a study of the relationship of the church to the social problems which clamored for solution. With the initiative coming from some of the Brazilians who had been active in the youth movement and had now come from the Evanston assembly of the WCC, the group formed in 1955, with Benjamin Moraes as President and Waldo Cesar as Executive Secretary. Proposing to stimulate the church to witness to its faith in the centers of social and political influence,[96] the department expressed interest in three areas. It hoped to prepare Evangelicals for participation in political life; it proposed to study the proper attitude toward Roman Catholic and Communist activity; it aimed at generating social action by Protestants, especially among industrial and rural workers.[97]

The reaction in the Presbyterian Church was mixed. The Executive Committee asked the Confederation to explain who had taken the initiative in forming the group and why the church had not been officially invited to designate its delegates to the first meeting. It appeared that the organizers of the new entity were careless about seeking official sanction from the member churches of the Confederation.[98] Still, formation of the department represented a badly needed breakthrough for Brazilian Protestant ethics, which might have been impossible had the organizers waited for a consensus of all the churches. The beginning of a new orientation in part of the church, at least, was indicated by José Borges dos Santos, Jr., President of the Supremo Concílio and pastor of São Paulo's Igreja Unida. After attending the Church and Society Conference in 1957, he called attention to the growing concern for "problems now affecting the Brazilian people which were vital for human life, and the responsibility of the Church in their solution." Noting that the tragic orientation of the past had led many believers to condemn politics and politicians while shirking their duty as citizens, he continued:

> A church isolated from the world is a church which has denied its call. . . . Because only the Church as the instrument of the power and grace of God has the resources to save the world, including industry, agriculture, work, and all that is of man . . . the Church must bring these areas to herself and ransom them for the service of her Lord and the benefit and salvation of man.[99]

Agreeing that the basic problem was man's character, he pointed out that the new man in Christ faced a series of complex problems as he attempted to serve God in the world. Thus the church must orient its children and present Christian solutions to specific problems. He concluded with a call to both study and action.

The following year the department issued a comprehensive and thoughtful document, orienting Evangelicals in regard to elections. Reminding its readers that "the believer who does not accept his responsibility to participate in political life is not completely converted," it referred to the long-standing Brazilian practice of selling votes for favors and reminded Protestants that they should not "trade their votes for anything except the good of society."[100]

Both Borges' statement and those of the Department of Church and Society went beyond the simplistic ethic of most of Brazilian Protestantism and opened new perspectives for the church. Only the future could tell if they would soon change the traditional views of Brazilian Presbyterians.

The Restructuring of Church-Mission Relations

The Brazil Plan, adopted in 1917, had left the church and the missions almost completely separated from each other, to the detriment of all concerned. It often led to less than optimum use of missionary resources and personnel, while contributing to the increasing isolation and ingrown character of the church. At the same time it hindered the work in most cities with the premature withdrawal of the missionaries and their concentration in the hinterland. Because the Modus Operandi Committee was inoperative during most of the intervening years, the church and missions were scarcely acquainted with each other's efforts.[101] If the missions were to fulfill their potential in mid-twentieth-century Brazil, they would have to structure a new relationship with the church which would allow greater flexibility in choice of geographical areas and types of ministry.

Important progress came with the founding of the *Junta de Missões Nacionais* in 1940, the Committee on Cooperation in Portugal in 1945, and the ceding of Miss Gammon to the church for youth work in 1946. All three represented innovations in making North American resources and personnel available to the church without compromising its autonomy and independence. Significantly, each resulted from the initiative of the church, at least in part.

But the stimulus for radical restructuring of church-mission relations came not from within Brazil but from the postwar conferences of the IMC, especially those at Whitby, in 1947, and Willingen, in 1952. In the first, the new concern for the ecumenical church, which now existed in nearly every nation in the world, combined with reactions against paternalism to bring the demand that missionaries be fully integrated into the churches with which they worked. The committee declared:

> It is essential that the missionary . . . while retaining the closest fellowship with the church of his origin, become in every respect a member of the church which he is to serve, and during the period of his service, joyfully give his allegiance to that church and regard himself as subject to its direction and discipline.[102]

Delegates from the "younger churches" at the Willingen meeting, held after the Communists had expelled foreign missionaries from China, added: "We are convinced that mission work should be done through the Church. We should cease to speak of missions and churches and avoid the dichotomy, not only in our thinking, but also in our actions."[103] The New York Board accepted the recommendation, and in 1953, J. C. Smith, a staff member, told the CBM that integration of the missions into the life of the national churches was to begin as soon as possible.[104] By 1956 missions of that board in a number of countries were merging with the churches with which they worked.[105]

There were several valid reasons for desiring the step in Brazil. From a theological standpoint a mission is an anomaly once a church has been formed. Ecclesiology clearly dictates that all those working in a given region should be part of the same church, and it would be difficult if not impossible to find New Testament justification for the existence of separate judicatories for missionaries and national pastors. It is also true that the resources and personnel used by missions on the geographical frontiers and in some educational institutions often could have served better in other areas. Theoretically, integration would facilitate more effective use of all resources, national and foreign, as the needs of Brazil as a whole were examined, priorities determined, and men and funds assigned without the traditional division of territory. It would also diminish the isolation of pastors and missionaries from each other, giving each a more complete vision of the whole church and its task throughout the nation. Consequently, some hoped that a more flexible structure of church-mission relations would contribute to renewal.

There were still pragmatic questions, however, coming out of traditional missiology, which seemed to justify separation, and these loomed large in the minds of most missionaries. Could North American resources and personnel be used within the structures of the national church without robbing it of its autonomy and financial independence? If it believed that funds would be forthcoming from Nashville and New York, would it be as zealous in raising money in Brazil and utilizing those resources carefully? It is true that through the years the boards should have provided more financial support and men for the seminaries, especially Recife, having awakened to this responsibility only after decades had passed. But many feared that integration would open the gates so wide that the church would become too dependent on North American sources. Missionaries also feared that if national churchmen began to determine allocation of resources, the work in the interior, to which the North Americans had committed themselves but which was relatively unknown to Brazilian leaders, would suffer. Naiveté on the part of some board leaders about the use of power in the church should have been shattered with receipt of requests from First Church, Rio, and the Igreja Unida in São Paulo, each for a loan of US$100,000 for building programs. The pastors of the two congregations, the wealthiest in the denomination, were the Executive Secretary and President of the Supremo Concílio, respectively.[106]

Historical factors important to Brazilian leaders were ignored by some staff members of the New York Board. While leaders of a number of younger churches saw integration as a means of achieving greater autonomy, the Brazilian church had enjoyed independence from missionary interference since 1917. Although the Brazil Plan had resulted from the initiative of the Central Brazil Mission, most Brazilians now defended it vigorously, believing it to be the product of their own nationalism. Thus, they were afraid that integration, instead of increasing their autonomy, would destroy it. Additional suspicion was aroused by the fact that the Brazilian church had not profited from ideas which the New York Board had attempted to introduce in past decades.[107] The struggle over theological education and missionary domination had led to the split of 1903; the controversy over the United Seminary had nearly caused another in 1928; more recently, the question of WCC membership, which some felt New York advocated, had caused agitation. Some churchmen were apprehensive that the missionaries of that board, once inside the judicatories, would attempt to lead the church in ecumenical and theological directions foreign to its traditions.[108] The isolation resulting from the Brazil Plan only fired such suspicion. Brazilians also pointed out the problems sometimes caused by the foreign missionary who had more funds available to him, either from the mission budget or from special sources, than his national colleague. With a larger salary and special financing he often displayed generosity in creating new projects which the Brazilian, who worked in an adjacent area or succeeded him, could not match. Would this not become worse in the case of integration, giving the missionary influence out of proportion to that of the Brazilian pastors?[109]

Thus, little interest was shown in integration in Brazil. In 1947 representatives of all four missions expressed a desire that the Modus Operandi Committee meet at least once a year and prepare an overall strategy for Presbyterian work, within the customary pattern of relationships.[110] Although one pastor recommended missionary participation in the judicatories of the church and called for national representation in the missions,[111] most Brazilian leaders were skeptical. Commenting on the Whitby meeting, Goulart noted that while the policy already in effect safeguarded the dignity of the church, the new orientation presented serious difficulties along with its possible advantages. Recalling Brazilian experiences with international gatherings in the past, he cautioned: "We always look at the results of this type of congress with reserve."[112] After the President of the church visited the fields of the CBM in 1952, he urged closer relationships between the church and the missions, but warned: "The Church is absolutely not thinking about organic union between the two bodies."[113]

The following year, C. Darby Fulton, Secretary of the PCUS Board, made it clear that he opposed any joint structure. Development of church-mission relationships should follow precisely the steps taken in Brazil, he wrote. First came the stage of the mission alone; then the mission-church, with missionaries taking part in the national judicatories; third, the point at which the missions were separate from the church; finally, when the latter was sufficiently strong, withdrawal of the North Americans from the country. He argued that the return of missionaries and their institutions to the church would hinder self-government and self-support, place it under a crushing administrative load, increase the possibility of friction between nationals and missionaries, and, perhaps, diminish evangelistic outreach.[114]

By a strange irony of history, the New York Board, whose missions had been primarily responsible for bringing about mission-church separation and formulating the Brazil Plan, was now most eager to reverse the situation, while the church and the PCUS missions were united in their determination to maintain the wall of division. The Central Brazil Mission was placed in the precarious position of attempting to interpret the respective positions of its board and the church to each other, often incurring the wrath of both as a result.

It had been obvious for years that the Modus Operandi Committee needed restructuring, and the Executive Committee of the church made such a recommendation in 1950.[115] The crucial question was how far change should go. After joint planning and preparation, forty delegates representing the church, the two boards, and the four missions, met in 1954 to create the *Conselho Inter-Presbiteriano* (CIP), to be composed of twelve church representatives and six missionaries from each board. Meeting at least once a year to serve as an intermediary between the church and the missions, it was empowered to approve new programs proposed by the missions or to suggest their initiation. The constitution of the CIP declared that while it was the responsibility of the church to evangelize Brazil, the participation of the missions in this task was joyfully accepted. The church was to have exclusive jurisdiction over fields occupied by the presbyteries and to participate in supervision of mission work through the new body. This would include not only evangelism and church development but spheres of action such as radio, schools, and publishing. A basic provision of the Brazil Plan continued in the stipulation that no worker of the church or a mission could be a member of both entities simultaneously. This was amended in 1958 to allow missionary membership in a Brazilian presbytery when it was necessary to complete that body's quorum.[116]

Although the new structure did not satisfy the proponents of integration, it did open the door to closer cooperation. In 1957, after CIP had approved a request of the Presbytery of Salvador, the CBM assigned Rodger Perkins to Feira de Santana, Bahia, a large and growing city which the presbytery was unable to serve effectively. It was a promising step toward return to the coastal cities which had been left prematurely.[117]

After the new plan was accepted by the cooperating entities and began to function in 1955, misunderstandings arose as to its ultimate purpose. Was it merely an updated form of the Modus Operandi Committee, continuing indefinitely the same basic structure of separation, or was it to be a short-lived stepping stone toward full integration of the missions into the church? Without question, the PCUS Board and the church considered it to be the former, while the New York Board saw it as the latter. Relationships were strained when some members of the staff in New York either did not listen to what Brazilian leaders were saying, or refused to believe that their viewpoint could not be changed. The Pan-Presbyterian Conference, which met in Campinas in 1956, declared itself against any one plan of mission-church relations, while José Borges dos Santos, Jr., President of the Supremo Concílio, asked that the traditional Brazilian structure be maintained.[118] Even so, the following year, when the New York Board published a book on its Lake Mohonk Consultation, at which Borges had been present, it said: "Every church represented in the Consultation wants the complete integration within the work of the national church of missionary endeavors. . . within five years."[119] The CBM, under pressure from its board, took a somewhat contradictory action: "Whereas it is recognized that integration of the CBM with the Presbyterian Church of Brazil can come about only as rapidly as the national Church desires, it was voted to defer any such action on a plan of integration and to suggest to Inter-Presbyterian Council that it prepare such a plan."[120] CIP replied that it was too soon to abandon the recently adopted structure,[121] and the 1958 Supremo Concílio agreed.[122]

But W. S. Rycroft of the New York Board continued to argue for the interim nature of the scheme. He based his position on a statement accepted by all the cooperating entities: "The final goal is that the Presbyterian Church of Brazil have the responsibility for all of the work in the country."[123] Rycroft understood achievement of the goal to be imminent; afterward, missionaries would continue to work within the structures of the church. The interpretation of the PCUS Board and Brazilian leaders was that total responsibility would be assumed only in the more distant future when no more missionary aid was needed. It was only through a series of meetings which took place after the Presbyterian World Alliance meeting in 1959 that board leaders finally recognized the difficulties caused in church-mission relationships by their attempts to force integration and changed their stance.

Suspicion of the plans and motives of the New York Board which affected a number of church leaders, combined with the memory of unfortunate disagreements between the two, would not quickly disappear, and any attempt to force the issue would only make matters worse. The very isolation of Brazilian Presbyterians from their missionary colleagues, caused by the Brazil Plan, had become self-perpetuating, and change could only come gradually, as the church willed it.

A related issue emerged when Robert L. McIntire of the CBM established the *Centro Audio-Visual Evangélico* in São Paulo in 1951. The project was sponsored by the Evangelical Confederation of Brazil, although most of the equipment and funds came from Presbyterian sources in the United States through the Committee on Cooperation in Latin America. The venture had the enthusiastic support of a number of pastors, but it lacked the official sanction of the church. If the Brazil Plan covered such a situation, it did so only in article nine, which stipulated that missionaries and pastors would not "sanction the invasion of fields or functions of the other."[124] The President of the Supremo Concílio voiced resentment in 1952 because the church had not been consulted officially and because Presbyterian money had come to Brazil to finance an interdenominational project, while the institutions of the Presbyterian Church lacked adequate funds.[125] Thus, although they were the first to be invited to join the Center in 1951, Presbyterians did not do so until two years later. In connection with this and other projects,[126] the question also arose as to the mission's authority to initiate any kind of work in geographical areas occupied by the church without its official approval. Up to that time the assumption had been that article nine of the Brazil Plan referred only to pastoral and evangelistic work. On that basis, the mission had established the Colégio Dois de Julho in Salvador and the Instituto JMC near São Paulo in the 1920's. But now it was evident that, even though the church agreed with the purpose of the audio-visual center, it felt that the CBM should have sought its approval before becoming involved in the project and that the center should be Presbyterian rather than interdenominational.

The Constitution of the Conselho Inter-Presbiteriano specifically included, within the missionary work it was to supervise, cooperation with the national church in audio-visual and educational activities,[127] but it did not clarify the status of missionaries related to interdenominational projects. Finally, at a meeting in August, 1959, with Brazilian leaders, CBM representatives, and COEMAR[128] staff members present, it was agreed that "no cooperative projects should be initiated without consultation with the Presbyterian Church of Brazil."[129]

The structure of church-mission relationships adopted in 1954, which some hoped would insure closer relationships and more creative use of North American funds and personnel, in reality perpetuated the old Brazil Plan and even narrowed the missions' sphere of action in some areas. Henceforth, new projects of the missions in Brazil would be limited by the traditional thinking of the national church, in which missionaries had no voice. While this decision appeared correct at the time, it left unanswered important questions which could become sources of friction in the future. New geographical frontiers would become more scarce as mission fields in the hinterlands organized into presbyteries. Many were finally realizing that coastal cities and new towns springing up in the territory of the church were seriously undermanned. Some missionaries would begin to feel that they could make a greater contribution in these areas than in the traditional mission fields. In addition, with broadening concepts of mission and ecumenical relations developing in the United States and, especially, with the growing concern for the cities, it was inevitable that missionaries would arrive who were more urban oriented and conceived of their mission in terms unacceptable to Brazilian leaders. If the activities of the North American Presbyterians were limited to those which fitted into the narrower concept of mission espoused by the national church, frustration would soon result. On the other hand, if missionaries disregarded the orientation of their Brazilian colleagues in undertaking new programs, valid as they might be, a new crisis might very well come. This would be one of the dilemmas facing the church and missions as they began the second century.

The Centennial Campaign and Renewed Evangelistic Growth

As it anticipated commemoration of its first centennial, the church began to plan a campaign which it hoped would bring evangelistic renewal. Projections were that by 1959, membership would double and union with the Independentes would become a reality. Natanael Cortez, the veteran pastor from Ceará, who was elected President of the Supremo Concílio in 1946, traveled widely, advertising the five goals of the campaign. These were to deepen spiritual life, increase evangelistic activity, improve stewardship in order to strengthen the institutions of the church, broaden its teaching function and reaffirm its creedal position, and, finally, to pay homage to the leaders of the past as an inspiration for the present.[130] But the Centennial Commission, with six Brazilian and six missionary members, struggled against inertia and lack of resources during most of the period. Efforts toward union with the Independentes failed once more over the Masonic question. Steps were taken to consolidate the seminaries, and funds raised in Brazil plus grants from the mission boards made it possible to construct badly needed buildings in Campinas and Recife. However, despite a large grant from New York for the purpose, the leadership of the *Casa Editora Presbiteriana* made no attempt to improve its facilities or publications.

Although the church formally reaffirmed its adherence to the Westminster Symbols in 1950, it undertook no special project to orient local congregations toward more effective religious education or more meaningful liturgy. Worship, even in the cities, tended toward stereotyped reproduction of forms used decades earlier in a Brazil that was quite different; often it did not speak to the new generation. Nor did the leadership of the church show interest in translation and publication of Calvin's *Institutes* when the Presbyterian World Alliance initiated the plan. Alleging that the translators chosen by the Alliance—T. H. Maurer, Jr., and I. Salum—were of dubious orthodoxy, the Supremo Concílio nominated another committee which never completed the task. It was apparently more important to avow one's adherence to creeds which had tried to interpret Calvin in the past than to study his thought and its relevance for the present.

The Centennial Campaign was more successful in stimulating evangelism and the organization of new churches. The Irish evangelist, J. Edwin Orr, and William Dunlap, a North American, spoke to large audiences all over Brazil in 1952 under the auspices of the campaign, and a new interest in evangelism grew in many churches. Paulo Rizzo wrote that in Campinas, ". . . where there had been a period of ten years in which no church had succeeded in successfully holding an evangelistic campaign, now all are full for an entire week."[131] After the Orr visit similar campaigns continued in all parts of the nation under the leadership of Brazilian pastors, notably Antônio Elias and Alfredo Stein from 1953 to

1958, with large numbers of decisions reported and a substantial proportion of young men offering themselves for the ministry.[132]

Despite those who expressed interest during the campaigns but soon drifted away, permanent results were seen in rising seminary enrollment and church growth. Influenced by the youth movement as well as the campaign, the total number of seminarians in Campinas and Recife rose from approximately 70 in 1950 to 150 in 1959. Membership did not double, but the total number of communicants in the church and mission fields grew from 61,000 in 1946 to 102,000 in 1959,[133] a rate of 4.3 per cent per year. This was appreciably better than the 1930's but still far below the church's potential. Clearly, after nearly a century of life, the Presbyterian Church of Brazil was beginning to feel the problems of middle age.

Analysis of the statistics for 1953, a typical year, shows that the Eastern Minas-Espirito Santo area continued to enjoy the greatest growth.

Synod	Ministers	Candidates	Churches	Prof. of Faith	Communicant Members[134]
Central	64	8	76	734	12,613
Minas-E.S.	38	30	111	1,714	23,161
Western	49	9	40	480	6,860
Southern	82	19	103	739	17,626
Northern	62	30	51	584	10,541
Bahia-Se.	18	2	24	98	3,831
Totals	313	98	405	4,349	74,632

Despite migration to other areas, that largely rural synod now contained one-third of the total membership of the church, provided nearly that proportion of its ministerial candidates, and accounted for 40 per cent of its professions of faith, even though served by only 12 per cent of the pastors. On the other hand, the Synod of the South, including densely populated São Paulo, numbered 17,626 communicants served by eighty-two pastors, but received only 739 people on profession of faith during the year. Its net growth from all sources from 1947 to 1959 was only 57 per cent, or slightly less than 4 per cent annually. This was not significantly greater than population growth in the area.[135]

Unquestionably, the church continued to achieve its most rapid increase in rural areas, while a noteworthy proportion of the growth of urban churches came through transfers from interior congregations, rather than by evangelism. In 1946 the Campo Formoso Church in the interior of Bahia lost fifty members by transfer, while during the first eight months of the following year the church in Salvador, the state capital, gained twenty members by transfer and only ten by profession of faith.[136] In 1957 a writer told of visiting a church in the city of São Paulo which had over two hundred members only two years after it had been organized. When asked where they all came from, the lay leaders replied, "from the interior."[137] Not only members, but much of the leadership of the city churches came from the same source. When Maria Madalena Regis of the Campo Formoso congregation died in 1954, it was noted that of her four surviving children, one was an elder and another was choir director in First Church, Rio.[138] The Presbyterian Church of Brazil, as it completed its first century, often failed to be at home in the cities. It was establishing new churches in Rio, São Paulo, and other urban centers, but overall growth there was not appreciably greater than that of the population.

One reason was the Brazil Plan, the missionary mentality which had produced it and the reluctance to change it. Continuing to direct the missions toward the hinterland and emphasize rural work, it made it impossible for them to cooperate in evangelism in the urban centers, which were growing far more rapidly. Noting the heavy migration from the interior of Pernambuco to Recife and adjacent areas, a writer asked in 1951 if the Presbyterian churches in the cities were keeping up with their demographic growth. In the previous decade, Recife had grown 55 per cent, adding 200,000 inhabitants, while nearby Paulista had grown from 12,843 to 23,000 and Olinda had increased to 38,700.[139] Recife had only a handful of Presbyterian churches; the other two cities had none. The resources and personnel of the North Brazil Mission were concentrated either in secondary schools or in the hinterland

A second, related influence was the rural ethos of the church. Most pastors were from rural areas, and, out of the ninety-eight ministerial candidates reported in 1953, sixty were from the predominantly rural synods of Minas-Espirito Santo and the North. A writer in 1964 called the rural churches the "backbone of Brazilian Presbyterianism," estimating that 80 per cent of them were congregations of about one hundred communicants. The young men leave and go to the cities, he said, while the churches maintain themselves by adding the children of believers and converts from outside Protestantism.[140] Some of the immigrants to the cities found churches in their new homes, while others drifted away. But the rural roots and orientation of most city churches, which sometimes made them attractive to new arrivals from the interior, made it difficult for them to speak to the new urban-oriented generation.

The traditional pattern of ministry, too, increased the social and geographical distance between the church leadership and the poor, who made up 80 per cent of Brazilian society. This, allied with the social mobility characteristic of Presbyterianism, helped to shape the church into a middle-class movement in many areas, sharply limiting its outreach among the masses. Benjamin Cesar, one of the most effective pastor evangelists, accused Presbyterianism of digging its own grave by becoming too concerned with prestige and the inclusion of the elite among its membership. "Damned elite," he cried.[141] Telling of the astonishment expressed by a visiting Presbyterian from another city when he baptized a black and a white together, he commented, "I discovered that it was not only in the American churches that there is racial prejudice."[142] Statistics of church membership among Baptists, Presbyterians, and Pentecostals in a number of cities in 1959, show that not only in the large centers, but especially in their satellites, Presbyterians were falling further behind.[143] (See chart, p. 238.)

By the end of its first century, it became apparent that if the Presbyterian Church were to utilize its full potential in evangelizing and serving modern Brazil, new patterns of outreach, pastoral preparation, and ministry were essential. Two attempts were made: one in the cities, and the other in rural areas. The first was the *Instituto de Cultura Religiosa*, founded by Miguel Rizzo, Jr., in São Paulo in 1931 and in Rio two years later. While it did not envision a different pattern of ministry, it did seek to reach those not linked to any local church through publications and by meeting in religiously neutral buildings. Rizzo and a small group of collaborators met some success, and large numbers became interested in their message. At one time 17,000 were receiving the Instituto's correspondence course on religion.[144] The church, however, often did know how to receive them, and when Rizzo became inactive

City	Denomination	Churches	Members
Rio de Janeiro	Presbyterian	24	8,864
	Independente	4	628
	Baptist	91	22,560
	Assembly of God	17	19,083
Nova Iguaçu	Presbyterian	4	838
(Satellite city near Rio)	Baptist	28	4,342
	Assembly of God	11	5,478
São Paulo	Presbyterian	14	6,919
	Independente	9	4,069
	Baptist	47	11,366
	Assembly of God	23	29,138
	Congregação Cristã	59	67,565
Salvador	Presbyterian	2	671
	Independente	1	62
	Baptist	10	2,757
	Assembly of God	1	4,153
Recife	Presbyterian	7	2,253
	Fundamentalist Presbyterian	3	1,631
	Baptist	40	8,366
	Assembly of God	59	8,921

because of age, there was no one of his ability and vision to carry on.

Various attempts were made to prepare lay evangelists for the interior. Some worked for presbyteries, but most were employed by the missions. Many did an effective job, penetrating areas where ordained men were not available, but because of traditional ideas about a well-trained clergy, most could not look forward to ordination. Even though they did the work of a local pastor, they could not administer the sacraments or preside over the local session. Their position was theologically indefensible and psychologically untenable. If the position of the lay evangelist, paid or not, had become the first step in an alternative path to ordination, the system might have opened up new possibilities for ministry in the interior and even in the cities.

The one region in which the church indicated interest in laymen and put them to work successfully to some degree was the Synod of Minas-Espirito Santo. Intensive lay activity was characteristic there, most of it unpaid and informal. However, when the synod cried for help in preparing its lay leadership more effectively, it was not heeded. The missions felt a prior commitment to the areas where they were working, and church leaders gave low priority to the project.[145] Thus, despite somewhat increased growth in the last decade of the first century, the church continued to maintain a traditional pattern of ministry and evangelism which was inadequate in newly industrialized urban Brazil.

The Centennial Celebration: Brazilian Protestantism Come of Age?

A century after Simonton's arrival, the Presbyterian Church of Brazil numbered over 100,000 communicant members,[146] gathered into 526 churches and nearly 1000 unorganized congregations, served by 414 ordained pastors, and scattered from the Amazon to Rio Grande do Sul. It was no longer a small group, struggling for recognition and equal status before the law; and it was no longer a stigma in public life to be known as a Protestant. If it aroused opposition from some, it attracted the support of others, who believed a Protestant was more likely to be honest.

Protestants, especially Presbyterians, were beginning to occupy positions of responsibility out of proportion to their number. In Bahia, a Presbyterian elder, Edgar Regis, became Secretary of Agriculture, and a pastor, Basilio Catalá de Castro, sat in the State Legislature.[147] The veteran pastor, A. T. Gueiros, was President of the Legislature and Vice-Governor of Pará.[148] Along the Ribeira River, in Willis Banks' former field, a Presbyterian was Mayor of Juquiá, another was President of the City Council of Iguape, while a third presided over the valley's agricultural society.[149] The first woman ever elected to head the Brazilian Society of Medicine and Surgery was Dr. Carmen Escobar Pires, an active Independente laywoman.[150] Examples were multiple, as Protestants gained elective office at all levels of government.

But the new status of Protestants was best symbolized when João Café Filho was elected Brazil's Vice-President in 1951, despite strong opposition by the *Liga Eleitoral Católica* and threats of excommunication against those who voted for him.[151] When Vargas shot himself in August, 1954, Café Filho, the son of a Presbyterian elder in Natal, and former student in the Presbyterian school in that city,[152] became Brazil's first Protestant president.[153] The dream of church leaders, that Evangelicals would eventually occupy important positions in government, was being fulfilled sooner than any had dared hope.

Religious pluralism was fast becoming a national trait, breaking down the myth of unity based on Roman Catholicism. São Paulo, the nation's largest city, counted 208 Roman Catholic, 99 Protestant, and five Orthodox churches, along with 244 Spiritist centers in 1952.[154] And when construction was begun on Brasilia, the new federal capital, a number of Protestant groups gathered members of their respective flocks who had arrived to help construct the city and established churches before the first priest got there.

Nowhere was the new status of Protestantism made more clear than in festivities surrounding the centennial celebration of Presbyterianism. The Presbyterian World Alliance, which met in São Paulo in July, 1959, was the first world gathering of a specific Protestant tradition ever held in Latin America, and it honored Brazilian Presbyterianism, a part of the largest Protestant community in any traditionally Catholic nation in the world. On August 12, the anniversary of Simonton's arrival, speeches were made in Congress by Catholics as well as Evangelicals, paying tribute to the contribution made by the nation's Protestant churches. It was pointed out that they were sending more men into the ministry than were Roman Catholics. Among those who stressed Presbyterian impact on education were Congressmen Paulo Freire de Araujo, a Presbyterian pastor and graduate of the Instituto Ponte Nova, and Pimenta da Veiga, a graduate of Gammon. Speakers even pointed out that Brazil's most popular sports, soccer and basketball, had been introduced by Mackenzie Institute and the YMCA, respectively. Freire indicated the growing power of Protestantism: "The time has ended in Brazil when to be a Protestant was to be a demon. Today we enjoy the friendship, the respect, and the admiration of all men of good will in our country. Not even the government can forget that the nation now counts a Protestant community of approximately four million."[155]

In a sense, Protestantism, especially Presbyterianism, had "come of age" in Brazil. After a century of suffering, abuse, and even persecution, it had become a recognized part of the nation's religious establishment. It was no longer assumed that the clergyman taking part in civic events must always be a Catholic priest, and pastors were often invited as well. In addition to the traditional thanksgiving Mass for university graduations, a Protestant baccalaureate service was becoming common.

The centennial celebration of Presbyterianism was climaxed when President Juscelino Kubitschek attended a worship service in Rio's Presbyterian "cathedral." The first time in Latin American history that a chief of state had officially attended a Protestant worship service, the event received widespread publicity in the nation's press.[156] With a note of triumph Presbyterianism was entering its own Constantinian era in Brazil. But triumphalism could easily obscure the need for renewal. The new century would present the church with magnificent opportunities, but these would be accompanied by new and different temptations. The difficulty would be to distinguish between the two.

Epilogue

Issues for the New Century

As the Presbyterian Church of Brazil began its second century, it could justly feel a sense of accomplishment and thanksgiving. It had increased tenfold in fifty years; its seminaries were growing stronger; it had established churches in nearly all of the nation's major cities; and it included many professional men, a few intellectuals, and even some political figures among its members. Several pastors were known and respected well beyond Protestant circles, and among the youth there were many capable university students.

However, the church was called not only to give thanks for the blessings of the past but to ask itself some basic questions about its nature and mission in the future. French historian Emile Leonard had called Brazil "the greatest victory which the Reformation had won after the sixteenth century in a people of European origin."[1] He exhorted Protestants to be truly Brazilian and avoid slavish imitation of the decadent European and North American churches. Boanerges Ribeiro, writing in the centennial year, sounded the same note:

> We have now been in Brazil one century. We are the spearhead of the Reformation. We have not reached an ideal form, we are seeking the Presbyterian expression of Christianity in Brazil. We have roots in the people, we are . . . a popular movement of reformation, a lay movement, with competent national leadership. We are interested in the life and thought of the Church in other countries, but we are not little monkeys who merely imitate the grimaces of others.[2]

While most Presbyterians would agree that the church should seek the Presbyterian or Reformed expression of Christianity in

Brazil, a number of prior questions required consideration. What was the genuinely Brazilian expression of the Reformed Faith? How could it be discovered? How might it be attained? Was it sufficient merely to continue following the inherited form of Presbyterian government under Brazilian leadership and reaffirm the Westminster Symbols, now translated into Portuguese, with even greater vehemence? Or did "Reformed" not mean adoption of the principle *Ecclesia Reformata semper reformanda* and "Brazilian" imply application of this principle specifically to the country, its problems, and its psychology?

There were several areas in which it was essential that this basic question be raised as the second century began. One was that of ecclesiastical structures. Brazilian Presbyterianism had inherited a form of government and ministry originally produced in a relatively stable sixteenth and seventeenth-century European "Christendom," then filtered through the North American experience. It is questionable whether either the form of government or pattern of ministry were adequate for the dynamic missionary setting in Brazil. All too quickly the church tended to harden into a rigid ecclesiastical institution and lose its missionary character, especially in the cities. The minister, with his university-level education, soon became the religious authority in the congregation, and although Church government at all levels theoretically assumed lay participation, cases where the clergy did not dominate were rare. And since no local Christian community could celebrate the sacraments unless an ordained man were present, it was not fully a church until it had enough resources to secure his services. Thus, the pattern of ministerial preparation, which served both to foster clericalism and to limit the number of pastors, became a factor in separating the church from the urban poor.

To be truly Calvinist in its second century, the church was called to discover more flexible structures of government open to participation by the whole Christian community, including the youth. New concepts of ministry and pastoral preparation which would recognize gifts of leadership in those who did not have the traditional level of formal education were also urgent necessities. If these two tasks were accomplished the church would be better prepared to reach out to the urban masses. This might also bring a richer and more Brazilian liturgy and style of worship expressing the joy and note of celebration characteristic of so much of Brazilian life.

A second major area of concern was theology. It was laudable for the church to nourish its heritage from the past. But this is never enough. Having reaffirmed its faith in the Bible as the word of God, it now had to help its people study the scriptures more profoundly than ever before, applying their word to the contemporary Brazilian situation. It was important to conceive of theology not as a list of doctrines but as a guide enabling the believer to discover his mission in the light of God's activity in the world. Without a proper understanding of theology, Brazilian Presbyterianism was in danger of becoming a middle-class ideology in which belief in correct doctrine would insure personal salvation.[3]

The ethical stance of the church was another important issue. Having been denounced for decades as a foreign-dominated and un-Brazilian institution, the church had finally become an accepted part of the religious establishment. A number of factors now combined to create new temptations for Presbyterianism in its newly won position of respectability: the necessity of defending itself from charges of Communism in the recent past, the fear and repulsion its middle-class leadership felt toward that ideology, and the traditional emphasis on separation of church and state and submission to the constituted authorities. These combined with a theology concerned almost exclusively with personal salvation and an individualistic moralistic ethic, making it extremely difficult for the church to raise a prophetic voice against the centers of power in an unjust society. Presbyterians in Brazil were not indifferent to the well-being of the nation. But they believed that the traditional democratic liberties—separation of church and state, education, and the personal moral improvement which would theoretically accompany conversion to Protestantism—would insure progress and a greater degree of justice for all. It was their own form of nineteenth-century optimistic liberalism. At the same time, their insecurity as a minority group, especially when Roman Catholic pressure was great, led them to support the government uncritically, even with suspension of certain liberties, as long as Protestant churches were allowed to function freely. But Brazilian Presbyterianism would have no ethic to guide it when liberal democracy collapsed. Presbyterians in government and the professions quite often had reputations for personal honesty and morality, but in few cases did they apply the special insights which Calvinist theology should have evoked.

Thus, a major challenge to the church in its second century would be to move beyond moralism and its belief that progress would inevitably come with the growth of Protestantism, to an ethic both broader and more realistic. This would necessitate moving beyond a theology of personal salvation to one of the redeemed life, in which the goal of the Christian life was seen as serving God in human society.

Finally, the Presbyterian Church would have to face the question of its relationship to the whole Church of Christ throughout the world. The schism of 1903 had yet to be healed, and the major Presbyterian churches of Brazil continued to go their separate ways, weaker because of the continuing separation which nearly all hoped would end. The church would also need to relate more fully to other Protestant groups in Brazil, not just through the Evangelical Confederation but at the local level. It would be especially important to achieve closer relations with the Pentecostals, who now constituted two-thirds of the nation's Protestants. As barriers were lowered on both sides, each could learn from the other. Use of foreign missionary personnel and resources in ways which would better enable the church to meet new opportunities without becoming unduly dependent on the mission boards was another important issue.

Outside of its traditional ecclesiastical sphere of interest, the church would be called to enter into a more positive relationship with worldwide Christianity. Participation in the World Council of Churches was secondary. More crucial was the necessity that the Brazilian church learn from the faith and experience of its brethren on other continents, those in "younger" as well as older churches, and in turn make its own contribution to them.

Finally, the Presbyterian Church of Brazil, existing in the largest nominally Roman Catholic nation in the world, had no choice but to come to terms with renascent Catholicism, especially after Vatican II. Would Evangelical, the favorite self-designation of Brazilian Protestantism, mean primarily anti-Catholic, as many seemed to believe, or would it imply a constant struggle to rediscover the good news of the Biblical message and proclaim it to those inside as well as outside the church? If the latter were the case, Brazilian Presbyterians would find a way to break out of their sterile antagonism toward the Roman Catholic Church, giving thanks for new evangelical tendencies within it, without losing their missionary spirit toward the nominally Catholic masses. It might even find ways, through dialogue, friendship, and example, to encourage renewal within the Roman church and learn from it in the process.

To confront the challenges of the new century positively and constructively would mean following directions which were sharply divergent from those of the past in a number of areas, and the church could not do so without struggle. But if it could accept the necessity for change, it might overcome both its superiority and its inferiority complexes—the belief that it was the holiest group within society even while it felt that it was a despised minority. Only then would it be a truly Reformed church, functioning as leaven in Brazilian society as it had done on many occasions in the past.

Notes

CHAPTER I

[1] Daniel P. Kidder, *Sketches of Residence and Travels in Brazil* (Philadelphia: Soren & Ball, 1845), I, p. 143.

[2] William R. Read, V. M. Monterroso, and H. A. Johnson, *Latin American Church Growth* (Grand Rapids: Eerdmans, 1969), p. 65.

[3] Gilberto Freyre, *The Masters and the Slaves*, tr., Samuel Putnam (New York: Alfred Knopf, 1946), p. 41.

[4] Roger Bastide, "Religion and the Church in Brazil," *Brazil, Portrait of Half a Continent*, eds., T. L. Smith and A. Marchant (New York: Dryden Press, 1951), p. 335.

[5] Thales de Azevedo, "Catholicism in Brazil, a Personal Evaluation," *Thought*, XXVIII (1953), p. 257, quoted in Charles Wagley, *An Introduction to Brazil* (New York: Columbia University Press, 1963), p. 234.

[6] Freyre, *op. cit.*, p. 336.

[7] Bastide, *op. cit.*, pp. 338–9. This is an interesting parallel to the struggle of the vestrys to control the Anglican churches in colonial Virginia.

[8] Pascoal Lacoix, *O Mais Urgente Problema do Brasil, O Problema Sacerdotal e sua Solução* (Vozes: Petropolis, 1936), p. 64.

[9] G. Freyre, *Ordem e Progresso, O Processo de Desintegração das Sociedades Patriarcal e Semi-Patriarcal no Brasil sob o Regime de Trabalho Livre* (Rio de Janeiro: José Olimpio, 1959), II, p. 526. He does not indicate whether or not this ratio represents the total number of priests, or only those who were active, but the latter was probably the case. The problem continues. A recent article said that in 1967 there were 13,000 priests for a population of 87 million, or one for every 6,000 people. But because only 42.2 per cent of the priests work in parishes, the ratio rises to one for every 14,200 Brazilians. When it is considered that approximately half the clergy in Brazil are foreign, the magnitude of the problem can be seen. Conrado Pallenbergo, "Motim na Igreja," *Visão*, São Paulo (May 9, 1969), pp. 53–9.

[10] Kidder, *op. cit.*, II, pp. 399–400.

[11] *Ibid.*, pp. 190-91.

[12] Alceu Amoroso Lima, *A Igreja e o Novo Mundo* (Rio de Janeiro: Typografia Coelho, n.d. [ca. 1943]), p. 24.

[13] Kidder, *op. cit.*, II, p. 227.

[14] Lima, *op. cit.*, p. 20.

[15] Kidder, *op. cit.*, I, p. 246.

[16] Cf. Euclides da Cunha, *Rebellion in the Backlands* (Chicago: University of Chicago Press, 1945), and Maria Isaura de Queiroz, *La Guerre Sainte au Brésil; Le Mouvement Messianique du Contestado*, São Paulo, 1957.

[17] José Carlos Rodrigues, *Religiões Acathólicas no Brasil*, 2nd ed. (Rio de Janeiro: Jornal do Comércio, 1904), pp. 104–07.

[18] Emile G. Leonard, *O Protestantism Brasileiro*, São Paulo, ASTE, 1963, p. 48.

[19] Robert L. McIntire, *Portrait of Half a Century: Fifty Years of Presbyterianism in Brazil (1859–1910)* (Cuernavaca: CIDOC, 1969), p. 94.

[20] Kidder, *op. cit.*, I, p. 298.

[21] Lima, *op. cit.*, pp. 19–20.

[22] Freyre, *Ordem e Progresso*, II, p. 518.

[23] M. Cardozo, The Holy See and the Bishop-Elect of Rio, 1833–1839, *The Americas*, X, no. 1 (July, 1953), p. 16, quoted in J. L. Mecham, *Church and State in Latin America*, rev. ed. (Chapel Hill: University of North Carolina Press, 1966), p. 267.

[24] Leonard, *op. cit.*, p. 38.

[25] Kidder, *op. cit.*, I, pp. 321–27.

[26] David G. Vieira, "Some Protestant Missionary Letters Relating to the Religious Question in Brazil: 1872–1875," *The Americas*, XXIV, no. 4 (April, 1968) pp. 341–42.

[27] Teodoro Magalhães, *A Liberdade dos Cultos no Brasil* (Rio de Janeiro: Oscar Soares, 1919), p. 7.

[28] Janus (J. J. I. von Dollinger et al.) *O Papa e o Concílio, com Introdução de Rui Barbosa*, 3rd ed., I (Rio de Janeiro: Elos, n.d.), p. 312.

[29] Freyre, *Ordem e Progresso*, II, p. 523.

[30] Emílio de Laveleye, *Do Futuro dos Povos Católicos*, Tr., Miguel V. Ferreira (São Paulo: Casa Editora Presbiteriana, 1950).

[31] Vieira, *op. cit.*, pp. 344–46.

[32] *Ibid.*, pp. 351–52.

[33] Freyre, *Ordem e Progesso*, II, p. 515.

[34] Lima, *op. cit.*, p. 27. Article 72, paragraph 3, of the Constitution stated, "All individuals and religious confessions may exercise publicly and freely their worship, associating themselves and acquiring property, for this end."

Paragraph 7 of the same article stated, "No cult or church will receive any official subvention nor will it have relations of dependence or alliance with the government of the Union or the states."

Articles 185 to 188 made it a crime, punishable by up to sixteen months in prison, to attack, threaten, profane, or prevent the realization of the worship of any religious confession.

[35] Cited in João C. de Oliveira Torres, *História das Idéias Religiosas no Brasil* (São Paulo: Editora Grijalbo, 1968), p. 178.

[36] Thales de Azevedo, "Catolicismo no Brasil?" *Vozes*, Petropolis, LXIII, 2 (Feb., 1969), pp. 117–24.

[37] Many such cases are recorded. The *Norte Evangélico*, Feb. 2, 1912, told of one of the first converts in the interior of Pernambuco, father of the first Presbyterian martyr in the North, who was an avid Bible reader before the missionaries arrived.

[38] Aníbal Nora, *Relatório Pastoral, 1908–1912* (Alto Jequitibá, Minas Gerais: Typografia 'O Manhuassu,' n.d.), pp. 19–21.

[39] Maria de Melo Chaves, *Bandeirantes da Fé*, Belo Horizonte, 1947, pp. 48–52.

CHAPTER II

[1] Ashbel G. Simonton, *Journal*, cited in P. S. Landes, *Ashbel Green Simonton, Model Pioneer Missionary of the Presbyterian Church of Brazil* (Fort Worth: Don Cowan Co., 1956), p. 11.

[2] McIntire, *op. cit.*, p. 85.

[3] *Ibid.*, pp. 97–98.

[4] *Ibid.*, p. 301.

[5] Cf. Leonard, *op. cit.*, pp. 27–34.

[6] McIntire, *op. cit.*, p. 105.

[7] Boanerges Ribeiro, *O Padre Protestante* (São Paulo: Casa Editora Presbiteriana, 1950), p. 207.

[8] Quoted in Vicente T. Lessa, *Padre José Manoel da Conceição*, second edition (São Paulo: Cruzeiro do Sul, 1935), p. 89.

[9] José M. da Conceição, "Por Que Ignoramos a Eternidade?" *Ibid.*, p. 75.

[10] Leonard, *op. cit.* He is unduly harsh in his criticisms of the North American missionaries, even to the point of misinterpreting the use of certain terms in Portuguese in order to discover attitudes in the Americans which were not necessarily there. And while Conceição did open up great new possibilities, one cannot suppose that all or even a majority of those who expressed interest in his message would have gone to the point of becoming active Protestants, even if there had been adequate pastoral care. After Conceição had sent Blackford a list of ninety interested persons in Sorocaba in 1866, and after visits to that city by the missionary, the church organized there in 1869 still had only five members.

[11] McIntire, *op. cit.*, p. 164.

[12] *Ibid.*, p. 203.

[13] *Ibid.*, p. 262.

[14] *Ibid.*, p. 274.

[15] *Ibid.*, p. 275.

[16] Emilio Willems, *Followers of the New Faith* (Nashville: Vanderbilt University Press, 1967), p. 11.

[17] Ashbel G. Simonton, "Entrai pela Porta Estreita," *Sermões Escolhidos* (Garanhuns: Norte Evangélico, n.d.), pp. 12–14.

[18] Lessa, *Annaes da 1ª Egreja Presbyteriana de São Paulo* (São Paulo: 1938), p. 289.

[19] McIntire, *op. cit.*, p. 247. The census for 1901 would report 84 per cent illiteracy. McIntire, p. 187.

[20] Leonard, *op. cit.*, pp. 95–100.

[21] Júlio A. Ferreira, *História de Igreja Presbiteriana do Brasil*, I (São Paulo: Casa Editora Presbiteriana, 1959), pp. 178–79.

[22] Leonard notes that the cornerstone of the permanent building of the *'Escola Americana'* in São Paulo was laid on July 4, 1885, the date chosen by Rui Barbosa, who was invited to speak on the occasion. Later, when Pereira succeeded in bringing the seminary to São Paulo, it opened for classes on Jan. 25, 1895, the anniversary of the founding of the city. "Paulistanism against Americanism," he observes. Leonard, *op. cit.*, pp. 135, 143.

[23] McIntire, *op. cit.*, p. 321.

[24] Charles M. Brown, "A History of the Presbyterian Church, USA, in Brazil" (unpublished Ph.D. dissertation, Ohio State University, 1947), pp. 123–124.

[25] Leonard, *op. cit.*, p. 143.

[26] *Ibid.*, p. 144.

[27] *Ibid.*, pp. 152–53.

[28] *Ibid.*, p. 152.

[29] *Annual Report of the Board of Foreign Missions of the Presbyterian Church in the USA* (New York: 1910), p. 398. At the same time the Independent Church had fourteen ministers, sixty churches and preaching points, and approximately five thousand communicants.

CHAPTER III

[1] The first *Annuário Estatístico do Brasil*, published in 1927, gave a total of 103,365 Protestants in the country in 1912. The statistics, probably incomplete, listed 72,146 Lutherans, 3,713 Anglicans, 12,341 Presbyterians (including Independentes), 8,691 Baptists, 3,709 Methodists, 1,384 Evangelicals (Congregationalists), 971 Episcopalians, and 410 Christians. The Lutherans and Anglicans were not missionary either in origin or program. T. L. Smith, *Brazil: People and Institutions*, Baton Rouge, Louisiana State University Press, 1946, p. 223.

Official statistics for the Presbyterian Church of Brazil showed 10,588 communicant members in 1911. *O Puritano*, Jan. 18, 1912.

[2] *Revista das Missões Nacionaes*, April, 1910; hereafter referred to as *RMN*. The term Evangelical is preferred to Protestant by most non-Roman churches in Brazil.

[3] *Actas da Assembléia Geral da Egreja Presbiteriana do Brasil*, 1910, p. 43, hereafter referred to as *Actas da A.G.*

[4] *RMN*, Nov., 1919.

[5] In 1905 when the seminary, with only one professor, asked the New York Board to cede a missionary to the institution, Waddell wrote Speer that it did not need a second man "anymore than a cat needed two tails." "Board Letters of the Presbyterian Church in the United States of America," XIX, March 1, 1905. Presbyterian Historical Society, Philadelphia (Microfilm), hereafter referred to as "Board Letters."

[6] *Ibid.*, XXII, Feb. 6, 1908, Porter to Speer.

7 *Ibid.*, June 6, 1908, Porter to Speer. Cf. other letters of Porter to Speer, April 10 and April 28, 1908, and Lennington to Speer, Feb. 22, 1909, *ibid.*

8 R. F. Lennington, "Annual Personal Report," 1912.

9 "Minutes," SBM, 1914, p. 142.

10 *RMN*, Sept. 1915.

11 The seminary curriculum included psychology, ethics, history of philosophy, Greek, Hebrew, hermeneutics, textual criticism, introduction to Old Testament, introduction to New Testament, archeology, sacred geography, exegesis of Old and New Testament books including the Psalms, the Gospels, and Hebrews; Bible history, church history, history of doctrine, homiletics, pastoral theology, ecclesiology, and two years of systematic theology. *RMN*, Oct. 1910.

12 *Christian Work in Latin America, Reports of the Commissions and Discussions, Congress on Christian Work in Latin America, Panama, February, 1916*, I, New York, Missionary Education Movement, 1917, p. 455, hereafter referred to as Christian Work in Latin America.

13 *RMN*, July, 1913.

14 *O Puritano*, Dec. 30, 1915.

15 *Norte Evangélico*, July 21, 1916, hereafter referred to as *NE*.

16 *Actas da A.G.*, 1910, p. 8.

17 "Actas do Presbytério Bahia-Sergipe," Nov., 1913, *RMN*, Feb., 1914.

18 *Actas da A.G.*, 1915, p. 15.

19 "Minutes," CBM, 1903, p. 9.

20 "Board Letters," XXIV, March 13, 1909. Waddell to Speer.

21 Porter, "Annual Personal Report," 1915.

22 McIntire, *op. cit.*, p. 293.

23 Ferreira, *op. cit.*, I, pp. 401–2.

24 Porter, *op. cit.*, 1911.

25 *O Puritano*, Feb. 9, 1911.

26 *Ibid.*, Feb. 1, 1912.

27 Cf. the articles by Jerônimo Gueiros, *RMN*, Nov., 1912; Benjamin Marinho, *NE*, Aug. 16, 1912; and Antônio Almeida, *ibid.*, Jan. 3, 1913.

28 "Actas, Presbytério de Pernambuco," *RMN*, Feb., 1913.

29 A. Almeida, "Os Dois Seminários," *NE*, Jan. 3, 1913.

30 A Presbyterian couple in Belém named their son, "Scofield." *NE*, Feb. 29, 1916. The paper also published a translation of the notes from the Scofield Reference Bible on Mt. 24:3, 16; Dan. 9:24–27; Romans 11:5; and Rev. 7:14.

31 *O Puritano*, May 13, 1915.

32 *Ibid.*, May 17, 1917.

33 *Ibid.*, Oct. 18, 1917.

34 *Ibid.*, May 13, 1915.

35 *Ibid.*, Sept. 20, 1913.

36 "Minutes," SBM, 1916, pp. 5, 25.

37 Smith, *Brazil: People and Institutions*, pp. 145, 152.

38 Willems, *op. cit.*, p. 28.

39 Ferreira, *op. cit.*, I, p. 347.

40 *O Puritano*, Dec. 20, 1930.

41 *Ibid.*, Feb. 19, 1912; July 24, 1913.

42 *Ibid.*, Feb. 6, 1913.

43 *Ibid.*, May 5, 1910; May 25, 1911; Oct. 26, 1911.

44 Nora, *op. cit.*, p. 22.

45 *O Puritano*, April 30, 1914.

46 *RMN*, July, 1914.

47 Letter to the author from the Reverend Apolinário Sathler, Oct. 27, 1969. Sathler was the son-in-law of Cabral and served as pastor in the area for many years.

48 By 1940 the state of São Paulo, with a population of 7,239,711, would have grown over fivefold since 1890. Smith, *Brazil: People and Institutions*, pp. 138, 143.

The city of São Paulo grew from 239,820 in 1900 to 3,307,163, in 1960. Instituto Brasileiro de Geografia e Estatística, *Censo Demográfico, Sinópse Preliminar* (Rio de Janeiro: Imprensa Nacional, 1962), pp. 4–5.

49 Cf. W. R. Read, *New Patterns of Church Growth in Brazil* (Grand Rapids: Eerdmans, 1965), pp. 22–23.

50 Porter, *op. cit.*, 1913.

51 Descalvado, one of the towns occupied at this time by the WBM in preference to São Paulo, eventually declined so much that its church was closed as the coffee cycle moved on.

52 Porter, *op. cit.*, 1912.

53 C. A. Carriel, "Annual Personal Report," 1914.

54 "Minutes," SBM, 1915, p. 271; 1916, p. 5.

55 *Ibid.*, 1917, p. 2.

56 *Ibid.*, p. 44, 45. The plan was never carried out.

57 Ferreira, *op. cit.*, II, p. 122.

58 *O Puritano*, Aug. 13, 1914.

59 *Ibid.*, March 2, 1916.

60 *RMN*, Sept., 1921.

61 J. E. Bear, Jr., *Mission to Brazil*, Nashville, Board of World Missions, PCUS, 1961, p. 52.

62 *Ibid.*, p. 56.

63 Smith, *Brazil: People and Institutions*, pp. 139–40.

64 "Board Letters," XXV, March 13, 1909, Waddell to Speer.

65 *O Puritano*, June 22, 1911.

66 "Minutes," CBM, 1912, pp. 56–57.

67 The population of Mato Grosso in 1900 was 118,025, and in 1920 it was 246,612. The figures for Goiás for the same years were 255,284, and 511,919. Smith, *Brazil: People and Institutions*, p. 138.

68 Instituto Brasileiro de Geografia e Estatística, *op. cit.*, pp. 2–3.

CHAPTER IV

1 *Livro de Ordem da Egreja Presbyteriana do Brasil*, edição revista (São Paulo: Irmãos Ferraz, 1924), pp. 6–8.

2 Kyle, one of the most perceptive missionaries, reported that he tried to

establish contact with the local priest for over sixteen years, but that the man refused to speak to him. He added, "It must not be assumed that every missionary goes out with brick in hand to attack the Roman Catholic Church. We go to preach the Gospel. When the people have the Gospel, it is no use to tell them about the evils of the Roman Catholic Church. They know better than we do. They can tell you more about the priests than you want to know." Foreign Missions Conference of North America, *Conference on Missions in Latin America, New York, 1913* (Lebanon, Pa.: Sowers Printing Co., n.d.), pp. 100–01.

3 Leonard, *op. cit.*, pp. 119–20.

4 *Ibid.*, p. 108; *O Puritano*, July 12, 1917.

5 Cf. *O Puritano*, Aug. 28, 1914.

6 George W. Butler, "High Water Mark in Canhotinho," *Missionary Survey*, IV, 6 (June, 1915), p. 459.

7 Cf. *NE*, June 21, 1916, in which Natanael Cortez told of the scattering of the congregations in Iguatu and Senador Pompeu, Ceará because of the persecution and added that Padre Cícero, the priest and political chief of Juazeiro, had hired killers to eliminate Protestants. Cf. also H. S. Allyn, "The Dynamiting of the School at Bom Sucesso," *Missionary Survey*, IV, 7 (July, 1915), pp. 504–05.

8 *NE*, Oct. 6, 1916.

9 *O Puritano*, Feb. 24, 1910.

10 *NE*, Nov. 1, 1912; Juventino Marinho, "Memorias," *NE*, Dec. 1956.

11 Jeffrey L. Klaiber, "Pentecostal Breakthrough," *America*, CXXII, 4 (Jan. 31, 1970), p. 99.

12 *O Puritano*, Feb. 23, 1911.

13 *RMN*, Dec. 1915.

14 *O Puritano*, Sept. 15, 1910.

15 *Ibid.*, July 11, 1912.

16 *Ibid.*

17 *Ibid.*, Jan. 14, 1915.

18 *NE*, July 7, 1916.

19 *Ibid.*, July 14, 1912.

20 *Pastoral Collectiva dos Senhores Arcebispos e Bispos das Provincias Ecclesiásticas de São Sebastião do Rio de Janeiro, Marianna, São Paulo, Cuyabá, e Porto Alegre* (Rio de Janeiro: Martins de Araujo, 1915), p. xxxiv.

21 *O Puritano*, Apr. 22, 1917.

22 F. Lennington, "Annual Personal Report," 1914.

23 *O Puritano*, Dec. 20, 1917. Cf. *ibid.*, Feb. 2, 1915; Feb. 11, 1915.

24 *Confissão de Fé e Catecismo maior da Igreja Presbiteriana do Brasil*, 2ª edição (São Paulo: Casa Editora Presbiteriana, 1955), p. 60.

25 SBM, "General Report," 1914.

26 Charles Hodge, "The General Assembly," *Biblical Repertory and Princeton Review*, XVII, no. III (1845), pp. 428–471.

27 *Minutes of the General Assembly of the Presbyterian Church in the USA*, 1875, N.S. III (New York: Presbyterian Board of Publication, 1875), p. 514.

28 Landes, *op. cit.*, pp. 39–41.

29 *Actas do Synodo*, 1891, pp. 17–18.
30 *O Puritano*, June 26, 1915.
31 *RMN*, Jan., 1915. Cf. *O Puritano*, Sept. 2 and Oct. 25, 1915.
32 *O Puritano*, July 15, 1915.
33 *Ibid.*
34 *RMN*, Sept., 1915.
35 *O Puritano*, Nov. 11, 1915.
36 *Ibid.*, Oct. 21, 1915.
37 *Ibid.*, Sept. 23 and Oct. 21, 1915.
38 *Ibid.*, Jan. 21, 1915.
39 *NE*, Jan. 8, 1916; *O Puritano*, Jan. 27, 1916.
40 *Actas da A. G.*, 1916, pp. 11–13.
41 *NE*, March 23, 1916.
42 Information from the Solomão Ferraz file, historical archives of the Presbyterian Church of Brazil, Campinas, hereafter referred to as Campinas archives.
43 Leonard, *op. cit.*, p. 129.
44 *NE*, Feb. 19, 1916.
45 *O Puritano*, July 6, 1911; Nov. 26, 1912.
46 *Ibid.*, March 23, 1911.
47 *Actas do Synodo*, 1888, p. 11.
48 Leonard, *op. cit.*, pp. 129, 130.
49 *RMN*, May, 1913.
50 *Ibid.*, June, 1913.
51 *O Puritano*, July 28, 1910.
52 *Actas da A. G.*, 1915, p. 52.
53 *Ibid.*
54 Leonard, *op. cit.*, p. 73.
55 *O Puritano*, Aug. 6, 1912.
56 *Ibid.*, Nov. 24, 1910.
57 "Actas da Assembléia Geral de 1912," *RMN*, Feb. 1912.
58 Read, Monterroso, and Johnson, *op. cit.*, pp. 65, 66, say that the Congregação Cristã no Brasil has 500,000 communicant members and the Assembléia de Deus, 1,400,000, out of a total of 3,257,501 in all of Brazil's Protestant churches.
59 *O Puritano*, Feb. 1, 1912.
60 Emílio Conde, *História das Assembléias de Deus no Brasil*, Rio de Janeiro, 1960, pp. 12–25.
61 *NE*, Feb. 14, 1913.
62 *O Puritano*, Sept. 9, 1915.
63 *NE*, Feb. 23, 1912; Aug. 29, 1913.
64 *O Puritano*, July 7, 1915.
65 J. A. Ferreira, *Galeria Evangélica: Biografias de Pastores Presbiterianos que Trabalharam no Brasil* (São Paulo: Casa Editora Presbiteriana, 1952), pp. 153–55.
66 *Actas do Synodo*, 1907, pp. 20, 37.
67 *O Puritano*, Nov. 2, 1911.

[68] Ferreira, *História*, II, p. 132.

[69] *O Puritano*, Nov. 9, 1915.

[70] *RMN*, Dec., 1915.

[71] *O Puritano*, Oct. 28, 1915.

[72] *Actas da A. G.*, 1916, p. 12.

[73] *O Estandarte*, Feb. 24, 1915, cited in *RMN*, Nov., 1915.

[74] *Actas da A. G.*, 1916, p. 46. An anonymous writer said that Pereira returned from Panama "with a full desire to heal the breach that had been caused by the schism. His advances in this sense were received in a most ungenerous manner. An unfortunate knowledge of history permitted some of his opponents to hail them with the cry, 'Eduardo comes to Canossa,' which put an end to the effort on his part." "A History of the Brazil Mission," n.d., [ca. 1934], mimeographed, WBM archives, Patricinio, Minas Gerais.

[75] *O Estandarte*, Feb. 24, 1916.

[76] "Actas do Synodo da Igreja Presbyteriana Independente," *O Estandarte*, Jan. 25, 1917.

[77] *O Puritano*, July 1, 1915.

[78] Brown, *op. cit.*, p. 92.

[79] S. H. Chester, Secretary of the Nashville Committee, writing to Erasmo Braga on Dec. 12, 1916, said: "By referring to the Manual of the Executive Committee . . . you will see that an arrangement by which our missionaries retain their ecclesiastical connection with the presbyteries at home, is regarded as the normal one, and that it is only by a special permission granted by the missionary's own presbytery that he can transfer to a presbytery in the field." *Appêndices às Actas da A. G.*, 1917, p. 7.

[80] *Actas do Synodo*, 1888, p. 6.

[81] Brown, *op. cit.*, p. 119.

[82] Although it was the policy of the PCUS for the missionaries to leave the presbyteries, they were less eager to do so than their PCUSA counterparts. Alva Hardie, of the WBM, was elected Moderator of the General Assembly of the Presbyterian Church of Brazil in 1922, and in 1926 there were still seven missionaries listed on the rolls of the Brazilian presbyteries, five of whom were from the PCUS. *O Puritano*, May 1, 1926.

[83] A study of the biographical data of twenty-six missionaries who went to Brazil from the PCUSA from 1859 to 1930 showed that all but two were from small towns or rural areas, mostly from western Pennsylvania and the Mid-West. CBM biographical files, typed manuscript, CBM archives, São Paulo.

[84] One pioneer, recommending the establishment of a school in Goiás, wrote, "The school should be out of town and away from influences opposing the Gospel." F. F. Graham, "Annual Personal Report," 1914.

[85] Porter, "Annual Personal Report," 1915.

[86] In asking the Board for more evangelists in 1924, the SBM said they "should have the physique and spirit of the old time circuit riders who struggled with human nature along the border and crowded our frontier into the Pacific Ocean." "Minutes," SBM, 1924, pp. 173–74.

It is ironic that board and mission personnel were probably influenced, directly or indirectly, by F. J. Turner's thesis on the role of the frontier in American history. The thesis, which dominated much of American historical studies for three decades after it was expounded in 1893, has been seriously challenged by contemporary scholars. Cf. George R. Taylor (ed.), *The Turner Thesis Concerning the Role of the Frontier in American History* (Boston: D. C. Heath & Co., 1949).

87 C. Viana Moog, *Bandeirantes and Pioneers*, tr. by L. L. Barrett (New York: George Braziller, 1964), p. 92.

88 *Annual Report, Board of Foreign Missions of the Presbyterian Church in the USA*, 1890, pp. 224–25.

89 Brown, *op. cit.*, p. 129.

90 "Minutes," SBM, 1913, p. 195.

91 "Minutes," Executive Committee of the Brazil Mission, Dec., 1913, p. 9.

92 "Board Letters," XXIII, Feb. 22, 1909, Lennington to Speer. Cf. *Ibid.*, XXII, June 6, 1908, Porter to Speer.

93 *RMN*, Dec., 1912.

94 Edward Lane said the plan was forced on the WBM. Cf. his comments on J. R. Woodson, "History of the West Brazil Mission," typed manuscript, WBM archives, Patricinio, Minas Gerais.

95 Cf. "Board Letters," XXV, Dec. 1, 1897, Waddell to Ellinwood, and Oct. 9, 1901, Ellinwood to the CBM.

There are indications that the request in 1892 that the missionaries withdraw from the presbyteries was made by Waddell. Cf. A. C. Salley, "Account of the Brazil Plan," typed manuscript, CBM archives, São Paulo.

96 "Minutes," CBM, 1903, p. 4.

97 "Board Letters," XXI, May 1, 1907, Waddell to Speer.

98 "Minutes," SBM, 1912, pp. 165, 166. *O Puritano*, Jan. 29, 1914.

99 *RMN*, Nov., 1912.

100 "Minutes," SBM, 1913, p. 190.

101 "Minutes," Executive Committee of the Brazil Mission, Dec., 1913, p. 12.

102 *RMN*, July, 1914.

103 *O Puritano*, Jan. 29, 1914.

104 "Minutes," SBM, 1915, p. 255.

105 The term originally used in the motion was *pesar*. It was changed to *sentimentos*. *Actas da A. G.*, 1915, pp. 23–24.

106 *Ibid.*, p. 25.

107 *Ibid.*, 1916, p. 22ff. The question arises as to the origin of this policy. There is no evidence of initiatives in this direction by Brazilian churchmen until well after the movement toward separation had been started by the CBM and followed by the SBM. In 1912 the latter spoke of "the definite policy of the Board and the Mission looking to the ultimate separation of the Mission from the Brazilian Church." "Minutes," SBM, 1912, p. 165.

When a copy of the 1916 resolution was sent to missionaries by the Stated Clerk of the Brazilian church an accompanying letter said, "Under the influence of your own counsel, and obeying instructions which came forth from the mission boards, it seemed good to the Supreme Council of your church in this country to adopt the principles which will regulate harmonious action of the Brazilian Church with the mother churches." E. Braga, *Mensagem ao "Board of Foreign Missions of the Presbyterian Church in the USA," ao "Executive Committee of Foreign Missions of the Presbyterian Church in the US," e aos missionários enviados ao Brazil pelas mencionadas corporações,* 1916, p. 8.

However, it is clear that the withdrawal of the missionaries from the Brazilian Church did not represent a general policy of the New York Board. On the contrary, it had refused to permit the step as late as 1902, and Speer's letter to the Brazilian Church after the 1916 resolution stated: "The Board continues to leave the determination of the question to the judgement and desires of the national churches and of the missionaries on the field." At the same time he said that the Presbytery of Allahabad, India, had asked that the missionaries remain as members, and added that in both cases, the Board respected the decision of the national church. *Appéndices às Actas da A.G.,* 1917, pp. 5–6.

Thus it is indisputable that the initiative in formulating the Brazil Plan and pressure for its acceptance came from the field, not from New York. Waddell's influence on Speer was undoubtedly the greatest factor in leading the Board to abandon its insistence that the missionaries remain in the presbyteries.

[108] *Actas de A.G.,* 1917, pp. 11–16. Cf. Appendix C for full text.

[109] *NE,* Dec. 5, 1916; Dec. 13, 1916.

[110] *Ibid.,* Dec. 5, 1916.

[111] *Appéndices às Actas da A.G.,* 1917, pp. 18, 19.

The entire motion is worth quoting: "Considering that the whole plan of removal of the missionaries from our judicatories was adopted with no previous notice to the presbyteries, without consulting them, and with imperfect representation on their part in an assembly composed of a small number of ministers, this presbytery having been represented by only one member who for over twenty years has been absent from our territory;

Considering that especially here in the North the move is unnecessary, bringing no advantage, but on the contrary comes to perturb our happy relations and the progress of the evangelical work;

Considering that to us, Brazilian ministers, it does not seem consistent with the spirit of the gospel to dismiss and eliminate from our judicatories, those who are our fathers in the faith, our educators, our guides, and our intimate and inseparable friends, and this without any reason which might justify such an act;

We. . . . Brazilian ministers and elders, members of this presbytery, propose that the Presbytery of Pernambuco request that the General Assembly either:

(1) Reconsider its resolution of 1916 regarding the relations of the missionaries and the national judicatories, permitting that those who are members of presbyteries remain where missionaries and natives mutually desire it;

or (2) That the Presbytery of Pernambuco be excepted from the plan because of its special circumstances;

or (3) That if this plan is adopted as the model for the future, this presbytery be allowed to refrain from putting it into effect as long as present conditions continue."

[112] It is of interest to note that the missionaries remained as members of the presbyteries in the Korean Church and do so still. That church has long been considered a model of self-support, despite the extreme poverty of the country.

[113] Cf. Joseph R. Woody, "The Brazil Plan of Mission-Church Relations: An Experience in Partnership" (Unpub. Th. M. thesis, Union Theological Seminary, Richmond, Va., 1961); Edward Lane, "History of the West Brazil Mission," typed manuscript, WBM archives, Patrocínio, Minas Gerais; *Christian Work in South America*, II, New York, Revell, 1925, pp. 258ff, 292.

[114] John A. Mackay, who served for a time as Secretary for Latin America for the New York Board, said the plan "brought disaster to the development of the Presbyterian Church of Brazil and to creative relations between Brazilian churchmen and American missionaries." Letter to the author, Aug. 26, 1969.

[115] *World Missionary Conference, 1910, Report of Commission II, The Church in the Mission Field* (London: Revell, n.d.), p. 27.

[116] *RMN*, July, 1914.

[117] Erasmo Braga, "The Future of the Church in Latin America," handwritten manuscript, n.d. [ca. 1928], Braga file, Campinas archives.

[118] Smith, Brazil, *People and Institutions*, pp. 147–49. Elsewhere Smith wrote that "the rush of people from rural districts to urban centers which took place during the second quarter of the twentieth century and which continues at a more accelerated pace during the third quarter, may well be considered the most important current demographic fact in Latin America." T. L. Smith, *Latin-American Population Studies* (Gainesville: University of Florida Press, 1961), p. 53.

[119] Instituto Brasileiro de Geografia e Estatística, *Culto Protestante no Brasil, 1960*, Departamento da Imprensa Nacional, 1963, p. 26.

[120] "Minutes," WBM, 1931, p. 55.

[121] "Minutes," Brazil Council, Dec., 1928, p. 4.

[122] "Minutes," SBM, 1927, p. 238.

[123] *O Puritano*, May 22, 1926.

[124] *Ibid.*, June 25, 1945.

[125] W. R. Hogg, *Ecumenical Foundations* (New York, Harper & Brothers, 1952), pp. 120, 131–32.

The importance of Edinburgh in the modern ecumenical movement is shown by Hogg when he says, "As a result of Edinburgh's far-reaching influence, it has become customary to speak of 1910 as the beginning of modern missionary cooperation, indeed, of the Ecumenical movement itself—a largely justifiable argument." *Ibid.*, p. 98.

[126] *Actas da A.G.*, 1910, p. 44. Cf. also the protest of the SBM, "Minutes," SBM, 1910, p. 70.

[127] *O Puritano*, July 2, 1910.

[128] Hogg, *op. cit.*, p. 132.

[129] *RMN*, June, 1915. This was the first meeting of the Evangelical Al-

liance since 1903 and was apparently called to define the Brazilian position on this question.

130 *Ibid.*

131 *Christian Work in Latin America,* I, p. 16.

For an account of missionary fears on the question, cf. Clara Gammon, *Assim Brilha a Luz, a Vida de Samuel Gammon,* tradução de Jorge Goulart (Lavras: Imprensa Gammon, 1959), p. 187.

132 *Christian Work in Latin America,* I, p. 19.

133 *O Puritano,* May 10, 1916.

134 Erasmo Braga, *Panamericanismo, Aspecto Religioso* (New York: Missionary Education Movement, 1917), p. 88.

135 John Fox, "Christian Unity, Church Unity, and the Panama Congress," *Princeton Theological Review,* XIV, no. 4 (Oct., 1916), pp. 550.

136 The paper, with an expanded treatment of the problem, was included in E. C. Pereira, *O Problema Religioso da America Latina* (São Paulo: Imprensa Editora Brasileira, 1920).

137 Fox, *op. cit.,* p. 551.

138 Harlan Beach, *Renaissant Latin America,* New York, Missionary Education Movement, 1916, pp. 198, 199. Braga wrote, "There prevails among Latin American Evangelicals the notion that the union of Romanism and Evangelicalism is possible only with the abandonment of the apostolic message on the part of Protestantism, or with the 'deromanization' of Roman Catholicism." Braga, *Panamericanismo,* p. 163n.

139 Beach, *op. cit.,* pp. 198–99.

140 *Christian Work in Latin America,* III, pp. 65–66.

141 *Ibid.,* pp. 79–82.

142 *Ibid.,* pp. 36–37.

143 Francisco de Souza, (ed.), *Congresso Regional da Obra Cristã na América Latina; Recomendações, Actas, e Theses do Congresso Regional, Rio, 14–18 de Abril de 1916* (Rio de Janeiro: Casa Editora Batista, 1917).

144 Braga, *Panamericanismo,* pp. 174–75.

145 Pereira, *op. cit.,* pp. 200–01.

146 *O Puritano,* April 27, 1916.

147 Pereira, *op. cit.,* p. 413.

148 *O Puritano,* June 27, Aug. 17, 1916

CHAPTER V

1 Cf. *O Puritano,* June 20, 1920; NE, Jan. 26, Dec. 13, 1926.

2 V. F. Araujo, *Seitas Protestantes em Pernambuco* (Recife: Typographia do Jornal do Recife, 1906), p. XI.

3 A non-Protestant merchant in Corumbá, Mato Grosso, told the writer that he did not require a cosigner for an active Protestant who bought an article on time, although he did for Roman Catholics.

4 Bear, *op. cit.,* p. 37.

5 A. Reis, *As Sete Palavras de Christo na Cruz* (Rio de Janeiro: O Puritano, 1917).

6 *O Puritano,* Oct. 29, 1914.

7 *Ibid.*, July 18, 1912.

8 *Ibid.*, Jan. 25, 1937. For an extensive treatment of the subject cf. Carl J.Hahn, "Evangelical Worship in Brazil, its Origins and Development," Unpublished doctoral dissertation, University of Edinburgh, 1970.

9 *Ibid.*, Dec. 20, 1917.

10 *NE*, Oct. 6, 1916. Cf. D. Ribeiro, "As Causas Principais da Reforma," *O Puritano*, Oct. 31, 1917 which places justification by works as the last in a list of fourteen Roman Catholic "errors," and E. C. Pereira, *O Problema Religioso da América Latina*, pp. 404–415, who left out the question of justification in his criticism of Roman Catholicism.

11 *Actas da A.G.*, 1918, p. 26.

12 *NE*, June 20, 1922.

13 This is one of the themes of the excellent novel by Josué Montello, *Os Degraus do Paraíso*, São Paulo, Martins Editora, 1965. Montello, a member of the Brazilian Academy of Letters, is the son of a deacon in the Independent Presbyterian Church. In one of the scenes of the book, the pastor says to the leading figure, a devout Catholic who has had her faith shaken, "Now I ask you, can a Church which disobeys the Word of God be the Church of Christ? No!, no!, and no! The true Church is that which follows rigorously all that is found in this Holy Book." pp. 137–38.

14 C. Gammon, *op. cit.*, p. 198.

15 *O Puritano*, March 4, 1915.

16 The writer had a student in seminary who, illiterate at the age of twenty, learned to read after his conversion, using the Bible as his primer.

17 *O Puritano*, Nov. 26, 1914.

18 *RMN*, Nov., 1915; Jan. 1916.

19 *O Puritano*, Aug. 17, 1916. Cf. *Minutes of the General Assembly of the PCUSA*, 1916, pp. 131–32.

20 Cf. *O Calix Eucharístico* (Rio de Janeiro: O Puritano, 1913).

21 *NE*, Oct. 3, 1917.

22 *O Puritano*, June 21, July 5, 1917.

23 *NE*, March 22, 1913.

24 Nora, *op. cit.*, pp. 6, 7. The Synod of 1900 had requested that judicatories do all in their power to lead church members to refrain from the use, sale, and manufacture of alcoholic beverages, except as medicine. *RMN*, May, 1920.

25 *O Puritano*, March 2, 1911.

26 *Ibid.*, April 3, 1913.

27 Nora, *op. cit.*, pp. 24–25.

28 *O Puritano*, Feb. 23, 1911; June 19, 1913; *RMN*, June, 1913.

29 *O Puritano*, Nov. 29, 1917.

30 *NE*, Oct. 24, 1913.

31 *O Puritano*, July 9, 1914.

32 *Actas da A.G.*, 1910, p. 45; 1912, pp. 20–21; 1915, p. 23.

33 *O Puritano*, March 29, 1917. The same article quoted a Rio newspaper as saying that the statue of St. Anthony in the church in Ouro Preto, Minas Gerais, still received an annual stipend from the federal government.

34 *Ibid.*, July 4, 1912.

35 *NE*, Oct. 10, 1913.

36 *O Puritano*, April 22, 1915.

37 *NE*, Aug. 4, 1916; *O Puritano*, April 24, 1910, Nov. 20, 1913.

38 Nora, *op. cit.*, pp. 13–15.

39 Melo, *op. cit.*, pp. 72–86.

40 *Ibid.*, pp. 191–92.

41 A. Nora, *Sermões Pequenos, Primeira Série*, 1932, p. 92.

42 Izaltina Banks Leite, *Willis Roberto Banks, O Pioneiro da Evangeli-zação do Litoral Sul-Paulista*, 2ª ed. (São Paulo: n.p., 1963), pp. 25–26.

43 *Actas da A.G.*, 1910, pp. 20–22.

44 *O Puritano*, Oct. 12, 1912; Feb. 19, 1914.

45 Á. Reis, *As Sete Palavras de Christo na Cruz*, pp. 48–49. The motto on the Brazilian flag is "Order and Progress."

46 Cf. *Actas da A.G.*, 1912, p. 16; *RMN*, Oct., 1910, Dec., 1912, Nov., 1914.

47 *O Puritano*, June 10, 1909; May 11, 1911.

48 A. A. Lino da Costa, *Conferencias Religiosas*, Rio de Janeiro, 1913, pp. 12–20.

49 *Christian Work in Latin America*, I, p. 346.

50 *NE*, March 22, 1917.

51 *O Puritano*, Dec. 4, 1913.

52 *NE*, Dec. 15, 1916.

53 *O Puritano*, Nov. 15, 1917.

54 Costa, *op. cit.*, p. 19.

55 *O Puritano*, April 22, 1915.

56 Melo, *op. cit.*, pp. 110–11.

57 *Ibid.*, pp. 111–15.

58 E. Willems, *Cunha, Tradição e Transição em uma Cultura Rural do Brasil*, p. 70, cited in T. H. Maurer, Jr., "Protestantismo e Cultura Brasileira," *O Estandarte*, Dec., 1954. An example of the interest in education among Presbyterians was seen in 1939 when twenty-four young people from the Curitiba church finished *ginásio* (secondary school), while sixteen were graduated from other institutions, including medical school. The church probably had no more than two hundred members. *O Puritano*, March 25, 1940.

59 *NE*, Oct. 11, 1912. A retired missionary told of a grandmother and ex-slave who was converted. When the owners of the *fazenda* where she lived warned her not to become a Protestant, she replied, "I've lived on this place my whole life and all I've ever been taught is the hoe. Now I'm learning to read so I can sing hymns and read my Bible." K. Hardie, *On Eagles' Wings*, (Richmond: William Byrd Press, n.d.), p. 80.

60 "Minutes," SBM, Jan., 1910, pp. 79–82; Nov., 1913, pp. 197–98.

61 *Actas da A.G.*, 1915, p. 76.

62 R. Telles, "Protestantismo e Educação no Brasil," *O Puritano*, May 10, 1953.

63 *Christian Work in Latin America*, I, p. 454.

[64] *Appêndices às Actas da A.G.*, 1924, pp. 109–10.

[65] *Christian Work in Latin America*, I, p. 437.

[66] Personal interview with J. N. Wright, former director of the institution, Feb. 15, 1970.

[67] *Christian Work in Latin America*, I, p. 491.

[68] *NE*, Nov. 10, 1916; Dec., 1956.

[69] *Ibid.*, Jan. 17, 1913.

[70] Melo, *op. cit.*, pp. 180–81.

[71] Maurer, *op. cit.*, p. 41.

[72] Willems found the same strong interest in education among Presbyterians and Methodists in the rural communities he studied. But he found that Pentecostals, although they improved the quality of their houses significantly over those of non-Protestants in the same community, showed no special interest in education. Willems, *Followers of the New Faith*, pp. 181–89.

[73] F. R. Teixeira, *Coronel Joaquim Ribeiro, Político, Filântropo, Educador* (Campinas: n.p., 1965), pp. 55–56.

[74] Melo, *op. cit.*, p. 194.

[75] *O Puritano*, July 1, 1915.

[76] The future Cardinal Archbishop of São Paulo called it the "fruit of a bad tree," and "a disguised Protestant movement." Agnelo Rossi, *Directório Protestante no Brasil* (Campinas: Tipografia Paulista, 1938), pp. 37–38. A Catholic paper in João Pessoa accused it of attempting to denationalize Brazil and make Protestants and Communists of those whom it taught to read. *O Puritano*, June 25, 1941.

[77] *O Puritano*, June 25, 1943; Oct. 7, 1946.

[78] Leite, *op. cit.*, pp. 26–28.

[79] Willems, *Followers of the New Faith*, pp. 180–86.

[80] *Ibid.*, p. 189.

[81] Álvaro Reis cited the case of J. C. Braga, a shoemaker, when converted, who became a pastor and professor. His children all completed university courses, one becoming a pastor, seminary professor, and member of the Brazilian Academy of Letters; another, a physician; one, a journalist; another an engineer. *O Puritano*, July 8, 1915.

[82] *Livro de Ordem, Egreja Presbyteriana do Brasil*, 1924, p. 52.

[83] In 1910 there were forty-two pastors for ninety-one churches; in 1932, 120 pastors for 250 churches plus many more unorganized *congregações*. E. Braga and K. Grubb, *The Republic of Brazil, A Survey of the Religious Situation* (London: World Dominion Press, 1932), p. 86.

[84] *O Puritano*, March 28; Aug. 29, 1912.

[85] *NE*, Oct. 24, 1913.

[86] *Constituição da Igreja Cristã Presbiteriana do Brasil* (Rio de Janeiro: O Puritano, 1938), p. 50.

[87] *RMN*, April, 1914.

[88] *O Puritano*, Aug. 21, 1913. The Campos church was established by Blackford in 1877 with ten members and had grown to forty-three by 1884. For twelve years it had no active pastor, and most of its members became

Baptists. When Porter went there in 1907 he found that the church building had been sold, even though the city had grown to 40,000. From 1907 to 1928 the church had a total of fourteen pastors, almost none of whom resided there. Finally, in the latter year, Benjamin Cesar began a pastorate there which was destined to be long and fruitful. *O Puritano*, July 4, 1931. In 1960 there were thirty-nine Baptist and ten Presbyterian churches in the city and surrounding rural area. *Culto Protestante no Brasil, 1960*, pp. 44–45.

89 *O Puritano*, Nov. 22, 1923.

90 *NE*, April 14, 1926.

91 A. W. Halsey and G. H. Trull, *Panama to Paraná* (New York: Board of Foreign Missions of the PCUSA, 1916), p. 63.

92 W. W. Sweet, *The Story of Religion in America*, rev. ed. (New York: Harper & Brothers, 1950), pp. 214–15.

93 Cf. J. Kolb, "Annual Personal Report," 1912.

94 *O Puritano*, Dec. 7, 1916.

95 *NE*, May 17, 1912.

96 *O Puritano*, Nov. 14, 1931.

97 *Ibid.*, July 4, 1931.

98 *Ibid.*, May 25, 1936.

99 A missionary noted in 1910 that after fifty years of work there were only about half a dozen churches that supported their pastors without outside help. "Minutes," SBM, Jan., 1910, pp. 82–83.

100 *NE*, July 21, 1916.

101 *O Puritano*, March 25, 1936. The Presbytery of Rio declined the services of three ministers who wished to transfer there in 1946. One of them became a Congregationalist and remained in the city. *Ibid.*, April 10, 1946.

102 The *RMN*, Feb., 1915, told of a young pastor who refused to accept any salary from his church but had already organized three of them. The writer had a colleague in Recife who organized five churches while supporting himself as an accountant.

103 *O Puritano*, Nov. 13, 1913.

104 *Ibid.*, Aug. 2, 1913.

105 *Actas da A.G.*, 1910, pp. 11–12.

106 *NE*, July 4, 1913.

107 J. M. Davis, *How the Church Grows in Brazil* (New York: International Missionary Council, 1943), p. 125. Of fifty students in Recife Seminary in 1970, 60 per cent came from towns of less than 5,000 population, and of the other 40 per cent, over half were from the interior. Letter to the writer from Dr. Aúreo Bispo dos Santos, Oct. 16, 1970.

108 It is worth noting, as Davis points out, that very few pastors' sons entered the ministry. Presumably one reason was that it was not a means of social mobility for them. While many remained in the church, they usually entered the liberal professions or teaching. Davis, *op. cit.*, p. 126.

109 In 1959 the pastors of the two largest Presbyterian churches in Rio, First and Copacabana, as well as the pastors of the largest churches in São Paulo, Campinas, Salvador, and Recife, were all from small interior towns or rural areas.

CHAPTER VI

[1] *O Puritano*, Jan. 9, 1919.

[2] Braga and Grubb, *op. cit.*, p. 97.

[3] An extreme example of this was seen in João Pessoa. The *NE*, July 28, 1926, mentioned a visit by the pastor of the Central Church to the "flourishing *congregação*" in the Jaguaribe district. But it was not organized into an independent church until 1965, when a recent seminary graduate became its pastor. Beginning with sixty-five communicants, it doubled its membership in two years.

[4] Braga and Grubb, *op. cit.*, p. 86.

[5] *Christian Work in South America: Official Report of the Congress on Christian Work in South America at Montevideo, Uruguay*, April, 1925, I (New York: Revell, 1925), p. 138.

[6] *O Puritano*, Jan. 20, 1921.

[7] *Ibid.*, July 4, 1931.

[8] *Ibid.*, Feb. 23, 1929.

[9] *Ibid.*, June 6, 1931; April 20, 1932.

[10] *Ibid.*, July 4, 1931.

[11] *Ibid.*, March 20, 1932.

[12] Egreja Presbyteriana Unida, *Annuário Estatístico, 1925–1926* (São Paulo: Typographia Pallas, 1926).

[13] *O Puritano*, Feb. 5, 1920; March 3, 1921.

[14] *Ibid.*, Jan. 8; June 18, 1927.

[15] *Ibid.*, Feb. 20, 1930.

[16] *Ibid.*, June 18; July 2, 1927.

[17] *Appêndice às Actas da A. G.*, 1928, pp. 56–57.

[18] *O Puritano*, Jan. 8, 1927.

[19] Data is insufficient to determine how many of the area's pastors did not go to seminary. But because some names of those ordained did not appear in the published lists of seminary students during the period, it is clear that several received no formal theological study.

[20] Mário Neves, *Meio Século* (São Paulo: Casa Editora Presbiteriana, 1955), pp. 29–30.

[21] *Ibid.*, pp. 33–36.

[22] *O Puritano*, Sept. 30, 1932.

[23] *Ibid.*, Nov. 13, 1924.

[24] *Ibid.*, Oct. 22, 1927.

[25] *NE*, March 15, 1917. The Synod of the North could not function legally, for lack of a quorum, from 1910 to 1917. *Ibid.*, Dec. 12, 1917.

[26] *Actas da A. G.*, 1930.

[27] *O Puritano*, April 3, 1919.

[28] *Ibid.*, March 9, 1929; *NE*, Feb. 2, 1928.

[29] Cícero Siqueira wrote that almost no churches in the North contributed to General Assembly causes in 1922. *NE*, Dec. 11, 1922.

[30] *Ibid.*, April 12, 1921.

[31] *O Puritano*, May 10, 1932.

[32] *NE*, May 6, 1921. Common-law marriages were common in Brazil, especially among the poor.

[33] Bear, *op. cit.*, p. 81.

[34] *Appêndices às Actas da A.G.*, 1930, p. 46.

[35] *NE*, Dec. 29, 1926.

[36] *Ibid.*, Feb. 10, 1930.

[37] *Ibid.*, Feb. 20, 1930.

[38] *Ibid.*, Feb. 10, 1930.

[39] *O Puritano*, April 25, 1931.

[40] *NE*, Jan. 5, 1912.

[41] *Ibid.*, Feb. 10, 1930.

[42] *Appêndices às Actas da A.G.*, 1928, pp. 68–69.

[43] "Minutes," SBM, Jan. 1931, pp. 316, 324–25.

[44] *Culto Protestante no Brasil, 1960*, pp. 2–6. Figures for the Assemblies of God in Acre and the Adventists in Amazonas in the source are incomplete. Those given here are conservative approximations based on comparison with statistics for 1966.

[45] *O Puritano*, Feb. 20, 1919.

[46] *Ibid.*, March 13, 1924.

[47] *Appêndices às Actas da A.G.*, 1928, pp. 69–78. Cf. J. Goulart, "Pascoal Luiz Pita," *Revista Teológica*, XXII, 26 (Dec. 1960), pp. 118–20.

[48] Sociedade Missionária Pro-Evangelização de Portugal, *Boletim*, n.d. [ca. 1931], Portugal Mission File, Campinas archives.

[49] *O Puritano*, Dec. 28, 1929.

[50] *Christian Work in South America*, I, p. 88.

[51] The population of northern Minas Gerais decreased from 1920 to 1940. Smith, *Brazil: People and Institutions*, p. 152.

[52] "Minutes," Brazil Council, 1928, p. 7.

[53] *O Puritano*, Feb. 2, 1929.

[54] *Ibid.*, Oct. 31, 1931.

[55] "Annual Report," CBM, 1928.

[56] Letter from F. Graham to M. Lyman, April 11, 1921. Irwin Collection. But when Alfredo Marien visited the town in 1946 he did not find any believers there. A. Marien, "Relatório Anual," 1947, Irwin Collection.

[57] *O Puritano*, Sept. 25, 1942.

[58] A. Reese, *The Approaching Advent of Christ, An Examination of the Teaching of J. N. Darby and His Followers* (London: Marshall, Morgan and Scott, 1937).

[59] R. F. Lennington was away from his station for two hundred days in 1919 but still could not visit all his field. The Xanxerê church and its out-stations, totalling 250 members, had not been visited for eighteen months. "Minutes," SBM, 1919, pp. 73–74.

[60] Smith, *Brazil: People and Institutions*, p. 140.

[61] "Minutes," Brazil Council, 1922, p. 6.

[62] "Minutes," SBM, 1928, pp. 271–72.

[63] *Ibid.*, 1930, p. 322.

[64] J. E. Bear, Jr., "The Missionary Work of the PCUS in Southern Brazil,

1869-1958," II (Unpublished manuscript, Union Theological Seminary, Richmond, Va., 1960), p. 107.

[65] "Minutes," SBM, 1929, pp. 296–97.

CHAPTER VII

[1] J. P. Calógeras, *A History of Brazil*, tr., P. A. Martin (Chapel Hill: University of North Carolina Press, 1939), p. 342.

[2] "Minutes," Brazil Council, 1932, pp. 5–6.

[3] "Minutes," CBM, 1918, pp. 2–4.

[4] M. G. dos Santos, *Bispos e Pastores, ou a Conquista do Brasil pelos Norteamericanos* (São Paulo: Imprensa Metodista, 1928), p. 1.

[5] *O Puritano*, Aug. 4, 1921; *NE*, July 1; Sept. 30, 1927.

[6] *Christian Work in South America*, I, p. 247.

[7] *NE*, June 10, 1922.

[8] *O Puritano*, Jan. 15, 1920.

[9] *Ibid.*, Oct. 16, 1919.

[10] Santos, *op. cit.*, p. 1.

[11] A. Delamare, *As Duas Bandeiras, Catholicismo e Brazilidade* (Rio de Janeiro, Centro D. Vital, 1924), p. 111.

[12] Braga, *Panamericanismo*, p. 18.

[13] *NE*, May 17, 1921; May 21, 1922; July 23, 1923.

[14] Jerônimo Gueiros, *O Brasil Ameaçado e a Victória da Liberdade* (Recife: n.p., 1925), p. 28.

[15] *NE*, Jan. 20, 1923.

[16] Delamare, *op. cit.*, p. 104.

[17] *Ibid.*, p. 110.

[18] *O Puritano*, Aug. 12, 1920.

[19] *NE*, Feb. 28; March 12, 1923.

[20] *O Puritano*, Oct. 23, 1919; April 21, 1921; Nov. 30, 1922.

[21] Magalhães, *op. cit.*, pp. 19–20.

[22] Cited in Gueiros, *op. cit.*, p. 76.

[23] Magalhães, *op. cit.*, pp. 20–22.

[24] Cited in Delamare, *op. cit.*, p. 82.

[25] *Ibid.*, pp. 102–03.

[26] *Ibid.*, p. 115.

[27] Cited in *O Puritano*, Aug. 9, 1923.

[28] Gueiros, *op. cit.*, p. 5.

[29] *Ibid.*, p. 15.

[30] *O Puritano*, Aug. 27, 1925.

[31] M. A. O'Neill, *Tristão de Athayde and the Catholic Social Movement in Brazil* (Washington, D.C.: The Catholic University of America Press, 1939), pp. 62–64.

[32] Tristão de Athayde (A. A. Lima), *As Repercussões do Catholicismo* (São João del-Rei: Centro D. Vital, 1932), p. 26.

[33] O'Neill, *op. cit.*, pp. 99–102.

[34] *Ibid.*, pp. 137–38.

[35] F. R. dos Sanctos Saraiva, *O Catholicismo Romano, ou a Velha e Fatal*

Illusão da Sociedade, Introdução de como a Egreja de Roma tem Actuado no Brasil, com Abundante Documentação Histórica, por Eliezer dos Sanctos Saraiva (São Paulo: Empresa Editora Brasileira,1932), pp. 49–50.

[36] *Diário Popular*, June 8, 1931; cited in *ibid.*, p. 43.

[37] José M. Bello, *A History of Modern Brazil, 1889–1964*, tr., James Taylor, new concluding chapter by R. E. Peppino (Stanford, Calif.: Stanford University Press, 1966), pp. 294–95.

[38] *O Puritano*, Feb. 28; June 6, 1931.

[39] M. G. dos Santos e G. Moreira, *Memorial Apresentado pela Egreja Presbyteriana do Brasil ao Governo Provisório* (Rio de Janeiro: Papelaria Cruzeiro, 1930).

[40] *O Puritano*, May 16, 1931.

[41] Sanctos Saraiva, *op. cit.*, p. 8.

[42] O'Neill, *op. cit.*, p. 138.

[43] Lima, *A Igreja e o Novo Mundo*, p. 28.

[44] Erasmo Braga cited Rauschenbush and McConnell in writing of the need to support workers in their drive for justice. Cf. Braga, *Religião e Cultura*, E. M. do Amaral, ed. (São Paulo: União Cultural Editora, [ca. 1932]), pp. 92–93.

[45] Guilherme Kerr urged the Church to evangelize workers and help them achieve greater justice to prevent Communism from winning their allegiance. *O Puritano*, Feb. 26, 1925.

[46] *RMN*, Aug. 1918.

[47] *Actas da A.G.*, 1918, pp. 49–50.

[48] *O Puritano*, Feb. 14; Feb. 21, 1924.

[49] *Ibid.*, March 20, 1926.

[50] *Ibid.*, March 25, April 10, 1933. The missionaries have been criticized at times for not taking greater interest in political action. However, it would have created great problems for their work and exposed them to even greater criticism had they done so. Thus they were advised against such action by their board. "Why should a missionary ever meddle with the local politics of the land he has adopted? It is neither wise nor safe to do it. . . . It was the bane of mission work in Syria in the early years of the mission, that the Syrians thought that becoming Protestants would secure them English or American consular protection. . . . Let the local civil authorities understand that Protestant Christians are as amenable to the laws as others. Above all, do not attempt to browbeat the officials, or carry a case by foreign influence. . . . Let the officials know you are a man of peace, and of inflexible integrity and respect for the law." Daniel McGilvary *et al.*, *Counsel to New Missionaries from Older Missionaries of the Presbyterian Church* (New York: Board of Foreign Missions of the PCUSA, 1905), p. 136.

In 1931 the Brazil Council expressed its view on the matter in similar terms: "It is the judgment of the Council (1) that foreign missionaries in Latin America must be very discreet in some of these matters owing to intense nationalism; and (2) that our main work, as missionaries, is the sowing of the seed that ultimately will produce the social changes." "Minutes," Brazil Council, 1931, pp. 6–7.

51 *O Puritano*, Sept. 9, 1934.

52 *Ibid.*, June 20, 1919.

53 *Ibid.*, June 27, 1919.

54 *Ibid.*, April 17, 1924.

55 *Ibid.*, March 24, 1928.

56 *Ibid.*, Oct. 19, 1929.

57 *Ibid.*, Oct. 10; Nov. 10, 1934.

58 *Ibid.*, Sept. 9, 1920; *NE*, Dec. 11,; Dec. 20, 1922.

59 *NE*, June 30, 1922.

60 *O Puritano*, May 3, 1932.

61 *Ibid.*, June 26; July 24, 1924. The latter citation reads: "Synods and other judicatories should not discuss nor determine anything other than ecclesiastical questions. They should not involve themselves in the civil affairs of the State except for humble petition in extraordinary cases, or through counsel . . . if the civil magistrate invites them to do so."

62 M. G. dos Santos wrote, "Protestantism is not a party, but all of its members, by their very nature, belong to the liberal wing which defends everywhere, freedom of conscience and equality of religious groups before the law." *Ibid.*, Nov. 10, 1932.

CHAPTER VIII

1 S. G. Inman, *Christian Cooperation in Latin America* (New York: CCLA, [ca. 1917]), pp. 34–35.

2 J. A. Ferreira, "Erasmo Braga, Sábio Brasileiro, Ministro Evangélico, Líder Ecumênico," unpublished manuscript, 1965, p. 18.

3 *Ibid.*, p. 26.

4 E. Braga, *Religião e Cultura*, p. 149.

5 Ferreira, "Erasmo Braga," p. 72.

6 E. Braga, *Panamericanismo* (New York: Missionary Education Movement, 1916).

7 *O Puritano*, Oct. 11, 1917.

8 C. Gammon, *op. cit.*, pp. 197–98.

9 *Appêndices às Actas da A.G.*, 1922, p. 41.

10 *Ibid.*, 1918, p. 47; *O Puritano*, Oct. 27, 1921.

11 "Minutes," SBM, 1921, pp. 104–05.

12 Bear, "The Mission Work of the PCUS in Southern Brazil," II, pp. 417–24.

13 M. Sydenstricker, "History of the East Brazil Mission," unpublished manuscript, 1965, pp. 72–76.

14 *O Puritano*, Aug. 27, 1925.

15 *Ibid.*, March 22, 1930.

16 E. M. do Amaral, "Erasmo Braga," *O Estandarte*, May 20, 1932.

17 *Appêndices às Actas da A.G.*, 1934, p. 147.

18 Inman, *op. cit.*, p. 143.

19 Bear, "The Mission Work of the PCUS in Southern Brazil," II, p. 91.

[20] Personal interview with J. A. Mackay, former Secretary for Latin America, Board of Foreign Missions, PCUSA, Oct. 15, 1970.

[21] Ferreira, *História*, II, p. 175; *O Puritano*, Nov. 2, 1922.

[22] *O Puritano*, Oct. 4, 11, 18, 1923.

[23] *Ibid.*, Oct. 3, 1925.

[24] *Ibid.*, July 17, 1927.

[25] John R. Mott, *Addresses and Papers*, VI, p. 442, cited by Jorge C. Mota, *Christianismo*, May, 1957.

[26] Kerr, the paladin of orthodoxy in the church who occupied Braga's former chair in Campinas Seminary, wrote that Braga "kept the faith." Ferreira, "Erasmo Braga," p. 80.

[27] *O Puritano*, May 4, 1929.

[28] Braga, *Religião e Cultura*, pp. 78–79.

[29] *Ibid.*, p. 95.

[30] *Ibid.*, p. 11.

[31] Braga, "Union on the Foreign Field" (a paper prepared for the World Reformed Alliance, 1929), unpublished manuscript, Campinas archives, p. 10.

[32] Braga, *Panamericanismo*, pp. 57–58.

[33] Braga, *Relatório Annual, Comissão Brasileira de Cooperação, 1924*, Rio de Janeiro, 1924.

[34] Ferreira, *História*, II, p. 175.

[35] *RMN*, Aug., 1924.

[36] *Christian Work in South America*, I, p. 379.

[37] Braga, *Relatório Annual, Comissão Brasileira de Cooperação, 1927–1928*, Rio de Janeiro, 1928.

[38] *Ibid.*, 1924.

[39] Braga, "Union on the Foreign Field," p. 11.

[40] In 1933 a writer asked, "Is this most modern movement of organic union a new instrument of Satan to corrupt the Church and secularize, if possible, the Kingdom of God? Does it not come exactly from those communions which are closest to Rome?" *O Puritano*, Oct. 25, 1933.

[41] Braga, "Union on the Foreign Field," pp. 3–10.

[42] *O Puritano*, March 4, 1919.

[43] *RMN*, June, 1921.

[44] *NE*, Feb. 10, 1922.

[45] *Ibid.*, March 12; June 20, 1923,

[46] *Ibid.*, March 11, 1925.

[47] *Ibid.*, April 29, 1925; Feb. 17, 1926.

[48] *Ibid.*, Dec. 8, 1926.

[49] *Appêndices às Actas da A.G.*, 1928, pp. 147–48.

[50] *NE*, Feb. 20, 1930.

[51] "Minutes," CBM, 1929, pp. 4, 7.

[52] *O Puritano*, Sept. 10, 1932; *NE*, Sept. 1, 1932.

[53] Benjamin Marinho, a pastor in the interior, criticized both the move to Recife and the interdenominational nature of the institution. "A united seminary," he wrote, "is not compatible with Presbyterianism and much less is a sign of our progress and spiritual zeal." *NE*, May 31, 1923. Cícero Si-

queira defended the plan, but when he left Pernambuco for Alto Jequitibá in 1930, the institution lost one of its strongest supporters. *Ibid.*, June 20, 1923.

[54] Two articles in 1913 showed the *Paulista* spirit. One spoke of "the state of the *bandeirantes* and coffee, the tree of riches, the state which has more merchants and farmers and politicians, more factories and schools and Evangelical churches, the state which does not love the tutelage of *cariocas* (natives of Rio), either political or ecclesiastical." *RMN*, April, 1913. The other spoke of the "nation of São Paulo," the "brains of the Republic," and noted that a former President of the Republic was now governor of that state. *Ibid.*, May, 1913.

[55] *Actas da A.G.*, 1917, p. 20.

[56] *RMN*, Nov., 1918; *O Puritano*, March 7, 1918.

[57] *O Puritano*, Dec. 18, 1918.

[58] *Ibid.*, Nov. 22, 1917.

[59] *RMN*, April, 1918.

[60] *O Puritano*, Sept. 6, 13, 1917.

[61] *O Estandarte*, Sept. 9, 1917.

[62] "Minutes," Executive Committee of the Brazil Missions, PCUSA, 1917, p. 26.

[63] *RMN*, April, 1918.

[64] *Actas da A.G.*, 1918, p. 19.

[65] *RMN*, April, 1918; April, 1919.

[66] *Appêndices às Actas da A.G.*, 1917, pp. 73–76.

[67] José C. Nogueira, "A Questão do Seminário Unido," *Revista Teológica*, XXII, 26 (Dec., 1960), p. 111.

[68] *RMN*, Aug., 1919.

[69] *Ibid.*, May, 1921.

[70] *Ibid.*

[71] *O Puritano*, July 10, 1919.

[72] *RMN*, Aug., 1919.

[73] *Ibid.*, April, 1918.

[74] *O Puritano*, Jan. 11, 1920.

[75] *RMN*, Oct., 1919.

[76] *O Estandarte*, Nov. 3, 18, 21, 1921.

[77] *O Puritano*, July 14, 1921.

[78] *Ibid.*, Feb. 17, 1921.

[79] *RMN*, Nov., 1920.

[80] *Appêndices às Actas da A.G.*, 1922, pp. 24, 28, 29.

[81] *RMN*, Feb., 1922.

[82] "Minutes," Brazil Council, 1922.

[83] *O Puritano*, Dec. 4, 1924.

[84] W. R. Wheeler to the Brazil missions: Board of Foreign Missions, PCUSA, letter no. 74, July 16, 1925. Presbyterian Historical Society, Philadelphia. The fundamentalist-modernist controversy in the PCUSA at the time might have been an additional factor which made the New York Board wary of appearing to impose the United Seminary, which seemed to have a more open theological stance, on the Brazilian church.

85 *O Puritano*, March 26; April 2, 1927.

86 *O Estandarte*, April 10, 1926.

87 *Appêndices às Actas da* A.G., 1926, pp. 76–78.

88 *O Puritano*, Aug. 16, 1927.

89 J. A. Ferreira, "Um Capítulo de História; Seminários," *Revista Teológica*, X (1948), p. 48.

90 *O Puritano*, March 17, 1928.

91 *Ibid.*, Nov. 14, 1931.

92 *Actas da A.G.*, 1932, pp. 13–14.

93 *O Puritano*, March 9; July 6, 1929.

94 *Ibid.*, Nov. 10, 1932; April 25, 1933.

95 *Ibid.*, March 31, 1928.

96 *Actas da A.G.*, 1934, p. 96.

97 "Minutes," SBM, 1929, p. 302.

98 E. Braga to F. R. Lennington, May 2, 1932, Braga file, Campinas archives.

99 *Cristianismo*, May, 1957.

CHAPTER IX

1 Bello, *op. cit.*, pp. 311–13.

2 A government report at the time said that half the officers in Brazil's navy and one third of the army officers had either joined the group or sympathized with it. J. W. F. Dulles, *Vargas of Brazil, a Political Biography* (Austin: University of Texas Press, 1967), p. 155.

3 M. G. dos Santos, *O Cincoentenário da Faculdade de Teologia da Igreja Cristã Presbiteriana do Brasil, 1888–1938* (Campinas: n.p., 1938), p. 14.

4 R. M. Levine, *The Vargas Regime, the Critical Years, 1934–1938* (New York: Columbia University Press, 1970), pp. 91–92.

5 M. G. dos Santos, *O Cincoentenário da Faculdade de Teologia*, p. 11. Cf. M. R. de Mello, *Varzia do Assu* (São Paulo: 1940), which attributes Communist influence to Protestantism and free thinking.

6 M. G. dos Santos, *O Cincoentenário da Faculdade de Teologia*, pp. 11–13.

7 *O Puritano*, Oct. 25, 1942.

8 *Ibid.*, March 10, 1942.

9 *Ibid.*, Nov. 10, 1943; "Can Catholics Close a Continent?" *The Christian Century*, LIX, 51 (Dec. 23, 1942), pp. 1582–83; A Jesuit wrote that the Ambassador told him that the State Department was adverse to Protestant ministers entering Brazil but could do nothing about it. P. Dunne, *A Padre Views South America* (Milwaukee: Bruce Publishing Co., 1945), p. 138.

10 Smith, *Brazil: People and Institutions*, p. 148.

11 *O Puritano*, May 25, 1937.

12 *Ibid.*, Jan. 10, 1939.

13 *Ibid.*, May 25, 1940; July 10, 1943.

14 Figures for the Presbyterian Church come from the *Actas da A.G.* for 1910 to 1929, from Braga and Grubb, *op. cit.*, for 1931, and from the Sta-

tistical Archives of the church, Governador Valadares, for subsequent years. Those for the Baptists come from Leonard, *op. cit.*, p. 274, and others from Read, *op. cit.*, pp. 29, 90, 91, and 120.

[15] Smith, *Brazil: People and Institutions*, p. 139.

[16] *O Puritano*, June 10, 1945.

[17] *Ibid.*, Aug. 10, 1936; March 10, 1937; March 10, 1938; March 10, 1939.

[18] *Ibid.*, July 10, 1943.

[19] *Ibid.*, April 10, 1940.

[20] *Ibid.*, Sept. 10, 1945.

[21] *Ibid.*, Sept. 10, 1938.

[22] Letter from Domingos R. Hidalgo, present pastor of the Brás Church, to the author, Jan. 22, 1970.

[23] *O Puritano*, March 10, 1944.

[24] Statistical archives of the Presbyterian Church of Brazil, Governador Valadares, Minas Gerais.

[25] *O Puritano*, Feb. 10, 1940.

[26] *Ibid.*, Feb. 25, 1944.

[27] *Ibid.*, June 25, 1945.

[28] *Ibid.*, Aug. 10, 1934.

[29] *Ibid.*, June 25, 1945.

[30] Although it met in 1932 and 1933, it apparently had no other meetings from 1917 to 1942. Cf. letter from A. C. Salley to L. K. Anderson, June 8, 1942, CBM archives, São Paulo.

[31] "Minutes," SBM, 1938, p. 108; "Minutes," new CBM, 1938, p. 123.

[32] A. C. Salley to L. K. Anderson, June 3, 1942, CBM archives.

[33] *O Puritano*, Feb. 25, 1940.

[34] *Ibid.*, Oct. 10, 1940.

[35] *Ibid.*, March 25, 1946.

[36] *Ibid.*, April 10; July 25, 1941.

[37] *Ibid.*, July 10, 1946.

[38] José C. Nogueira, "Resumo Histórico da Junta de Missões Nacionais" (unpublished manuscript, 1958, Campinas archives).

[39] *O Puritano*, Oct. 10, 1941; March 10, 1944.

[40] J. C. Nogueira *et al.*, "Relatório duma Visita a Amazonas" (handwritten manuscript, 1945, Campinas archives).

[41] *O Brasil Presbiteriano*, April, 1959; hereafter referred to as *BP*.

[42] *O Puritano*, May 10, 1942.

[43] *Ibid.*, March 10, 1944; Jan. 10, 1947.

[44] "Atas da Junta de Missões Estrangeiras," March, 1948, mimeographed.

[45] *Atas da A.G.*, 1934, p. 28f.

[46] *O Puritano*, March 10, 1935.

[47] *Atas da A.G.*, 1936, pp. 22, 77. Church leaders later declared that the Assembly did this only to keep peace between the church and the mission. Coriolano de Assumpção, "Comunicação da Comissão Executiva, Igreja Presbiteriana do Brasil, à Missão do Brasil Central (typed manuscript, Feb. 1941, CBM archives).

[48] "Minutes," Executive Committee, CBM, Dec., 1940, p. 16; Dec., 1942, p. 11.

[49] *Appêndices às Actas da A.G.*, 1934, p. 147.

[50] *O Puritano*, June 10, 1944.

[51] E. M. do Amaral, *O Magno Problema* (Rio de Janeiro, Comissão Brasileira de Publicidade, 1934), p. 14.

[52] *Ibid.*, pp. 168–69.

[53] *Ibid.*, p. 23.

[54] *O Puritano*, June 25, 1935.

[55] *Ibid.*, Aug. 25, 1935.

[56] *Ibid.*, Jan. 25, 1935.

[57] Leonard, *op. cit.*, p. 289.

[58] *Atas da A.G.*, 1934, pp. 32–33.

[59] *O Puritano*, Sept. 25, 1934.

[60] *Ibid.*, May 10; Aug. 25, 1934.

[61] *Atas do Segundo Concílio Geral da Igreja Metodista do Brasil*, 1934, p. 27, quoted in P. Landes, "Report of the Committee on Comity with the Methodist Church in Brazil" (typed manuscript, 1934 [CBM archives]).

[62] "Minutes," Brazil Council, 1935.

[63] *Atas da A.G.*, 1936, p. 32.

[64] *O Puritano*, Aug. 10, 1938.

[65] Leonard, *op. cit.*, p. 296.

[66] *O Puritano*, April 25, 1941.

[67] *Ibid.*, Jan. 10, 1945.

[68] *Ibid.*, July 10, 1934.

[69] *Ibid.*, Aug. 25, 1935.

[70] *Ibid.*, Feb. 10, 1937.

[71] *Ibid.*, July 10, 1934.

[72] *Ibid.*, March 10; April 25; May 10, 1938.

[73] *Ibid.*, July 10; July 25, 1938.

[74] *Ibid.*, Nov. 25, 1938.

[75] *Appêndices às Atas da A.G.*, 1936, p. 71.

[76] *Atas do Supremo Concílio*, 1938, p. 26.

[77] *Constituição da Igreja Cristã Presbiteriana do Brasil* (Rio de Janeiro, *O Puritano*, 1938), Pte. I, Cap. V, Sec. 2, art. 90h.

[78] *Ibid.*, Cap. IV, Sec. 2, art. 37d.

[79] *Ibid.*, Pte. III, Cap. XVII, art. 317.

[80] *O Puritano*, Dec. 10, 1942.

[81] *Ibid.*, Jan. 25, 1936.

[82] *Ibid.*, April 25, 1937.

[83] *Ibid.*, May 10, 1938.

[84] *Ibid.*, March 10, 1939.

[85] Leonard, *op. cit.*, p. 294.

[86] *O Presbiteriano Conservador*, July, 1940.

[87] Leonard, *op. cit.*, p. 296.

[88] E. M. do Amaral *et al.*, *Ao Protestantismo do Brasil*, São Paulo, 1942.

[89] "Minutes," Executive Committee, CBM, Dec. 1942, p. 11.

[90] *O Puritano*, June 25; Sept. 25, 1943.

[91] *Ibid.*, July 10, 1942.

[92] *Ibid.*, Oct. 25, 1942.

[93] *Ibid.*, March 22, 1930.
[94] *Constituição*, 1938, Pte. I, Cap. IV, Sec. 3, art. 59.
[95] *O Puritano*, May 10, 1943.

CHAPTER X

[1] E. B. Burns, *Nationalism in Brazil, a Historical Survey* (New York: Frederick Praeger, 1968), p. 89.

[2] Celso Furtado, *Reflexões Sobre a Pre-Revolução Brasileira* (Rio de Janeiro: Confederação Evangélica do Brasil, 1962).

[3] *O Puritano*, Sept. 10, 1951; Oct. 10, 1953.

[4] *Ibid.*, Oct. 25, 1946; *NE*, July, 1958.

[5] *O Puritano*, Aug. 25, 1946.

[6] The newspaper, *O Estado de S. Paulo*, reported that the state granted Cr$6.286.588 (US$315,000) for construction of the cathedral in São Paulo. (*O Puritano*, Oct. 10, 1949.) The Seminary of the Archdiocese of Rio, which graduated only ten priests per year, received Cr$3.000.000 (US$45,000) from the federal government in 1956. *Ibid.*, April 25, 1956.

[7] *Ibid.*, Aug. 25, 1955.

[8] *Mocidade*, Aug., 1953.

[9] Mecham, *Church and State in Latin America*, p. 279.

[10] *O Puritano*, April 4, 1950. But a few priests were beginning to show a different attitude. Helder Câmara, the future Archbishop of Recife and Olinda, spoke of the greatness of many Protestant missionaries, denied that they were mercenaries, and urged Catholic catechists to teach more of the Bible. *Ibid.*, March 10, 1939.

[11] *Ibid.*, June 10, 1950.

[12] *Ibid.*, Sept. 10, 1951.

[13] *Ibid.*, Feb. 10. 1952.

[14] *BP*, Oct., 1958; Jan., 1959.

[15] *Ibid.*, June, 1959.

[16] *Jubileu da Ordenação do Rev. Jerônimo Gueiros* (Recife: n.p., 1951).

[17] *NE*, July 1, 1949.

[18] *O Puritano*, Nov. 10, 1956.

[19] *Ibid.*, Aug. 25, 1951.

[20] *Ibid.*, Feb. 10, 1953.

[21] *Atas do Supremo Concílio*, 1946, p. 34. The only other Brazilian church to accept the invitation was the Methodist.

[22] Personal interview with S. Rizzo, Jan. 9, 1971.

[23] *O Puritano*, Feb. 10, 1948; Jan. 10, 1949; Feb. 10, 1949; S. Rizzo, "O Concílio Mundial de Igrejas," *Unitas*, X, 1 (Jan., 1948), pp. 715–21; XI, 4 (April, 1949), pp. 211–18; XI, 5 (May, 1949), pp. 285–90.

[24] Letter from B. Moraes to S. Rizzo, March 10, 1949, in the possession of S. Rizzo.

[25] C. McIntire, *The Struggle for Latin America, the First Missionary Journey* (Collingswood, N.J.: Christian Beacon Press, 1949), p. 7.

[26] *Ibid.*, p. 12.

27 *Ibid.*, p. 30.

28 *NE*, Nov. 1, 1949.

29 J. Goulart, "Carl McIntire, Seus Livros e Suas Obras," *Unitas*, XI, 9 (Sept., 1949), pp. 690–94.

30 *Mocidade*, Sept., 1949; Nov., 1949.

31 *NE*, Nov. 1, 1949.

32 *O Puritano*, Feb. 25, June 10, July 25, 1950.

33 *Ibid.*, July 25, 1950.

34 *NE*, May 1, 1950.

35 Letter from A. Reese to H. Midkiff, June 22, 1950. CBM archives.

36 *Atas do Supremo Concílio*, 1950, p. 32.

37 J. Goulart, "Ecumenismo," *Revista Teológica*, XII (1950), pp. 20–26; XIII (1951), pp. 47–55.

38 *Ibid.*, 1951, p. 50. For a serious discussion of the problem of how to be ecumenical and also evangelize nominal Roman Catholics, cf. M. R. Shaull, "Evangelism and Proselytism in Latin America," *Student World*, XLVI, 1 (Jan., 1953), pp. 14–20. The author was very skeptical about the possibility of a converted student finding a spiritual home in the Roman Catholic Church as it existed in Latin America at that time. Criticism of Shaull's view indicates that the fears of Latin Americans were not entirely unfounded. Cf. the letter from William Nicholls, *ibid.*, 3 (July, 1953), pp. 255–58.

39 *O Puritano*, Feb. 10, 1950.

40 Goulart, "Ecumenismo," *Revista Teológica*, 1950, p. 22.

41 *Atas da Comissão Executiva do Supremo Concílio*, Jan., 1956 p. 11.

42 "Minutes," CBM, 1957, p. 33

43 *O Puritano*, Oct. 25, 1955.

44 This is important in the light of Israel Gueiros' later charges that he was forced out of the seminary because of missionary pressure, as soon as he began to fight against modernism and associate himself with the ICCC. His uncle's opposition to him antedated McIntire's arrival. Jerônimo Gueiros did not figure in the 1956 controversy, having died in 1953. N. Cortez, *Carta Aberta aos Presbiterianos do Brasil* (Recife: n.p., 1956).

45 A. Reese, "Relatório do Reitor à Directoria do Seminário Presbiteriano do Norte, Janeiro-Junho, 1950," "Livro de Atas da Directoria do SPN, 1937–1952," handwritten manuscript, Presbyterian Seminary of the North, Recife, p. 67.

46 *Ibid.*, p. 77.

47 Personal interview with Professor Oton G. Dourado of Recife Seminary, Nov. 4, 1969. But Dourado affirmed that even Kerr taught that there were errors of history in the Bible.

48 *NE*, July, 1956.

49 Personal interview with the Reverend Victor Pester, a member of the Presbytery of Pernambuco at the time, Nov. 5, 1969.

50 *NE*, July 6, 1956.

51 *Ibid.*, July, 1956.

52 In a personal interview, Nov. 16, 1969, Gueiros said that a total of 2440 members went with a new group, but a more realistic figure would be one third or one half that number.

53 L. N. Bell, "Slander in Brazil," *Southern Presbyterian Journal*, XV, 16 (Aug. 15, 1956), p. 5.

54 Cf. M. R. Shaull and R. Alves, "The Devotional Life of Brazilian Protestantism," *Student World*, XLIX, 3 (July, 1956), pp. 360–66.

55 J. C. Mota, "A Evangelização dos Universitários," *Unitas*, XIV, 9 (Sept., 1952), pp. 44–48; B. Gammon, "Relatório da SGM, 1954–1958," mimeographed.

56 *Atas do Supremo Concílio*, 1946, p. 26. It is important to understand that "youth" in the Presbyterian Church of Brazil included those from twelve to thirty years of age. Thus the leaders were not adolescents but, usually, university students.

57 *O Puritano*, June 10, 1946.

58 Sydenstricker, *op. cit.*, p. 72.

59 Enrollment in Campinas Seminary, which was approximately 50 in 1950, grew to 122 in 1959. *Supre*, July, 1959.

60 *O Puritano*, July 10, 1950.

61 They were Benjamin Moraes, Domício de Matos, Billie Gammon, Irecê Wanderley, Jorge C. Mota, and Waldo Cesar. *Ibid.*, Oct. 25, 1954.

62 *Mocidade*, March–April, 1949.

63 *Ibid.*, Oct., 1949.

64 *Ibid.*, Aug., 1948.

65 *Boletim do Sínodo Setentrional*, Recife, 1952.

66 *Mocidade*, May, 1948.

67 *O Puritano*, April 10, 1948.

68 *Mocidade*, Feb., 1951; April, 1951.

69 A. A. Vassão, "Relatório do Secretário Executivo da IPB à Comissão Executiva," Jan., 1952, mimeographed.

70 *Mocidade*, May, 1952.

71 *Ibid.*, July, 1954.

72 *O Puritano*, Feb. 10, 1953.

73 *Mocidade*, March, 1951.

74 Presbytery of Bahia-Sergipe, *O Puritano*, Sept. 10, 1949; the presbyteries of Rio and São Paulo, *Mocidade*, July, 1951, May, 1952; the Synod of the North, *Atas do Sínodo Setentrional*, Feb., 1952.

75 "Atas da Comissão Executiva do Supremo Concílio," Feb. 1954, mimeographed.

76 *O Puritano*, Jan. 10, 1956.

77 "Atas da Comissão Executiva do Supremo Concílio," Jan., 1956, mimeographed.

78 *Atas do Supremo Concílio*, 1962, pp. 12–14.

79 *O Puritano*, April 25, 1958.

80 "Atas da Comissão Executiva do Supremo Concílio," July, 1952, mimeographed.

81 *Ibid.*, Feb., 1954.

82 J. C. Mota, *O Puritano*, Sept. 25, 1949. Cf. the replies by Kerr, *ibid.*, Feb. 10, 1950, and Goulart, *ibid.*, Feb. 25, 1950. Goulart noted that he had to teach ten different subjects in the curriculum and that both professors and students suffered from lack of preparation.

[83] Cf M. R. Shaull, *Oito Estudos de Preparo para o Testemunho*, Rio de Janeiro, 1956; *Somos Uma Comunidade Missionária*, Rio de Janeiro Secretaria Geral da Mocidade, 1957; *Cristianismo e a Revolução Social*, Rio de Janeiro, UCEB, 1954.

[84] Shaull, *Somos Uma Comunidade Missionária*, p. 10.

[85] Shaull, *Oito Estudos*.

[86] *O Puritano*, June 25, 1954.

[87] *Ibid.*, June 10, 1957.

[88] J. A. Ferreira, "Relatório do Reitor do Seminário Presbiteriano de Campinas, 1957," handwritten manuscript, in the possession of Sr. Ferreira.

[89] *Mocidade*, Aug., 1953.

[90] *O Puritano*, Dec. 10, 1954, tells of one such experiment. Another took place in São Paulo during 1956 and 1957.

[91] Cf. Shaull, *Cristianismo e a Revolução Social*, and *Mocidade*, Nov., 1954 to May, 1955.

[92] *O Puritano*, June 10, 1957.

[93] *Ibid.*, Sept. 10; Nov. 10, 1945.

[94] *Ibid.*, Dec. 10, 1945.

[95] *Ibid.*, Nov. 25, 1954.

[96] R. Anders and W. Cesar, *Relatório da Confederação Evangélica do Brasil, 1955–1956* (Rio de Janeiro: n.p., 1956), pp. 77–84.

[97] *O Puritano*, April 10, 1956.

[98] *Atas da Comissão Executiva do Supremo Concílio*, Jan., 1956.

[99] *O Puritano*, April 10, 1957.

[100] *Ibid.*, July 25, 1958.

[101] B. Moraes, "Relatório do Secretário Executivo do Supremo Concílio, 1949," mimeographed.

[102] International Missionary Council, *The Witness of a Revolutionary Church* (New York: IMC, 1947), p. 27. Cf. K. S. Latourette and W. R. Hogg, *Tomorrow is Here* (New York: Friendship Press, 1948).

[103] Norman Goodall (ed.), *Missions Under the Cross, Addresses and Findings of the Committee of the International Missionary Council, Willingen, 1952* (Edinburgh: Edinburgh House Press, 1953), p. 234.

[104] "Minutes," CBM, 1953, pp. 55–58.

[105] Cf. W. Wysham, "Toward an Ecumenical Mission," *Christian Century*, LXXIII, 30 (July 25, 1956), pp. 872–874.

[106] "Minutes," CBM Executive Committee, 1954, p. 5. The loan was granted to First Church, Rio, with a stipulation that the funds would be repaid into a building and loan fund for the entire church. None had yet been repaid in 1970.

[107] Cf. J. A. Ferreira and Américo Ribeiro, "A IPB no Quadro da Igreja Universal," *Revista Teológica*, July, 1962, p. 114.

[108] In Brazil it is assumed that a delegate to a meeting represents the views of the body which appointed him, even though they might be counter to his own position. Thus, it was generally believed that missionaries were under obligation to advocate policies of their boards whether they agreed with them or not, when, in fact, this has not been true in the writer's experience.

[109] Ferreira and Ribeiro, *op. cit.*, p. 117.

[110] "Minutes," Pan-Presbyterian Alliance, July, 1949.

[111] *O Puritano*, Nov. 25, 1946; Dec. 10, 1950.

[112] J. Goulart, "A Conferência Mundial de Canadá," *Unitas*, X, 3 (March, 1948), pp. 138–42.

[113] B. Moraes, "Relatório do Presidente do Supremo Concílio à Comissão Executiva," July, 1952, mimeographed.

[114] C. D. Fulton, "Developing Self-Government and Self-Support," *Presbyterian Survey*, XLIII, 2 (Feb., 1953), pp. 22–25, 32–33.

[115] *O Puritano*, April 10, 1950.

[116] "Estatutos do Conselho Inter-Presbiteriano," mimeographed.

[117] "Minutes," CBM, 1957, p. 27.

[118] Bear, "The Mission Work of the PCUS in Southern Brazil," II, pp. 444–45.

[119] W. R. Hogg, *New Day Dawning* (New York: World Horizons Press, 1957), p. 66.

[120] "Minutes," CBM, 1956, p. 22.

[121] Bear, "The Mission Work of the PCUS in Southern Brazil," II, p. 499.

[122] "Minutes," EBM, 1958, p. 23.

[123] *BP*, July, 1959.

[124] Cf. Appendix C.

[125] B. Moraes, "Relatório do Presidente do Supremo Concílio à Comissão Executiva," July, 1952, mimeographed.

[126] The same question was raised regarding a proposed youth hostel in São Paulo and Shaull's involvement in the Student Christian Movement.

[127] "Estatutos do Conselho Inter-Presbiteriano," Art. 13, par. 1.

[128] The Board of Foreign Missions of the PCUSA became the Commission on Ecumenical Mission and Relations (COEMAR) in 1958.

[129] "Commission, National Church, and Mission" (The 1959 Rio Agreement), mimeographed, CBM Archives.

[130] N. Cortez, *Relatórios e Mensagens* (São Paulo: n.p., n.d. [ca. 1951]), pp. 20–21.

[131] *O Puritano*, June 10, 1952.

[132] Garanhuns reported 213 decisions, and 64 young men indicated interest in the ministry. *Ibid.*, Sept. 10, 1953; Jan. 10, 1954. In Fortaleza there were 202 decisions (*ibid.*, Aug. 10, 1954), and in Governador Valadares, 250. *Ibid.*, Sept. 10, 1954.

[133] Statistical archives of the Presbyterian Church of Brazil, Governador Valadares, Minas Gerais.

[134] *Ibid.*

[135] The annual population growth of São Paulo was 3.4% from 1890 to 1940. It was probably greater from 1940 to 1960. Smith, *Brazil: People and Institutions*, p. 140.

[136] *O Puritano*, July 25, 1947.

[137] *Ibid.*, May 10, 1957.

[138] *Ibid.*, May 25, 1954.

[139] *NE*, Jan. 1, 1951.

[140] *BP*, July, 1964. Even in Governador Valadares, center of the area

where Presbyterianism has grown most rapidly, the three rural *congregações* of the city's First Presbyterian Church, containing only 20 per cent of its members, produced 33 professions of faith from January to November, 1969, while the central church, with 80 per cent of the members, had seen only 17 professions during the same period. Personal interview with Miguel O. de Freitas, pastor of the church, Nov. 21, 1969.

141 *O Puritano*, May 25, 1950.

142 *Ibid.*, July 10, 1950.

143 Instituto Brasileiro de Geografia e Estatística, *Culto Protestante no Brasil, 1959*, 1961. The number of churches listed for the Assemblies of God is low because their organization often included many semiautonomous congregations within one church.

144 *BP*, March, 1963.

145 *O Puritano*, July 10, 1947; July 10, 1950. In 1955 the *Conselho Inter-Presbiteriano* put funds for the project behind the loan for First Church, Rio, and a grant for an auditorium for Campinas Seminary. It was never funded. "Atas do CIP," 1955, mimeographed.

146 The figure includes members in the fields of the four North American missions.

147 *O Puritano*, July 25, 1947.

148 *Ibid.*, Aug. 25, 1947.

149 *Ibid.*, Jan. 10, 1951.

150 *The Christian Century*, LXVIII, 29 (July 18, 1951), p. 852.

151 *O Puritano*, Oct. 25, 1954.

152 Café Filho wrote that it was considered the best school in Natal at the time and added that it inculcated democratic ideas in its students which had been the basis of many of his decisions as a public servant. Letter from J. Café Filho do D. G. Vieira, March 4, 1965.

153 *The New York Times*, Feb. 21, 1970, called him this. He was not a church member but was considered a Protestant by the public.

154 *O Puritano*, Dec. 25, 1952.

155 Paulo F. de Araujo, *O Primeiro Centenário da Igreja Presbiteriana do Brasil* (Rio de Janeiro: Imprensa Nacional, 1959).

156 E. g. *O Estado de S. Paulo, Correio da Manhã*, and *Diário de Notícias*, Aug. 13, 1959.

EPILOGUE

1 *O Puritano*, June 25, 1951.

2 *Supre*, Feb., 1959.

3 Cf. R. A. Alves, "Latin American Protestantism: Utopia Becomes Ideology"; Jorge Lara-Braud (ed.), *Our Claim on the Future* (New York: Friendship Press, 1970), pp. 62–78.

Appendices

APPENDIX A

LIST OF ABBREVIATIONS AND PORTUGUESE TERMS

Bandeirante. Literally, a flag bearer, the name gaven to the early pioneers who pressed westward from São Paulo in search of riches.

Cachaça. A heavily consumed, cheap, sugar-cane rum.

Carioca. A native of the city of Rio de Janeiro.

Carnaval. The three days of celebration immediately before Lent.

Commissão Brasileira de Cooperação. The Brazilian Committee on Cooperation.

CBM. The Central Brazil Mission. It was the mission of the PCUSA in Bahia and the adjacent areas until 1938, when it absorbed the South Brazil Mission to include, in one body, all of the work of that church in Brazil.

CCLA. The Committee on Cooperation in Latin America.

CEB. Confederação Evangélica do Brasil. The Evangelical Confederation of Brazil.

CIP. Conselho Inter-Presbiteriano. The Inter-Presbyterian Council.

Colégio. A school, usually including the secondary level.

Compadre. A witness at the wedding of one's parents or at one's baptism; an intimate friend.

Congregação. In Brazilian Presbyterianism, a regularly worshipping community, not yet organized into an autonomous church, and thus ecclesiastically dependent on its mother church.

Crente. A believer, a common designation of Brazilian Protestants.

Doutor. Doctor, the term widely used in the interior for anyone with a university-level education.

EBM. The East Brazil Mission of the PCUS.

Eleitoral. Electoral.

Escola. School.

Faculdade. A specific faculty in a Brazilian university, e.g. a law school, usually with greater autonomy than is the case in a North American institution.

Fazenda. A large ranch or land holding.

Fazendeiro. The owner of a *fazenda.*

Feira. An open-air street market, usually held weekly.

Festa. A festival.

Ginásio. Formerly the entire secondary course which lasted five years; later the first four years of the seven-year secondary course; the term was abolished at the inception of the 1972 academic year.

ICCC. The International Council of Christian Churches.

IMC. The International Missionary Council.

Independente.   A member of the Independent Presbyterian Church, formed by the schism of 1903.

Instituto JMC.   The José Manoel da Conceição Institute.

IPB.   *Igreja Presbiteriana do Brasil.*   The Presbyterian Church of Brazil.

JME.   Junta de Missões Estrangeiras, the Board of Foreign Missions of the IPB.

JMN.   Junta de Missões Nacionais, the Board of National Missions.

Liga.   League.

NBM.   The North Brazil Mission of the PCUS.

Paulista.   A native of the state of São Paulo.

PCUS.   The Presbyterian Church in the United States, whose foreign mission board was located in Nashville.

PCUSA.   The Presbyterian Church in the United States of America, whose board was located in New York.

Pernambucano.   A native of Pernambuco.

SBM.   The South Brazil Mission of the PCUSA, which existed until 1938 when it was absorbed into the CBM.

SCM.   The Student Christian Movement.

Supremo Concílio.   The name of the highest judicatory of the Church after adoption of the 1937 Constitution.

UCEB.   União Cristã de Estudantes do Brasil, the Brazilian branch of the SCM.

Unida.   United.

WBM.   The West Brazil Mission of the PCUS.

WCC.   The World Council of Churches.

WSCF.   The World Student Christian Federation.

APPENDIX B

MAP OF BRAZIL, SHOWING STATES AND CITIES IMPORTANT IN THE HISTORY OF THE PRESBYTERIAN CHURCH IN BRAZIL

APPENDIX C

THE BRAZIL PLAN[1]

The purpose of missionary work is to establish an autonomous national Church and that purpose has already been fulfilled in Brazil. That fact has already been recognized by both national judicatories and by the missions. There are, however, vast regions and multitudes still unreached by the voice of the pure Gospel, which fully justify the continuing of missionary work. But it has become necessary to establish a new regime that will harmonize the interests and define the limits of the fields of action of the two forces, the missions and the Church, in Brazil. It was on the basis of these factors that the Assembly of 1916 made the resolution which is already known regarding the new structure.

In order to fulfill that which was proposed by the General Assembly regarding the new relations which should exist between the Presbyterian Church and the missions which cooperate with her, the joint committee recommends the following:

MODUS OPERANDI

Chapter I

Fields of Work

Art. 1. This vast territory is under the responsibility of the General Assembly and the Missions. The fields already occupied by the presbyteries will be considered fields of the Assembly, and those where the missions are working will be considered theirs.

Chapter II

Relationships Between Workers

Art. 2. No worker of the Presbyterian Church of Brazil or of the missions, may be a member of both bodies simultaneously, except in the cases specified below.

Art. 3. When any presbytery has less than five national pastors it may invite one or more of the oldest missionaries working in the same area, to become a member. This will not prejudice the relations of these

---

[1] *Actas da A. G.*, 1917, pp. 11–16. Unofficial translation by the writer.

workers with their respective missions, nor will it imply the transferring of their fields from the mission to the presbytery.

In no case will any minister belong to two presbyteries simultaneously.

Art. 4.   No missionary will serve as pastor of any church of a presbytery, and, equally, the missions will not employ members of the presbyteries in evangelistic work. These bodies will have the right to concede, one to the other, for short periods of time and for specified work, the services of their members. The exchange of work and personal help will be freely arranged within the limits of ordinary courtesy.

Transitory clause: The missionaries who presently pastor churches in the presbyteries may continue to do so in the conditions which apply at present as long as they, the missions, and the presbyteries involved so desire.

Art. 5.   In respect to deliberation number three, in which the Assembly treated the case of Drs. J. R. Smith and Thomas Porter, the missionaries who are ceded by their missions for special work of the Church should maintain their relationship with their presbyteries in the United States, but should give to the proper judicatories all information and reports solicited, with their work remaining solely under the direction of these judicatories.

The concession of these workers will always be made through a request to the judicatory for a fixed period, and its renewal will depend on a new request.

Art. 6.   The missionaries should promote in their fields the support of the diverse causes presented by the judicatories of the Church and do all possible to develop a spirit of solidarity between their congregations and the churches of the presbyteries.

Chapter III

Jurisdiction

Art. 7.   The ecclesiastical authority of the missionaries will be final in their fields. They will have full power to receive members, organize them into *congregações* and churches, and maintain discipline over them.

Art. 8.   Jurisdiction over candidates for the Evangelical ministry and licentiates will belong exclusively to the presbyteries. The missions will not relate themselves to either candidates or churches ecclesiastically, except through the judicatories.

Art. 9.   Missionaries and pastors will mutually respect the limits of the fields and parishes, and neither will sanction the invasion of fields or functions of the other.

Art. 10. Letters of transfer and disciplinary acts will be mutually respected by the members of the presbyteries and missions.

Art. 11. It is highly convenient that the presbyteries and missions exchange, annually, detailed information about the general progress of their work.

Chapter IV

Subsidies

At times it happens that a missionary field is in a condition in which it may be incorporated into the national Church, but without sufficient means for pastoral support. In such cases it is necessary that the missions continue to subsidize the work and that it be done according to the following articles:

Art. 12. Because of the conditions in which the boards work, the aid given by the mission to any church or parish will be arranged for periods of one year.

The renewal, when it is conceded, will be decreased 8 per cent of the original amount, but this decrease may be suspended or modified in special cases by the permanent executive committee.

These payments will be made monthly by the treasurers of the missions directly to those of the presbyteries.

Art. 13. When a subsidized church is without a pastor or pastor evangelist, the money stipulated for it will be paid or not, depending on the judgment of the mission.

Art. 14. The presbyteries will inform the missions annually if the subsidized churches have fulfilled their pastoral contract and, at the same time, will send a detailed report of the general progress of these churches.

Art. 15. If any church fails to fulfill its contract, the mission may suspend aid the following year, until the presbytery responsible certifies rectification of the error.

Chapter V

Transfer of Fields of Work

Since the authority of the missionaries is transitory and the service of the national Church is permanent, facilities should exist for the transferring of mission fields to the presbyteries.

This should be done according to the following articles:

Art. 16. When a *congregação* or church in a mission field achieves a degree of development which promises permanent support of a pastor, the mission or the congregation will consult the presbytery, and, if its opinion is favorable, the mission and the presbytery will define the parish and arrange the terms by which the former will aid in pastoral support. Once the contract has been made, the presbytery will install the pastor and supervise the parish, while the ecclesiastical authority of the mission will cease at once.

Art. 17.   When a presbytery judges itself ready to assume authority over a mission field, it may show the resources which it has available for the purpose and request that the mission make the transfer indicated. The mission will have the right to accept or refuse the request.

Art. 18.   When a mission wishes to transfer any field of work to the care of a presbytery, it will so propose, indicating the resources which it offers to subsidize the work. The presbytery will have the right to accept or refuse the proposal.

Art. 19.   In case it is considered convenient to open missionary work in the capitals or other centers of population, the presbytery involved will determine the field which should be assigned to the missions.

Chapter VI

Permanent Executive Committee, Meetings and Powers

Art. 20.   In order to promote the greatest possible efficiency in the execution of this plan, a permanent committee will exist, composed of three representatives of the missions of the Committee in Nashville, three of those of the Board in New York, and six of the Presbyterian Church of Brazil, seeking as far as possible in its composition to consider the interests of the presbyteries which have relations with the missions.

This committee will meet annually in the month of December, with the place, day, and time determined by its president.

Art. 21.   The committee should:

1. Watch over the fulfillment of this plan and remove difficulties which may arise in its execution, receiving and channeling complaints, etc.;

2. Serve as an intermediary between the missions and the General Assembly;

3. Study the religious condition of the nation and promote the unification of the various bodies associated in this plan, in a general campaign of evangelization.

BIBLIOGRAPHICAL NOTE

The historical archives of the Presbyterian Church of Brazil, which are housed in Campinas Seminary, constitute the most important collection of sources for the study of its history. Compiled and classified by the Reverend Júlio A. Ferreira, the archives contain periodicals, minutes of the General Assembly (called the *Supremo Concílio* after 1937) and other judicatories, the various constitutions of the church, and addresses, sermons, reports, tracts, and other papers of a number of important figures, including Erasmo Braga. The statistical files of the church are now located in the Executive Secretary's office, Uberlândia, Minas Gerais. Another important source of statistical information on Brazilian Protestantism is the *Estatística do Culto Protestante no Brasil*, published by the *Instituto Brasileiro de Geografia e Estatística* for 1956 and subsequent years.

The most important collection for the study of mission policies and church-mission relations is to be found in the archives of the Central Brazil Mission in São Paulo. It contains the minutes of the missions of the New York Board and their executive committees for the period under study, in addition to annual personal reports of missionaries and the missions, correspondence, and other documents. While the two New York missions in Brazil were separate, a Brazil Council, consisting of representatives of each, met at times with certain overall responsibilities. Minutes of its meetings are also located in the CBM archives. Additional missionary sources are the minutes of the West Brazil Mission, to be found in its archives in Patrocínio, Minas Gerais; those of the East Brazil Mission, in the possession of Mr. Albert Coit of Campinas; and a collection of documents pertaining to the East Goiás field, in the possession of Mr. Richard Irwin, also of Campinas. Correspondence of the Board of Foreign Missions of the PCUSA is located in the Presbyterian Historical Society, Philadelphia. Additional documents pertaining to the history of the work of the Nashville Board are located in the Historical Society of the PCUS, Montreat, N. C.

The Campinas archives contain a complete collection of *O Puritano* (Rio de Janeiro, 1898-1958), the most important Presbyterian periodical of the period. In addition to publishing minutes and statistics of various judicatories, the paper provided a forum for the discussion of issues with which the church was concerned and usually expressed the viewpoint of its leadership. The *Revista das Missões Nacionaes* (Rio de Janeiro and São Paulo, 1887-1924), also to be found in Campinas, often provided vigorous debate, at times in opposition to *O Puritano*. Other important periodicals in the archives are the *Revista Teológica*

(Campinas, 1939 to the present); *Unitas* (São Paulo, 1939-1959, called *Fé e Vida* from 1939 to 1945), which often presented points of view different from those found in the official church publications; *Mocidade* (Rio de Janeiro, 1944-1964), which expressed the opinion of the youth organization; and *O Brasil Presbiteriano* (Recife and São Paulo, 1958 to the present), now the official organ of the church, which resulted from the merger of *O Puritano* and *Norte Evangélico*. The latter, published sporadically from 1910 to 1958 in Garanhuns and Recife, is to be found in the library of the Presbyterian Seminary of the North, Recife. *O Estandarte* (São Paulo, 1893 to the present), the official organ of the Independent Presbyterian Church, is available in its archives, located in São Paulo.

Significant secondary works on the history of Brazilian Presbyterianism, memoirs and biographies, and more general studies of Brazilian history and culture, are listed in the notes with their places and dates of publication indicated in the first citation. An important collection of works on the rise of Roman Catholic nationalism and the struggle against clericalism is in the possession of Dr. David Gueiros Vieira, of West Caldwell, New Jersey.

In addition to consulting these and other written sources, the writer had personal interviews with a number of important figures and corresponded with others.

A more complete bibliography, which lists all of the works cited in the notes, but not all of those consulted in the research, will be found in Paul E. Pierson, "A Younger Church in Search of Maturity: The History of the Presbyterian Church of Brazil from 1910 to 1959," unpublished Th.D. dissertation, 1971, Speer Library, Princeton Theological Seminary, also available through University Microfilms.

Index

About the Author:

Paul E. Pierson, after serving in the U.S. Navy in World War II, was graduated from the University of California at Berkeley in 1949 and worked for a time as an engineer. He then entered Princeton Theological Seminary, graduating in 1954. In 1971 he received the Ph.D. degree, Magna Cum Laude, from Princeton Seminary.

Dr. Pierson went to Brazil under the Board of Foreign Missions, Presbyterian Church in the U.S.A. in 1956. After language study, he served as evangelist and organizing pastor of new churches in Mato Grosso. In 1961 he became Professor of Church History and Missions at the Presbyterian Seminary of the North, Recife, Brazil, serving as Dean and President of that institution for part of the period. He was Visiting Professor of Church History at the Baptist Seminary of the North in Recife in 1969-70 and Professor of Old Testament and Practical Theology at the Evangelical Seminary of Lisbon, Portugal from 1971-73.

Now living in Fresno, California with his wife and four children, the author is senior pastor, First Presbyterian Church of Fresno.